For Jane, and for our children and their children,
in the hope that something will always turn up for them.

Something Will Turn Up

Britain's economy, past, present and future

David Smith

PROFILE BOOKS

First published in Great Britain in 2015 by
PROFILE BOOKS LTD
3 Holford Yard
Bevin Way
London WC1X 9HD
www.profilebooks.com

1 3 5 7 9 10 8 6 4 2

Typeset in Garamond by MacGuru Ltd
info@macguru.org.uk
Printed and bound in Great Britain by
Clays Ltd, Bungay, Suffolk

A CIP catalogue record for this book is available from the British Library.

ISBN 978 1 78125 322 9
eISBN 978 1 78283 095 5

Something Will Turn Up

Contents

Introduction

This is not my first book on the British economy, though it covers a longer time span than its predecessors and it is, I hope, a little different. I took my title, of course, from Charles Dickens, and his character Wilkins Micawber in *David Copperfield*. He is known for his simple but memorable recipe for household finance: 'Annual income twenty pounds, annual expenditure nineteen nineteen and six, result happiness. Annual income twenty pounds, annual expenditure twenty pounds ought and six, result misery.' Mr Micawber, however, was also the eternal optimist. However blighted his existence, however low he falls, he always believes that 'something will turn up'. This book is not written from the perspective of the eternal optimist, though as I have got older I have become more inclined to look for bright spots amid the bouts of frequent gloom than some other economic commentators and economists. But it is also an observation. Something does turn up, even in the darkest times and the deepest crises. The British economy is quite good at taking itself to the edge of the abyss and coming back again. Perhaps it is just a case of muddling through, although sometimes it has been rather better than that. And we should not think that it is just some invisible elastic, controlled by Adam Smith's invisible hand, that does this. Sometimes the economy has had to be pulled back from the edge by politicians, and their advisers, doing the right things when it was needed.

In this book I describe some of those people, as I saw them at first hand. After more than three decades writing about the economy for national newspapers, mainly the *Sunday Times*, chancellors of the exchequer and Bank of England governors were necessarily in my orbit. I have known them all over that period, though some better than others. I have also known most prime ministers along the way. If there has been a change over the time I have been doing the job, it is that we have moved beyond the age of the private indiscretion. Most politicians and other policymakers – not all – tend to operate on the principle now that what they say in private will be reported in public, in one form or another. That is a pity, but perhaps understandable.

I was born and brought up in the West Midlands, the Black Country, at a time when manufacturing industry was much more important than it is now. It dominated the Midlands, and it had a dominant role in the economy, and in popular perceptions of what constituted business. Business meant making things, and industrialists ruled the roost. No longer. Though most of my life has been spent in London, albeit with frequent visits to other parts of the country and abroad, I have tried to weave a thread from the manufacturing-dominated Black Country I grew up in – which at the time we believed was the permanent state of things – to today's service-based national economy. Along the way, the West Midlands went from being one of the most successful regions of the UK to one of the least, though there are signs of revival as I write this. I have also tried to tell the story of the ups and downs of the economy over more than half a century, as I saw them at the time, and how I see them now with the benefit of hindsight. Recessions and crises litter the story, but they are not the whole story. I also attempt, in the final chapter, to assess whether we should be optimistic or pessimistic looking forward.

This is not a blow-by-blow account of the modern economic history of Britain. To do that would require several volumes. There are, inevitably, things that I have left out for reasons of space, or out of personal choice. Some of these things are covered in detail in other books I have written. The aim has been to keep it flowing. I hope I have done so.

1

The workshop of the world

Indeed let us be frank about it – most of our people have never had it so good. Go around the country, go to the industrial towns, go to the farms and you will see a state of prosperity such as we have never had in my lifetime – nor indeed in the history of this country.

Harold Macmillan, Bedford, 20 July 1957

We are redefining and we are restating our socialism in terms of the scientific revolution ... The Britain that is going to be forged in the white heat of this revolution will be no place for restrictive practices or outdated methods on either side of industry.

Harold Wilson, Labour Party conference speech, Scarborough, 1 October 1963

I was born on 3 April 1954 at 24 Coronation Avenue, County Bridge, near Walsall, Staffordshire. The house, a neat three-bedroom 1930s' semi-detached, was in a street named, I think, after the 1936 coronation (and what turned out to be the short-lived reign) of Edward VIII, later the duke of Windsor. The address, which has changed over the years as a result of local government reorganisation, and acquired a postcode along the way, sounds almost rural. It was, however, part of a small estate just off the busy Walsall Road, which at the time carried most of the traffic between Walsall and Wolverhampton. It was, more to the point, in the heart of the industrial West Midlands, and in particular the Black Country, the collection of towns neighbouring Birmingham whose dirty prosperity was built on coal, iron and eventually every type of metalworking and manufacturing.

The back garden of our house sloped upwards, steeply for my young legs, to a small rockery and fence, beyond which the land sloped down again to a canal, the Bentley Canal. When I was born, the canal was still in use; it carried coal barges to feed coal-fired furnaces. By the time I was aware of it, however, it had fallen into disuse, but it was still filled with its characteristic bright orange water, said to be the result of a continuous discharge from a local firm, Ductile Steel, and later embellished by the rust of abandoned prams and other detritus. Later it was filled in, to the relief of residents. Another feature of our small estate was a sewage farm, fortunately a couple of streets away. One hot summer day some older children encouraged me to walk on its encrusted surface, with disastrous consequences for the Sunday school outfit my mother had carefully dressed me in that morning.

Definitions of the Black Country vary and are a source of local dispute, but most would agree that it encompasses the towns of Walsall, Wolverhampton, Wednesfield, Bilston, Darlaston and Willenhall in the north; West Bromwich, Oldbury, Dudley and Wednesbury at its heart; and Stourbridge and Halesowen in the south. Its name originated in the nineteenth century, when it became, if not the cradle of the Industrial Revolution – that was in Ironbridge, 25 miles or so away – then its beating heart. In the Black Country metals were made and forged, rolled, pulled, twisted, bent and bashed into every possible shape. The range of skills was wide, as was the range of industrial processes. Elihu Burritt, a travel writer and diplomat appointed US consul to Birmingham by Abraham Lincoln in 1864 (itself a reflection of the enormous economic importance of the West Midlands), described the area as 'black by day and red by night', a reference to the powerful and permanent glow from the furnaces and foundries. Burritt is credited with popularising the term 'Black Country', though the name dates back some years before he wrote. An 1851 book, *Rides on Railways*, by Samuel Sidney, described how

> in this Black Country, including West Bromwich, Dudley, Darlaston, Bilston, Wolverhampton and several minor villages, a perpetual twilight reigns during the day, and during the night fires on all sides light up the dark landscape with a fiery glow. The pleasant green of pastures is almost unknown, the streams, in which no fishes swim, are black and unwholesome; the natural dead flat is often broken by high hills of cinders and spoil from the mines; the few trees are stunted and blasted; no birds are to be seen, except a few smoky sparrows; and for miles on miles a black waste spreads around, where furnaces continually smoke, steam engines thud and hiss, and long chains clank.

Things were different a century later, when I was growing up, but not that much different. The throb, hum and thud of industry were all around. The air was thick with smoke and dust. The Clean Air Act had passed into law, but its effects had yet to show through. The fogs were frequent, and the autumn and winter smogs were choking. You could get stranded even a few miles from home. My school, Walsall Road, a former Victorian boarding-school bought by the council and converted into a state primary, now long demolished, had two sources of distraction. One was that it was a spot where the passing trolley buses regularly lost contact with the power supply, their poles becoming detached from the overhead wires. This required a tricky manoeuvre by the conductor, re-attaching the pole using a special tool stored under the bus's floor. The other distraction was the noise from the factory just yards away, across the road. I never found out exactly what was done in that factory – it was some kind of stamping process – but its sound will stay with me for ever. Think of a giant drum kit, a slow bass beat interspersed with a high-hat, all at maximum volume, and you have something like it. Black dust and iron filings blew into the corners of the school playground, from any number of nearby factories. By-products of industrial activity were commonplace. Every boy's set of marbles was embellished by at least a few shiny ball bearings. It was not a great primary school – only four out of my class of thirty-six passed our eleven-plus – but it did its best.

None of this is meant to suggest it was a grim existence: far from it. An industrial area is a great place to grow up in, if not necessarily the healthiest. Cinder banks were perfect for our version of motocross, on pedal bikes, while canal tunnels with their uneven paths offered fun, if risky, adventures. There were dark and dank air-raid shelters, from the relatively recent Second World War, to explore. Children were expected to come home dirty, and we did. An industrial landscape was and is fascinating, from the smoke billowing out of giant chimneys to the fire and steam glimpsed through factory gates. We knew, moreover, little else. My mother came from a farm in Cardiganshire, in Wales, and when we went there to visit our grandmother for holidays, the fields, fresh air and quiet added up to a strange environment, which took some getting used to, such was the contrast with the smoke and noise of the Black Country. Industry was all around us, and we expected it to be. We knew too that it was the source of prosperity. Manufacturing kept food on the table, and more.

Made in Britain

In the 1950s Britain was a world leader in manufacturing, and the Black Country was at the heart of its success. This is not to ignore the contribution of large swaths of the rest of the country, from the shipbuilding, steel, chemicals and process industries of the industrial north-east to the tin mines and china clay of the south-west. Birmingham, the great manufacturing city, competed with Manchester and Glasgow. South Wales, Scotland's highly productive industrial belt, the East Midlands and London and the south-east were all key parts of Britain's industrial base, as were Yorkshire, Merseyside and the Boltons, Blackburns, Burys, Wigans, Oldhams and all the other mill towns of Lancashire. Few parts of the country were untouched by industry. In the 1950s, in what was still a male-dominated workforce, 40 per cent of people – roughly 9 million – were employed in manufacturing. A further 900,000 were coal-miners. Manufacturing contributed at least a third directly to Britain's gross domestic product, and much more if its indirect contribution – via service and other sectors dependent on industry – was taken into account. In 1950 Britain had a 25 per cent share of world manufactured exports, more than war-ravaged Germany, France and Italy put together.

Britain's manufacturers sold to the world, and mainly to the world beyond Europe. Since the Industrial Revolution the country had run a surplus on manufacturing trade, a situation that was to persist until the early 1980s. It was the natural order of things. Britain was no longer the biggest economy in the world, and it had been badly weakened by two long world wars, but it was still the place many countries came to for their manufactured products. 'Made in Britain', or perhaps at least as often 'Made in England', was a badge of quality. In the 1950s the trade surplus in manufactured goods was often as much as 10 per cent of gross domestic product (GDP). That did not mean the overall balance of payments was healthy: far from it.

Food and commodities had to be imported, and the legacy of war meant overseas debts had to be serviced and repaid. Manufacturing kept the wolf from the door, though broader balance of payments pressures meant sterling had to be devalued in 1949, and again, after a long attempt to resist it, in 1967. That is for later. In the meantime, Britain's manufacturers did not just dominate the economy; in many ways they *were* the economy. The big manufacturers GKN (Guest Keen and Nettlefolds), ICI (Imperial Chemical Industries) and GEC (the General Electric Company) were household names. Dunlop, with its impressive Fort Dunlop headquarters in Birmingham, which can still be seen standing tall alongside the M6 motorway (it is now offices, shops and a hotel), was another. Investors, as they looked through the FT30 index of leading British shares, saw mainly a portfolio of industrial firms, in engineering, textiles, cars, trucks and construction materials.

It is important not to over-romanticise British industry in this period. Though the 1930s had seen enormous growth in the 'new' industries of cars and consumer durables, and though it had seen an important and necessary building boom (which saved Britain from the severity of the Great Depression experienced by the USA), it had also exposed some fundamental weaknesses in traditional British industries, including shipbuilding, textiles and steel. The war had provided temporary demand in all these sectors but had not altered the fundamental challenges they faced. Some of the industrial giants of the post-war era were more fragile than they seemed. Large-scale nationalisation by the 1945–51 Attlee government was driven by ideology, but also by a strong perception that rescue by the state was the only route to survival for many of these big employers. Some take a more critical view. The historian Correlli Barnett, in his book *The Lost Victory*, argued that Labour was keener to build the New Jerusalem – the post-war welfare state and National Health Service – than to provide the industrial and technological base needed to generate the wealth to fund it. Where it was ideological, moreover, it was damaging. Most of the steel industry was nationalised as the Iron and Steel Corporation of Great Britain in 1951, the year in which the Labour government was voted out of office. The incoming Conservative government, under Winston Churchill, set about returning it to the private sector, which was achieved by 1957. It was nationalised again in the 1960s, when the British Steel Corporation came into being in 1967. Steel was the ultimate political football, kicked between the public and private sectors in a way that squandered resources and was an enemy to long-term planning and investment.

Even so, this was an era of industry-led prosperity. The post-war 'golden age' for the world economy saw sharply rising output in the Black Country and in Britain's other industrial heartlands. By the end of the golden age, which ran from 1950 to 1973, manufacturing output had more than doubled. Even the steel industry, despite its nationalisation and denationalisation travails, enjoyed strongly rising production. Benefiting initially in the early 1950s from West Germany's struggle to rebuild its steelmaking capacity, the industry enjoyed a 50 per cent rise in output during the decade. By 1960 Britain's steel industry was comfortably bigger than those of France and Italy, though, perhaps ominously, it had already been overtaken by Germany again.

Industrialists, along with trade unionists, made the news. They were the household names of British business, not the men who ran the banks or City stockbrokers. The 1950s and 1960s were the era of the industrial magnate, of Lord Nuffield (the former William Morris), the first chairman of the British Motor Corporation (or BMC, formed from the merger of the Morris company with Austin), and Lord Rootes, of the Rootes Group, another car industry giant. Sir Michael Sobell made a fortune with his Radio and Allied Industries but was probably eclipsed by his son-in-law Arnold (Lord) Weinstock, for thirty-three years the managing director of the General Electric Company (GEC). Sometimes takeover battles brought industrialists to the fore. Frank Kearton's success as Courtald's deputy chairman in fighting off a takeover bid in the early 1960s from ICI brought his elevation to chairman. Newspaper readers (there was not much business or financial news on radio and television) knew the names of leading industrialists, and they knew the names of industrial designers, most notably Alec Issigonis, who designed the Morris Minor and, perhaps more significantly, the Mini. When, in the 1960s, first the Conservative government and then – more enthusiastically – Labour tried to adopt elements of France's successful post-war economic planning, industrialists took their place on the National Economic Development Council (which first met in 1962), alongside ministers and trade unionists. Industrialists were listened to for their pronouncements on whether times were good or bad. If you wanted to know what was happening in the British economy, industry provided the answer. As late as the 1980s ICI, which no longer exists, was regularly described as a barometer for the British economy. Sometimes industrialists made the news for other reasons, as with Sir Bernard Docker, the chairman of BSA (Birmingham Small Arms) and Daimler. Sir Bernard and his wife, the former dance hostess Norah, Lady Docker, made the headlines during the austere 1950s for their extravagant and flamboyant behaviour, which eventually led to a boardroom coup at BSA against Sir Bernard in 1956. Under Lady Docker's design guidance, Daimler produced a gold-plated limousine, along with other exotic and, at a time of austerity, very expensive creations.

Making everything

Everybody I knew had a father who worked in manufacturing

industry. Many of my friends had fathers who worked for Rubery Owen, a family firm which made components for the car and commercial vehicle industry and much more besides. The 'Ro' in Rostyle car wheels, once very popular, stands for Rubery Owen. The firm employed 17,000 people across Britain, many thousands of them at its nearby factory in Darlaston. It was a paternalistic and enlightened business, providing its workers with benefits that were ahead of the time, including sports facilities, subsidised canteens, day nurseries and retirement advice programmes. The day nursery at Darlaston, supervised by a matron and staffed by several nurses, provided for the children of the many working mothers who worked at the factory. Another benefit available to workers was Cadogan, a convalescent home at the seaside town of Barmouth, in Wales, for employees recovering from illness or injury. The benefits included the provision of housing. Rubery Owen owned and rented housing to its workers, including many of those on our estate. Two of the streets, Somerset and Devon Roads, were almost entirely houses owned by Rubery Owen, and the firm had plenty more in the district. These were not, in the main, the firm's steel-framed factory-built houses, which were sold in prefabricated form, mainly to local authorities, from the late 1940s onwards to help deal with the post-war housing shortage.

The factory was close enough for its bull-horn signalling the end of a shift, known as 'the Bull', to be clearly heard. It was a signal for wives (those who did not go out to work) to put the kettle on, or get the lunch (always known as 'dinner') on the table. Minutes after the bull-horn had sounded, a sea of men on bikes, and in the occasional car, would arrive. Rubery Owen, run by the formidable Sir Alfred Owen, exuded power and permanence. Privately owned, and one of the largest such firms in Britain, it did not have to dance to the tune of stock market investors. It had an adventurous spirit, perfectly illustrated by its ownership of the BRM (British Racing Motors) Grand

Prix team. At company open days, the racing-green BRM cars, driven at various times by Graham Hill, Jackie Stewart and Pedro Rodríguez, were a magnet for small boys and others. Rubery Owen, with engineering interests extending well beyond the motor industry, made just about everything. It manufactured stands for spectators at Twickenham and Old Trafford, Manchester. Its twenty constituent companies included Conveyancer, which made forklift trucks; Leabank, which produced office furniture; and Easiclene, acquired in the late 1930s, which made fridges, melamine kitchen units and other domestic equipment. Rubery Owen made equipment for the aerospace industry from two subsidiaries, as well as nuts, bolts, chains and agricultural tools and equipment. It had a finger in just about every industrial pie, and it appeared indestructible. In 2005 the firm produced a book, *Memories of Rubery Owen*, a collection of photographs, many of them from that era, and mainly taken from the company newspaper, *The Owen News*. As well as photographs of industrial processes – the manufacture of double-decker bus chassis, car wheels and the 100,000th Ferguson plough – there is an aerial view of Rubery Owen's 75-acre Darlaston site. It looks, as it seemed from the ground, vast. On that site there was the Sons of Rest workshop, for men of retirement age who did not want to give up work: skilled workers aged seventy or over who continued to make specialist parts and equipment. Included in the memories are a vast range of extra-curricular activities: the cricket and netball teams, the ladies' slow cycle race on sports day, the theatre groups, the children's Christmas party, the eighteen-coach works outing to the coronation in 1953 and many more. It was paternalistic in a way that barely exists any more. Many things have changed for the better since those days, but it is hard not to feel a little nostalgia for the time when these factories provided not just work but a rounded existence.

Sir Alfred Owen, who remained chairman until his death in 1975, was a considerable local and national figure. A

committed Christian and philanthropist, he was a local coun-
cillor for nearly forty years (his knighthood was for services
to local government), the first pro-chancellor of Keele University and a member of committees for Dr Barnardo's and
the Boys' Brigade, among other charities. He was chairman of
the National Road Safety Council and vice-chairman of the
National Savings Movement. Later in life he became a sup-
porter of the Billy Graham Christian crusades. Owen was not
unique. Many towns and cities had these big figures, heads of
big family firms, many of whom saw it as their duty to partici-
pate in local or national life. Industry carried with it power and
influence.

Industry and empire

My father, Charles Henry Smith, worked not for Rubery Owen
but for another large industrial firm, Metropolitan Cammell.
As its full name – the Metropolitan Cammell Carriage and
Wagon Company – suggests, it built railway locomotives, carriages and wagons, mainly from three factories in the West
Midlands: one at nearby Wednesbury and two in Birmingham,
at Saltley and Washwood Heath. Though a white-collar worker,
in the company's drawing office, my father was very much
involved in the manufacturing process, through engineering
design. Metropolitan Cammell supplied much of the rolling
stock still used on the London Underground (look for the
nameplate on the floor by the sliding doors). It was also a major
supplier to British Rail, including most of its workhorse diesel
units in the 1950s and the luxurious Pullman trains acquired by
the nationalised rail company during that decade. Many of the
company's most lucrative markets, however, were in the former
British Empire – from the late 1940s, the Commonwealth.
The Metropolitan Cammell factory my father worked at, Old
Park in Wednesbury, was big enough to occupy both sides of a

busy main road. As befitted the nature of its business, it had its own railway line running between the factory sheds, and across the road. When a carriage or locomotive had to be taken from one part of the factory to the other, across the road, the gates swung into position and the traffic on the busy road from Darlaston to Wednesbury was stopped. The firm built some superb rolling stock, including the Pullmans, and it was never seen better than when fresh from the paint shop. Locomotives and carriages produced there and in the other factories were sold across the world, including to the national railways of Nigeria, Pakistan, Mexico, Nyasaland (now Malawi) and the Trans-Zambezi Railway. Like Rubery Owen, Metropolitan Cammell laid on open days and outings for the families of its employees. I remember seeing a magnificent, gleaming, blue-liveried locomotive, huge and impressive, built for South African Railways and ready to be shipped off there. For firms like my father's, and for many others, the world was apparently their oyster. This was what they did, and the world wanted it.

Commonwealth markets were hugely important for British industry. The system of imperial preference was adapted and supplemented by bilateral trade arrangements as the British Empire evolved into the Commonwealth in the aftermath of the Second World War. Commonwealth countries were used to buying their industrial products from Britain, and to selling their agricultural crops, minerals and other commodities to Britain. In the early 1950s more than 40 per cent of UK exports went to the Commonwealth, while roughly 35 per cent of imports were from these countries. As late as 1960 a third of Britain's overseas trade was with the Commonwealth. Australia was the second most important destination for exports (after the USA), followed by Canada and, in fifth and sixth places after Germany, South Africa and India respectively.

It was a time of optimism, of belief. At that time, rightly or wrongly, we believed British was best. Victory in the Second

World War may have been achieved at a huge human and economic cost, but it was also a springboard for post-war revival. British industry's two big advantages – the damage to the industrial base in continental Europe and an apparently captive market in the Commonwealth – were formidable. Though the expression 'jerry-built' has nothing to do with Germany, it was cheerfully misused to mean that nobody in their right mind would want anything to do with German products. The threat from Asia, similarly, was no threat at all. 'Made in Hong Kong' was the pejorative term for anything cheap and plasticky, the throwaway things you might win at a fair or get in a Christmas cracker but would not dream of buying. Pride in things made in Britain may never have been higher than in the 1950s and early 1960s. Every town had its specialisation, and each one regarded itself as the best in the business. In nearby Willenhall, our local small town, my father, a voracious reader, took me to the library each week. Often we would wander into the adjoining lock museum and gaze on the exhibits, including some weird and wonderful products. The town, the centre of Britain's lock-making industry, had been home to hundreds of lock-making businesses in the nineteenth century, and the museum showed off their wares. Some of those businesses had merged over the years, but this was still a thriving trade. The Black Country was reaching out to the world. Even one of the local football teams, my team, Wolverhampton Wanderers, at the time one of the top clubs in the country, was reaching out by pioneering floodlit football against European opponents, against the wishes of the English football authorities. We believed we could take on the world and win. When the government made its first (unsuccessful) application to join the Common Market in the early 1960s, I asked my father what it was all about. It was, he said, so we could sell our things to the rest of Europe, not so that they would sell theirs to us. We believed in British, and we bought British, and we believed everybody else would want to buy British, and never was this more true than when it came to cars.

Driving on the right

There were just under 2 million cars on Britain's roads in 1950, meaning that the vast majority of households had no access to a car, and most of those that did were well-off. The rise of car ownership, having been interrupted by the Second World War and its austere aftermath, was, however, in full swing. By 1960 there were 4.9 million cars registered, and by 1970 there were 10 million. This was the era when the car began to replace the bicycle as the transport of choice for workers travelling to and from factories and offices. As petrol ceased to be rationed in May 1950 (rationing was briefly reintroduced in 1956–7 in response to the Suez crisis), people took to the roads in increasing numbers for pleasure and leisure. It was also the era of motoring holidays and the rise of the stately home. People needed somewhere to drive their cars, when they were not washing and polishing them, and entrepreneurs, including some of Britain's great aristocratic families, provided it. The rise in car use was, if anything, even more striking than the increase in the car population. From 16 billion vehicle miles in 1950, the number rose to 42 billion in 1960 and 96 billion by 1970.

Overwhelmingly, these miles were driven in British cars. Whether it was force of habit, restrictions on imported vehicles, including relatively high tariffs, or a genuine belief that British was best can be debated, but the vast majority of cars sold in Britain were British-made. In the mid-1950s the proportion of cars imported was a fraction over 2 per cent. To put that in perspective, though there are caveats I will explain later, in 2013 roughly 85 per cent of the cars sold in Britain were imported. Somebody in the area drove a Renault Dauphine, a 1950s' vehicle later listed by *Time* magazine as one of the fifty worst cars of all time. It was a brave choice of vehicle, even avant-garde, but mainly it was regarded as odd. Many foreign manufacturers regarded their prospects in the British market as so poor that they did not bother to manufacture right-hand-drive vehicles. Maybe, though, that Renault buyer was not so odd. He or she was certainly ahead of their time. Not only that but they probably got hold of their car more quickly. With the Conservative government (which in 1957 evolved into Harold Macmillan's 'you've never had it so good' government) keen to maximise export earnings from Britain's car industry, domestic buyers often had to wait for many months after ordering their British-made vehicle. Nicholas Comfort, in his book *The Slow Death of British Industry*, describes how his grandfather, having rung the local BMC dealer and been told he would have to wait a couple of months for a car, decided to get in touch with Renault. A car was outside his house that afternoon, and he bought it.

Almost without exception, however, people bought British, and the choice was a wide one. When, in the 1950s, German travel agents came up with the idea of the 'Romantic Road' in southern Germany, the *Romantische Strasse*, to encourage Britons and others to take motoring holidays – not an easy sell – those who did so toured in their MGs, Rovers and Jaguars. Though the market in Britain for Volkswagen Beetles gradually grew, it took a long time for British buyers to look favourably on German cars. The Beetle was famously rejected by Lord Rootes at the end of the war as 'quite unattractive to the average buyer' because it was 'too ugly and too noisy', though in his defence Henry Ford also rejected it as being not 'worth a damn'. But why would anybody want an odd-looking Volkswagen when, during the 1950s and 1960s, British cars appeared to be at the forefront of new and exciting design. There were Fords, including the daring Anglia and the American-influenced Classic, Zephyr and Zodiac. There was the Austin A40 Farina, the world's first hatchback, as well as solid executive transport such as the Austin Cambridge and Morris Oxford. There was the Mini, every bit as iconic as the Beetle eventually became and a much cleverer design. There were Vauxhalls, Rileys, Wolseleys, Standards, Triumphs, Sunbeams and many others. For bank managers there were solid Rovers. For business people who had made it there was the Jaguar, for those who had really made it the Rolls-Royce and Bentley.

Until he graduated to a company Ford Cortina, much later, my father drove Rootes Group cars. Brand loyalty was important as was the fact that his brother, who during the war had fought at Dunkirk and Monte Cassino, returned to work at the local Rootes dealer. In our dilapidated garage was a pre-war Singer Le Mans sports car, never driven in my lifetime but good fun to play in. When the time came to rebuild the garage, the car was taken away for scrap. There were then a succession of Hillmans, a marque that ceased to exist in the 1970s, as did Humber, my father's last privately owned vehicle before the arrival of the company car. Rootes, later absorbed into Chrysler and then Peugeot before its factories were eventually closed, had an 11.5 per cent share of Britain's new car market in 1955, well below BMC with its Austin, Morris and other badges, which had 39 per cent, and Ford, with 26.5 per cent, but ahead of Standard (9.5 per cent) and Vauxhall (8.5 per cent).

A golden age of sorts

The advantages Britain enjoyed in the 1950s did not last. The Commonwealth was less of a captive market than hoped, not least because Commonwealth countries wanted to build up their own manufacturing bases. Australia and South Africa imposed tariff barriers in order to protect their own embryonic car industries, and other countries followed suit, for cars and other industrial products. The old Empire relationship, in which manufactured products flowed one way and commodities the other, was one that many Commonwealth countries wanted to change. They wanted to be economically independent. Britain, it seemed, wanted to change too, with a growing if belated emphasis on trade relations with Europe. Within Europe, meanwhile, helped by Marshall Plan aid and the process of post-war rebuilding, industrial revival was surprisingly rapid, particularly in Germany. Indeed, within a few years some British manufacturers, still using Victorian equipment, were looking with envy on the gleaming machine tools and equipment their German counterparts were using. Germany's comeback, during its *Wirtschaftswunder* economic miracle, was indeed impressive and Britain's post-war industrial dominance short-lived. In 1938 Germany enjoyed a bigger share of global industrial production, though a slightly smaller share of manufacturing exports, than Britain. In 1950 Britain was well ahead on both measures, its share of manufacturing exports, almost 25 per cent, more than three times that of Germany. It did not last. By 1964 Germany accounted for almost a fifth of global manufacturing exports, just behind the USA, and well ahead of Britain's 14 per cent. Britain's car manufacturers made more than half a million cars in 1950, well above France (257,000) and Germany (219,000) combined. Germany quickly increased car production and really came into its own in the second half of the 1950s, boosting annual production from 762,000 in 1955 to 1.82 million in 1960. Production also rose strongly in Britain, from 898,000 to 1.35 million, but Germany was back in front, and was to remain there.

By any absolute measure, British industry did well over this period. Production rose strongly, by modern standards, in most years through the period of the golden age, 1950–73. Manufacturing was the biggest employer and the single most important sector of the economy. Despite often ill-judged government intervention, in the motor industry and in other parts of manufacturing, industry continued to be globally very important, only losing its position as the third-largest manufacturing power to France on the eve of the 1973 OPEC (Organization of Petroleum Exporting Countries) oil crisis. The old British Motor Corporation, which merged with the truck manufacturer (and Standard-Triumph owner) Leyland in the late 1960s, with the encouragement of the Labour prime minister, Harold Wilson, was unwieldy, inefficient and ravaged by internal rivalries and industrial relations problems. It still, however, had a third of the market in the early 1970s. It may have tested the loyalty of its buyers, with questionable designs and even more questionable quality, but people still tended to buy British. In the case of the growing trend towards company car fleets, many businesses demonstrated their patriotism and helped the domestic manufacturers by adopting a British-only policy. There are, in yellowing copies of the *Sunday Times Business News* from the 1970s, the early signs of the shape of things to come, with advertisements from BMW and Audi for 'executive' cars. They were merely dipping their toe in the water. Even they could not have guessed how successful they would be when they eventually dived in.

Envying the rest

While the absolute performance of British industry during the golden age was generally acceptable, its relative performance was not. For Britons, the easy eclipsing of the country's manufacturing by Germany and later Japan was galling. Increasingly, they sensed something was wrong, and they were right. If the story of the 1950s, the first half of the golden age, was one of growth and confidence, despite national humiliations such as Suez in 1956, the 1960s were when economic reality began to sink in. Harold Macmillan's 'most of our people have never had it so good' in 1957 was meant as much to reassure as to boast, but the fact that it could be said without ridicule showed the extent to which there was genuine optimism. The numbers for the 1960s, despite the very obvious pressures, looked good. Gross domestic product rose by 41 per cent and manufacturing output by 44 per cent, much better than later decades. Unemployment remained close to 'full' employment levels. Living standards rose. Swinging London was only a hundred or so miles away, and in many respects could have been on another planet, but the social revolution of the 1960s, most of it for the good, was undeniable.

Britain, however, was not doing as well as the rest. In his hugely influential book *The Stagnant Society*, published by Penguin in 1961, Michael Shanks, whom I later worked with, wrote that, as long as Britain was divided by class, its economy would struggle. The country was falling behind its competitors because of a class-defined social structure. In this he was anticipating another highly influential book, the American academic Martin Wiener's 1981 book (given to every member of Margaret Thatcher's Cabinet by Sir Keith Joseph) *English Culture and the Decline of the Industrial Spirit, 1850–1980*. Shanks was particularly critical of British industry. The backwardness of much of it, he wrote, was becoming 'a music-hall joke'. He was not alone. A few years earlier, on being shown BMC's model range by Leonard Lord, who ran the company, Prince Philip, the duke of Edinburgh, said he was not sure they were up to the foreign competition.

The statistics tell some of the story. By the 1960s Britain's productivity growth – the growth in output per worker – was quite strong in absolute terms, but at 4.1 per cent a year from 1960 to 1973 was eclipsed by France, 6.6 per cent, and Germany, 5.7 per cent. Britain's overall growth rate during this period, a respectable 2.6 per cent, compared unfavourably with the European Economic Community (EEC) average of 3.3 per cent. This was the era when governments embarked on a restless search for ways of ensuring Britain could keep up with the competition. After initially rejecting membership of both the European Coal and Steel Community (in Herbert Morrison's famous phrase 'the Durham miners won't wear it') and the EEC following the Treaty of Rome, the Conservative government nevertheless recognised that trade with the rest of Europe was likely to be more important in future than trade with the Commonwealth. As an alternative to the EEC, Britain was a founder member and driving force in the creation of the European Free Trade Association (EFTA) in 1960. The EEC had six members – France, Germany, Italy, Belgium, Luxembourg and the Netherlands – while EFTA had seven (Austria, Britain, Denmark, Norway, Portugal, Sweden and Switzerland). Europe, as one wag put it, was 'at sixes and sevens'. EFTA was never going to be enough for British industrialists eyeing the fast-recovering European market, or for Britain's politicians. Unfortunately, having rejected membership of the proposed EEC in the mid-1950s, there was no quick way back. General Charles de Gaulle's two rejections of British membership in January 1963 and November 1967 – 'England in effect is insular, she is maritime, she is linked through her exchanges, her markets, her supply lines to the most diverse and often the most distant countries; she pursues essentially industrial and commercial activities, and only slight agricultural ones' – was a blow to national pride. It was also a blow to British industry and the economy, which had come round to the view that Europe, not the Commonwealth, would be the source of future prosperity.

Geoffrey Owen, in *From Empire to Europe*, argues that British industry lost out by missing the benefits of European integration but also from persisting with what had been an increasingly creaky pre-war industrial model. Germany evolved a decentralised framework, with the centre taking responsibility for orthodox and anti-inflationary fiscal and monetary policy but industrial development and finance devolved to regional and local level, including large-scale employers but also the country's *Mittelstand* of medium-size business. France adopted a system of state-sponsored industrial modernisation, accompanied by economic planning, with the emphasis on technology and investment. The two models were, as Owen notes, very different but also successful. British governments did not stand idly by. Harold Wilson's 'white heat of technology', the memorable phrase he used in a speech to the Labour Party conference in Scarborough in 1963, was intended to convey a modernising zeal: a contrast with the sleepy Conservative Party and a firm nod across the Channel in the direction of France. The French influence was also evident when Wilson's 1964–70 government set up a Department of Economic Affairs (DEA) in 1965 and launched a French-style indicative plan with the aim of boosting industrial production and lifting Britain's annual growth rate to 4 per cent a year. The DEA, under George Brown, was short-lived, and so was the plan. By the time of sterling's 1967 devaluation, and the crisis management surrounding it, it had long gone.

The pound in your pocket

Shortly after the October 1964 election, which ushered in a Labour government with a wafer-thin majority, and the end of thirteen years of Conservative rule, Wilson, the new prime minister, spoke to his party. Though he probably did not know it, he gave a pretty good summary of many of the themes and challenges that would dominate the economic debate for the next half-century. Wilson, an economist who at twenty-one was one of Oxford University's youngest dons, wore his learning lightly, preferring to cultivate a 'man of the people' image. Britain, he said late in 1964, was prone to frequent bouts of financial uncertainty, particularly affecting sterling, but he was determined to pursue a strong currency policy and 'ruthlessly protect the pound'. The country needed to export and invest more, a common refrain now, and 'while our scientific effort is as good as that of any other country, we are still far too slow in applying technology to industry'. Britain was too often in 'the humiliating position of paying royalties on a British invention'.

The new prime minister was, however, optimistic. 'We have great reserves of skill and craftsmanship, of science and technology, of talent for production and design and sales, which now they have been called into battle will produce a result which will delight our friends and surprise the world', he said. 'This is the mood of Britain today, the determination, the readiness, the eagerness for change which ... will sweep our country to victory in the economic field.' To ensure that these reserves of skill and craftsmanship and what he had earlier called the 'white heat of technology' were converted into economic growth, Wilson put his rival George Brown in charge of the new DEA, with the aim of harnessing the country's energies and, as noted, in a direct steal from France, using a form of planning – so-called 'indicative planning' – to remove the economic bottlenecks and achieve a 4 per cent growth rate. Britain was doing well by later standards in the 1960s, but it was not doing as well as most other industrial countries, including the rest of Europe.

With the benefit of hindsight, and with decades of revisions to the GDP figures, we can see that one thing Wilson got badly wrong was his description of the economy as 'tired and spiritless'. On current data, Britain in 1964 was booming, with growth of 5.9 per cent, following 4.7 per cent in 1963. The problem with that growth was that it was unbalanced, a big current account deficit – at a time when it mattered – reflecting the economy's vulnerability.

That vulnerability set the tone for the economy. Growth was good in comparison with later decades, but turbulence and financial instability soon took over. The DEA soon became a footnote of history, killed off by the Treasury, George Brown's frequent bouts of drunkenness and a determined but ultimately unsuccessful attempt to avoid devaluation. The sterling devaluation of November 1967 from $2.80 to $2.40 was necessary but humiliating, mainly because the Labour government had spent so long denying it would happen. For this reason James Callaghan, the chancellor, felt honour-bound to resign. The pledges he had given, he recalled later, were so unequivocal as to leave resignation his only course of action. Wilson was left to explain it to the nation, in words that were to haunt him. The pound had been devalued, said Wilson in a television broadcast, but 'it does not mean that the pound here in Britain, in your pocket or purse or in your bank, has been devalued'. Wilson, it was said, knew this statement would expose him to ridicule, but he was simply following the Treasury's devaluation 'war book'. In 1949, when sterling had previously been devalued, from $4 to $2.80, there was a widespread belief that sterling's face value internally – the pound in people's pockets – had been reduced.

The 1967 devaluation was a pivotal moment in post-war British economic history. Immediately following the devaluation of sterling in November 1967, a Letter of Intent to the International Monetary Fund committed the government to growth in the money supply in 1968 at or below its rate of increase in 1967. The letter, published on 30 November 1967, the day after Roy Jenkins replaced James Callaghan as chancellor of the exchequer, was chiefly concerned with the balance of payments, and how quickly the devaluation would act on Britain's current account deficit. But it also represented the first formal commitment to monetary targets by a post-war British government – the first stirrings of the monetarism, the belief that the way to control inflation was by control of the money supply, that was to come later. It was also an early example of austerity. Cuts in planned public expenditure were announced shortly after the devaluation, to be followed, in the spring of 1968, by a tax-raising budget. Roy Jenkins's March 1968 budget stood out, at the time, as among the most deflationary in the post-war era, raising taxation by nearly £1 billion overall. Devaluation, Roy Jenkins's subsequent stern stewardship of the Treasury and the unfortunate timing of the delivery of a couple of jumbo jets (which distorted the trade figures) resulted in Wilson's surprise election defeat in 1970. But it was also an important moment for the world economy. Though the pound was second-best to the dollar, it was an important reserve currency. Its devaluation was a nail in the coffin of the Bretton Woods system of fixed-but-adjustable currencies, put together in the dying days of the Second World War. Within five years that system was no more.

The post-war system of fixed exchange rates, known as the Bretton Woods system after the village in New Hampshire where it was hammered out in 1944, finally collapsed in March 1973. Its survival for nearly thirty years, from the end of the war to the rise of OPEC, evokes a modern golden age of strong growth and steady prices. Reassemble Bretton Woods, it is said by some, and those conditions would return.

The system, to be fair, has had rather too good a press, conditioned by comparisons with the sharp currency swings and persistent instability of the floating rate era of the late 1970s and 1980s. It is often forgotten that the system envisaged in 1944 did not begin operating properly until the early 1960s, when the countries of Western Europe, as well as Japan, allowed free access to the foreign exchange markets for current account transactions. Even then, exchange controls on capital transactions remained firmly in place and, indeed, may have been essential for the preservation of fixed exchange rates.

In Britain a fierce debate over devaluation dominated economic policy for much of the 1960s, to an extent that, in retrospect, is hard to believe. The eventual decision to devalue the pound from $2.80 to $2.40, taken with a heavy heart by the prime minister, Harold Wilson, in November 1967, came after years of soul-searching. It provided, as noted, the first major blow to the Bretton Woods system. The decision to float the pound by the Conservative prime minister, Edward Heath, in June 1972 was the system's death knell.

Nobody growing up in the Black Country, surrounded by manufacturing industry, could be immune to these developments. The industrial relations climate was deteriorating, with the number of strikes increasing significantly in the second half of the 1960s (a prelude to the turbulent 1970s and 1980s). Everybody was aware of Britain's failed attempts to enter the EEC, sterling's 'pound in your pocket' devaluation and the general sense of national disappointment. Few, however, thought that a large manufacturing sector was anything but the norm. True, things were changing. My father's Metropolitan Cammell factory, the one where I saw those wonderful trains, was closed in the 1960s, and he was forced to travel further to the firm's only remaining factory in the West Midlands, at Washwood Heath in Birmingham. Not everything was permanent. The prospect of a huge manufacturing decline, however, seemed remote, almost fanciful, the idea of a service-based economy – seen from an industrial area – impossible to imagine. The factories were solid and unyielding. They were, it seemed, permanent. Civic and industrial pride, established in the Victorian era, was still very evident in the 1960s. In any case, what would workers do, if they did not clock in at the factory? Where else would the mass employment of the future come from other than industry? It was complacent, but it was born out of belief and historical precedent. Industry had been through ups and downs before, some of them of great severity, but had come through. Why should it be any different this time? Something, surely, would turn up.

2

Giving it all away

As Prime Minister, I want to speak to you, simply and
plainly, about the grave emergency now facing our
country. In the House of Commons this afternoon
I announced more severe restrictions on the use of
electricity. You may already have heard the details of these.
We are asking you to cut down to the absolute minimum
the use of electricity for heating, and for other purposes
in your homes. We are limiting the use of electricity by
almost all factories, shops and offices, to three days a week.

Sir Edward Heath, broadcast to the nation,
13 December 1973

The ten years from 1973 to 1983 marked the end of the post-war
golden age for the world economy, and few countries marked its
passing as painfully as Britain. This was the period of high inflation, which reached a peak of 26.9 per cent (retail price inflation) in August 1975 and averaged more than 14 per cent for
a decade. It marked the end of full employment, in a way that
few could have envisaged in the 1950s and 1960s. The number
of people claiming unemployment benefit, just over 500,000
in 1973, rose to above a million at the beginning of 1976 and

by the end of 1983 had reached 2.8 million, well on its way to the 3 million level it was soon to hit. It included two serious recessions, in 1973–5 and 1980–81, a sharp contrast with the mild downturns of the golden age. Though the economy recovered after both recessions, gross domestic product in 1983 was a mere 13 per cent above its level ten years earlier. This was a pale shadow of 1963–73, when GDP rose by 43 per cent, and 1953–63, when there was a rise of 37 per cent. The spell of strongly rising prosperity was broken in the 1970s, and it took time to come back. Perhaps because of this, or perhaps because this was the moment when the unions collectively decided to exert their economic and political power, it was an era of considerable industrial disruption, which at times verged on industrial anarchy. In the 1950s an average of just over 3 million working days were lost annually as a result of strikes, rising to just over 4 million in the 1960s. In the 1970s, 13 million working days were lost on average annually, peaking at 29.5 million in 1979, a strike wave that contributed to the defeat of the Labour government at the hands of Margaret Thatcher's Conservatives in 1979. Though this was the worst modern-day episode of industrial disruption (closely followed by the 27.1 million days lost as a result of the 1984 miners' strike), it should be said that the record was far worse earlier in the century: 162 million working days were lost in the General Strike of 1926, 86 million in 1921 and 41 million in 1912.

For Britain's manufacturing industry this combination of high inflation, two big recessions and a hugely disruptive industrial relations climate was toxic. This was the era of the three-day week, an abrupt rise in the cost of energy, the humiliating 1976 International Monetary Fund rescue of the British economy and the winter of discontent. The lights did not go out completely on British industry, but they dimmed. Manufacturing had driven the economy for nearly two centuries. This was the period when it went into a relative decline from which it has yet to recover. If the performance of the economy during the 1973–83 period was poor, the performance of manufacturing was disastrous. Despite its frequent travails in earlier decades, manufacturing had always achieved solid growth. That growth may have compared poorly with competitors, but in comparison with what followed it verged on the miraculous. In the ten years after 1973 manufacturing output fell by 16 per cent. At one stage, in the depths of the 1980–81 recession, manufacturing output was almost 25 per cent down on its early 1970s' peak. Industry was hit by a formidable double-blow. Before it had properly recovered from the 1973–5 recession the even more serious 1980–81 recession hit it hard. It took until the late 1980s, a decade and a half, for manufacturing output to recover to the level it had achieved in 1973. Even more sobering, perhaps, is that in January 2010 manufacturing was producing the same volume of output as it had done thirty-seven years earlier, in 1973. The dreadful decade of 1973–83 took its toll on manufacturing jobs, more than 4 million of which disappeared. By 1983 manufacturing employment was barely a quarter of the numbers employed in the rapidly growing services sector. The lights had gone out in factories across the nation.

Witness to decline

In the late 1960s we moved from the three-bed semi near Willenhall and Darlaston to West Bromwich. My mother, Elizabeth Mary Smith, a primary school teacher from rural Cardiganshire, had died young, from cancer, at the age of only forty-three, in August 1963. When I returned to school that September after the summer holidays, in grief, the only thing anybody wanted to talk about was the great train robbery, which also happened in August 1963. For a few years things were tough. My mother's salary was no longer coming in, and my father attempted to compensate for her loss by spending: too much, as it turned out. Soon we were in debt. To go to the corner shop and be told we could not have anything until the account was settled was a grim experience and put me off indebtedness for life. Fortunately my father remarried, to Molly Birks, a former colleague at Metropolitan Cammell, who was ready to return home after many years overseas. At the end of the war, as a secretary in a Birmingham law firm, she had responded to an advertisement from the United Nations Relief and Rehabilitation Administration (UNRRA), a job that took her to immediate post-war Germany, and the grim aftermath of the liberation of the concentration camps, and to China at the time of the Communist revolution in 1949. Her later postings with the United Nations Children's Fund (UNICEF) included Jakarta, Indonesia and Addis Adaba, Ethiopia, where she befriended Haile Selassie's daughters. At the time of her marriage to my father, she was based at UNICEF headquarters in New York.

They had both grown up in West Bromwich, so that is where we moved. Though it was leafier than our previous house, on the edge of a narrow strip of green belt (soon to be made even narrower by a motorway), beyond which was Birmingham, it was still very much the Black Country. It was also where I had my first direct experience of manufacturing industry from inside the factory gates. My education took me from West Bromwich Grammar School to Cardiff and Oxford universities. In those days – the early to mid-1970s – it was surprisingly easy, through temporary employment agencies, to get holiday jobs in factories, despite the economy's woes. Firms always needed labourers, sweepers, packers or, in one case, somebody who knew their way around a calculating machine (these days it would all be done by computer) to work out what should go into the employees' pay packets. Though these holiday jobs added up cumulatively to many months working in manufacturing, I would not pretend that they gave anything more than an impression. That impression, however, was almost without exception that it was no surprise that British industry was in trouble.

Jensen Motors, in West Bromwich, was a luxury car maker, established by two brothers of that name in the 1930s, and which moved to a purpose-built factory in the mid-1950s. It was known for big-engined sports saloons, most notably the Interceptor. It also made car bodies for other manufacturers, including the Austin Healey. The big Jensen cars, with beautiful bodywork and craftsman assembly, were collectors' items. Production was deliberately low: in the 1960s and 1970s not many people could afford such luxury. In the 1930s the firm had built a specially commissioned car for the Hollywood actor Clark Gable, then at the height of his fame, who came to the town to collect it, attracting huge crowds as he paraded down the high street. By the time I came to work at Jensen Motors, on two or three separate occasions, things were already difficult. It was a fascinating place to work, from the sumptuous leather sheets laid out in preparation for seating and trim, to the massive 7-litre Chrysler engines, imported from the USA, ready to slot into the elegant bodies. There was, however, another side to Jensen Motors. When the British Motor Corporation decided to discontinue production of the popular Austin Healey, a much smaller and cheaper sports car, at the end of the 1960s and Jensen lost the contract to build the bodies, it decided to build its own version of the car, the Jensen Healey, under the chairmanship of Donald Healey, following the departure of the two Jensen brothers from the business.

Unfortunately Jensen, in trying to produce sports cars in volume, quickly ran into problems. The cars, while attractive to look at, were poorly assembled, though some of the roughly 10,000 that were built are still around, particularly in the USA. Not only did the Jensen Healey suffer from quality issues, but the car-industry veterans that Jensen had imported to man the production line, many of them from the Austin factory at

Longbridge, brought with them industrial relations problems all too typical of the industry. Add to that the limited appeal in the wake of the oil crisis of the Interceptor, with its gas-guzzling 7-litre engine, and Jensen was in trouble. My abiding memories of working at Jensen were of how little work was done. There was, it seemed, always a tea break, a union meeting or a shutdown. Production was a fraction of what it could have been, and the mood grew more militant as the company was forced into a programme of redundancies. Jensen called in the receivers in September 1975 and ceased trading in May 1976, to nobody's surprise, though there have been various attempts to revive the brand, including one as I write this.

Tools to trust

Not every firm I worked at in that succession of temporary jobs in the 1970s suffered the same sad fate as Jensen Motors, though many had to restructure and close down some of their operations, including those in the Black Country. At one stage I worked at Spear & Jackson, the toolmaker, which owned and ran a large factory in nearby Wednesbury, said to be one of the oldest industrial sites in the area. The site, which later became a magnet for industrial archaeologists, was said to have housed a foundry as long ago as the reign of Elizabeth I. Tools had been made on the site for almost two centuries, following the acquisition of the Wednesbury Forge by Edward Elwell in the early part of the nineteenth century. Elwell Tools, later acquired by Spear & Jackson, was a prominent local firm for many years. When I worked there, briefly, Spear & Jackson needed temporary employees to pack crates of tools – shovels, forks, saws and garden implements – for export. The tools were packed first into large wooden boxes and then into shipping containers. As I packed, I noticed two things. The first was that most of these tools were bound for Commonwealth markets, particularly countries in Africa. The second was that all these consignments were desperately late. The tools I was packing for customers in Botswana, Nigeria and other countries were already typically eighteen months beyond their expected delivery date, and had not even left Wednesbury for their long sea voyage to Africa. How long they would have taken to get there I cannot tell, but it would be a fair guess that the tools would not be in the hands of the customers until close to two years after they were due. If an export strategy is at least partly based on on-time delivery, this one was failing. Too many British firms took these Commonwealth markets for granted. When those markets switched to German, Japanese or South Korean suppliers, as they inevitably did, it was no surprise. Spear & Jackson, however, lasted longer than many. It continued to operate on the Wednesbury site until 2006, before announcing its closure and demolition, consolidating its hand-tool business at a single site in Sheffield.

Motorcycle diaries

Other parts of the industrial landscape changed much more quickly. During that time I had a succession of motorbikes. This was a time when Britain's motorcycle industry was facing even more of a challenge from imports than the car manufacturers. British motorcycles were typically big, oily and unreliable. They were great for enthusiasts, who thought nothing of cleaning spark plugs or even stripping down an engine before embarking on a weekend trip. Japanese motorcycles of the time, which owed little to aesthetics – particularly the small 50, 70 or 90 cc machines – offered a simplicity and reliability that appealed to commuters. Later Japanese motorbikes began both to look good and, with larger machines, to appeal to the enthusiast. Britain's motorcycle industry, which in 1950 produced over 170,000 machines, was down to half that level by the late 1960s. The competition from imports, which increased from virtually nothing to more than 110,000, was compounded by the easy availability and increased affordability of cars. Why travel by motorbike, or the once ubiquitous motorcycle and sidecar, when it was possible to travel in the comfort of a car?

The motorcycle industry's decline (though there is a later story of limited revival) was abrupt. BSA (Birmingham Small Arms) was once Birmingham's biggest employer, with a history, as its name suggests, of arms manufacture, including Lee Enfield rifles, Lewis and Browning machine guns, Sten guns and air-craft cannons, including those used on Spitfires and Hurri-canes, and anti-aircraft manufacture. In peacetime it became better known for its manufacture of bicycles and motorcycles. BSA made big bikes with evocative names, such as the Gold Star, Spitfire, Rocket, Victor and Thunderbolt. At its Small Heath factory in Birmingham it also assembled Ariel, Sunbeam and some Triumph motorcycles. It was the heart of Britain's motorcycle industry. I did not have one of BSA's big bikes, but I did have a BSA Bantam, its version of the commuter bike, with a 175 cc engine. The sensible thing to do would have been to buy a Japanese motorbike but I still believed British was best. The BSA Bantam, bought second-hand, was not a great buy. In fact, it was trouble from day one. I took it back to the dealer I had bought it from to fix a persistent fault. Then, when the fault recurred, I took it back again, and again, and again. Finally, I decided to take it back to BSA. Its Small Heath factory was not far away, and the bike was working well enough to get me there. When I chugged around the corner of the street to this heart of Britain's motorcycle industry, however, what I mainly encoun-tered was a large pile of rubble. Parts of the factory were still standing, but something terrible had clearly happened. What had happened was the failure of BSA, which went bankrupt in 1973 and, despite a government-inspired rescue and con-solidation of the industry, failed to cling to life for very long. BSA, once run by Sir Bernard Docker – the husband of the flamboyant Lady Docker – reflected the collapse of a once proud British industry.

By 1975 the entire British motorcycle industry was producing just 20,000 machines a year. A single Japanese company, Honda, by contrast, was making 2 million bikes annually, and quite a few of them were being sold to British customers. Though some British bikers stubbornly refused to buy Japanese motorcycles, they were the exception. The market was easily captured: it fell without a serious fight. In his book *The Strange Death of the British Motorcycle Industry*, Steve Koerner cites the Boston Consulting Group report *Strategy Alternatives for the British Motorcycle Industry*, commissioned by the Department of Industry following the bankruptcy of BSA and the government's attempt to rescue and restructure the industry. The report was used by the Labour government, under Harold Wilson, to justify its refusal to continue supporting an industry in its death throes. Koerner also records that it has gone on to become a teaching tool at the Harvard Business School, as an object lesson in entrepreneurial failure, and how not to run what had been an important sector of the economy. As for my BSA Bantam, I did eventually get it working properly, though perhaps it was never meant for a long life. I sold it to a fellow student. The last time I saw it, a few months later, it was in pieces on the kitchen table in his university lodgings.

Rubery Owen: Making everything no more

Rubery Owen, the diversified manufacturing firm that was such a presence during my childhood – 'you name it, we made it' – was one of the casualties of this grim period for British manufacturing. The 1970s was, in every respect, a difficult time for Rubery Owen. Sir Alfred Owen, who had had a heart attack in 1969, died in 1975 while still chairman of the firm. By then it was clear that Rubery Owen faced a battle for survival.

The recession of 1973–5, triggered by the quadrupling of the oil price by OPEC following the Yom Kippur War in October 1973, exposed the vulnerabilities of British manufacturing. Even Rubery Owen, with its long record of employee engagement and a reputation as a very good employer, was not immune to the poisonous industrial relations climate. In 1976 the company's workers at Darlaston went on a six-week strike, shutting down production. That strike was settled relatively quickly, but the writing was on the wall. Jobs were cut in an attempt to reduce costs as the firm's customer base also struggled, but to no avail. The 'winter of discontent' of 1978–9, which included a long national strike by engineering workers, left the company badly weakened. Margaret Thatcher, in her speech to the 1979 Conservative conference, blamed the strike for the loss of sales and, ultimately, jobs. 'We may never make up those sales and we shall lose some of the jobs which depended on them', she said. 'And who will send up a cheer? The Germans, the Japanese, the Swiss, the Americans. Instead of exporting engineering goods we shall have exported engineering jobs.' The final blow was struck by the 'industrial' recession of 1980–81, which saw a huge shake-out in Britain's manufacturing capacity, a combination of an over-strong pound, high inflation and large pay settlements and a dramatic downturn in demand for British industrial products.

In 1981 the Darlaston factory, the bustling centre of so much industrial activity across so many different products, but by the end down to just over 1,000 workers, was closed. According to the company's own account:

In 1981 the Company took the momentous decision to close its main Darlaston factory, with over 6,000 jobs having been lost during the course of the previous 5 years, and from that point on the company took the decision that it would pursue a strategy of 'orderly exit' from its traditional manufacturing and engineering businesses – successful and growing manufacturing businesses were sold to organisations with access to larger amounts of capital and therefore better placed to drive their growth, whilst other operations were rationalised or even closed.

Rubery Owen, big for a family firm, was in the end not big enough to survive. The last official photograph of the factory, in 1982, shows Sergeant George Peake, one of the firm's security officers, standing outside the soon to be demolished works entrance. Though Rubery Owen retained its office on the site, which it uses to this day, a modern observer would be hard pressed to recognise that this was once a huge industrial site. Instead of a vast network of industrial buildings there is a large housing estate, an attractively landscaped open space and a children's playground. In 1981 the giant bull-horn that announced the end of shifts went silent. Workers who used to pour out of the factory either endured years of unemployment or found something else to do, often taking jobs outside manufacturing. The houses Rubery Owen provided for its workers near where I grew up were sold off, either to the tenants or, more typically, to housing associations. The world changed, in a way that even ten years earlier would have been unthinkable.

David Owen, the eldest son of Sir Alfred Owen, was group chairman of Rubery Owen Holdings until 2010, having joined the family firm nearly half a century earlier, in 1961. At the time of writing he was a consultant to the board. When I spoke to him about what had happened to Rubery Owen's manufacturing business, it was clear that, though we were talking about the events of more than three decades earlier, there was still considerable sadness and regret, particularly about the closure of the Darlaston factory. How had it happened? As he put it, the fortunes of Rubery Owen were closely tied to those of its biggest customer, British Leyland, the car industry conglomerate formed from the merger of the British Motor Corporation and Leyland Trucks. Suddenly, most of the car marques that Rubery Owen had traditionally supplied were under the same ownership, and most of them were struggling. In the 1970s the import share of the UK car market rose from just over 14 per cent to nearly 57 per cent.

The firm could not, as Owen pointed out, switch its business to the fast-growing car manufacturers of France and Germany, who had long-term relationships with their own component suppliers. Even though Rubery Owen itself escaped most of the industrial anarchy of the period, that anarchy provided the worst possible advertisement for buying British, either in export markets or among traditionally loyal domestic buyers. British Leyland struggled and eventually died, though well after it had dragged down Rubery Owen. Owen is proud of the fact that, when the decision was taken to close down the Darlaston factory, he struck a deal with the unions to produce enough components to tide British Leyland and other customers over until they could find alternative suppliers. Like everything else the firm did, it was important for it to be done properly.

Rubery Owen is still in existence today, but the firm that made everything no longer manufactures anything. 'For a whole variety of reasons, what the company used to do is no longer done in this country any more. Our fortunes, as a supplier of components and other assemblies under long term contracts to manufacturers of finished goods, were largely in the hands of others and in many ways our hands were tied', it says in its own history. It sees itself, quite rightly, as a 'microcosm' of the British economy, its manufacturing activities (the last of which were disposed of in 1993) replaced in a smaller company by property, investment and a series of independent operating companies outside manufacturing. It did what was best for the business. It is hard not to feel more than a tinge of sadness.

The world is our workshop

Britain's relative decline as a manufacturing power can be seen in many ways: a sector that was once easily the most important to the economy, reduced, by the 2010s, to providing little more than a tenth of gross domestic product. Or, on the official workforce in employment measure, an eventual reduction in manufacturing employment to just over 2.5 million, a decline of more than 70 per cent in less than four decades, which contrasted sharply with the march of private and public services, in which employment by 2013 was 27 million. Perhaps there is no better indicator of Britain's change of manufacturing fortunes, however, than the trade figures. Britain, along with its industrial competitors, was a country the rest of the world came to for manufactured products. Even when other parts of the economy could not be relied on to pay their way, Britain's manufacturing exporters came good. Since the Industrial Revolution in the eighteenth century, Britain sold more manufactured goods to other countries than it imported from them. 'Made in Britain' meant quality, products built to last. A trade surplus in manufactures was one of the few guarantees when it came to Britain's economy, or so it seemed. Nobody expected modern-day Britain to produce all its own food. Though the Industrial Revolution was built on coal, iron ore and other mineral deposits, nobody questioned that many commodities and industrial raw materials had to be imported. Manufactured products were different. This was where, to use the language of economists, the country's comparative advantage lay. Or at least it did, until everything changed in 1983.

Battered by high inflation, industrial unrest, a strong pound and the painful 1980–81 recession, British industry succumbed in 1983 to something people had not thought possible: a trade deficit in finished manufactures. Throughout the 1970s, despite everything, British industry ran a trade surplus. As late as 1980, the trade surplus on finished manufactures was one of the highest on record, £4.1 billion. Two years later, the surplus had sunk to just £1.3 billion. That smaller surplus in 1982 was, however, one to remember. It was the last one, as of 2014, to be recorded. There may never be another one. In 1983 that first trade deficit in finished manufactures was £2.6 billion. By the end of the decade, in 1989, it was £12.9 billion. Two decades later, Britain was running an annual manufacturing deficit of nearly £60 billion, and the centuries of guaranteed surpluses were a very distant memory.

Why did it happen? There is a straightforward economic explanation for the shift from surplus into deficit, based on declining manufacturing capacity, a loss of competitiveness and an increasingly patchy reputation for reliability of product and ability to meet delivery times. Britain's anarchic industrial backdrop and a failure to keep up with developments in manufacturing processes which had transformed industry in competitor countries, alongside a long-run history of under-investment, are all part of the story. There was also, however, another important shift. When manufacturing employment dominated the economy, buying foreign goods appeared to be the equivalent of shooting yourself, or your neighbour, in the foot. The connection between buying British and both local and national prosperity was as clear as it could be. That changed. British households, planning the purchase of a new car, or television set, or washing machine, no longer felt honour-bound to buy British. The industry they saw portrayed on the news and read about in their newspapers was dominated by trade unionists apparently committed to driving the firms they worked for into the ground, and run by weak management. The more that employment shifted to the service sector, and away from manufacturing, the less people felt any direct connection with industry. No longer were British buyers prepared to give home-produced products the benefit of the doubt. And once the psychology of buying British broke down, the flood of imports was unabated.

In some cases the shift was rapid. British consumers had little hesitation in switching to Japanese Sony, Toshiba and JVC televisions (and later to Samsung and LG, from Korea). The country that had given the world its first televisions, produced by John Logie Baird's Baird Corporation, and which had been happy with Bush, Decca, Pye and Marconi sets for many years, had little hesitation in switching to cleverer and more reliable Far Eastern products. Eventually mass manufacture of televisions in Britain died out altogether. In some cases the change took longer. For decades Marks & Spencer used the fact that the vast majority of its products were made in Britain as a marketing tool. The relationship with the retailer kept large parts of the UK textiles industry in business, though some observers of the sector argue that long and lucrative Marks & Spencer contracts ultimately undermined the suppliers. Instead of developing distinctive brands and designs, and exploring export markets, they were happy to be anonymous suppliers under the Marks & Spencer St Michael brand. Whatever the truth of that, eventually even Marks & Spencer was forced to bow to the inevitable as it was undercut on price by its high-street rivals, who were importing their clothing from low-cost locations overseas. It held on longer than most, and drew a storm of protest from the unions when it changed strategy. By the 1990s Marks & Spencer could not claim that most of its products were made in Britain. Its St Michael brand (at one time there was also a St Margaret brand) was also soon dropped.

Not such a Black Country

Well before the end of this disastrous decade for manufacturing I had left the Black Country, via university, for London. But I came back often. In fact, in my first job, with Lloyds Bank, we were given two free return train tickets home each month, to avoid homesickness. There was something of a trade in these tickets, with some people's home towns more popular than others. I cannot pretend that Birmingham, the closest mainline station to West Bromwich, was an easy sell. Perhaps it was that I was not living there all the time, or maybe the changes in the Black Country were even more visible to those experiencing them directly, but this was a period of economic transformation, overwhelmingly for the worse. In the mid-1960s the larger West Midlands region in which the Black Country was located had an unemployment rate of less than 1 per cent, indicating an extraordinarily tight job market. As late as 1975, during the first of the two big recessions of the period, unemployment was under 3 per cent, and thus within the 2–3 per cent range economists regarded as consistent with full employment. That was one reason why those holiday jobs were always so easy to come by. Unemployment in the West Midlands rose in the second half of the 1970s, but it soared as a result of the recession of the early 1980s. By 1983 the West Midlands was an unemployment black spot, with an overall unemployment rate of 12.2 per cent and a male jobless rate of 14.5 per cent. To put those figures in perspective, the national unemployment rate at that time was below 10 per cent and the rate for men was under 12 per cent.

The change in fortunes was dramatic. The Black Country, like other parts of the West Midlands, had been part of a zone of prosperity during Britain's post-war golden age. It was to Black Country towns that workers flocked from other parts of Britain because the jobs were there. It was also in the Black Country and Birmingham that many immigrants chose to live, for similar reasons. The Black Country always needed workers, skilled and unskilled. Until the abrupt decline of manufacturing brought it plunging back down to earth, the West Midlands was one of two regions in Britain, along with the south-east, in which regional policy was used actively to direct economic development elsewhere in the country. The 1947 Town and Country Planning Act legislated for industrial development certificates, required for new factories. The 1965 Control of Office and Industrial Development Act supplemented the earlier legislation by introducing office development certificates. In the 1960s roughly a quarter of applications for industrial and commercial development in the West Midlands were being rejected, in the hope that those applying for them would take their projects elsewhere in the country. Less than two decades later, admittedly in a period when regional policy was being downgraded, every town in the Black Country, and many others in the West Midlands, was eligible for assistance under regional policy, regional development grants being available for firms investing in the area.

Anybody who lived through that period saw the most profound change. One of the last jobs I did as a student, in the mid-1970s, was with Birmingham Dairies in nearby Great Barr, delivering milk to factories all over the West Midlands. The factories had refrigerated milk machines, and the job was to replenish them with fresh cartons. The dairy depot always reminded me of something out of a Norman Wisdom film from the 1950s, particularly in the mornings, when the vans and floats in their distinctive red and yellow livery set forth on their rounds. There were twelve milk machines in Fort Dunlop alone and dozens more in factories large and small, on what was a 60-mile daily round. It was a considerable test of memory, given the complex geography of some of these factories. When one of the machines at Dunlop went unfilled for a week, because I had forgotten where it was, the workers threatened to go on strike, a threat taken seriously enough for me to be dispatched on a Friday evening to remedy the problem. It was, to be honest, a pretty horrible job. It is still quite hard to think, however, that within a few years many of those factories – and the workers employed in them – were gone. Every factory was a community, and usually a vibrant one, a hubbub of noise and banter. In every one of those factories there were human stories: stories of men and women who believed they had a job for life, people who often complained but for whom work, and taking home a pay packet at the end of the week, was their life. The abrupt decline of manufacturing, centred on its collapse in the Black Country and Birmingham, was an economic story, but it was also a huge collection of personal ones.

The Black Country I grew up in was a place of optimism and, though we may not have been fully aware of it at the time, of very considerable prosperity compared with the rest of Britain. In 1966 GDP per head in the West Midlands was second only to the south-east, and within sight of it. The West Midlands and south-east were the only two regions with GDP per head higher than the national average, and the south-east – including London – was only 6.5 per cent higher than the West Midlands. It did not last. By 1976 GDP per head in the West Midlands had slipped below the national average and behind Scotland (which was beginning to benefit from North Sea oil). Much worse was to come. By 1987, even after the worst of the 1980–81 recession and several years of industrial recovery (though after the miners' strike), the West Midlands was poorer, measured by GDP per head, than the south-east, East Anglia, the East Midlands, Scotland, the south-west, the northwest and Yorkshire & Humberside. By then, GDP per head in the south-east was almost 30 per cent higher than in the West Midlands. Of all the industrial areas in Britain, only the northeast and industrial South Wales had a comparable experience.

The Black Country's decline was clear from the numbers, but it was also evident in other ways. Industry did not, of course, die out entirely, but in far too many places where there had once been the bustle of workers desperate to clock in on time there were now chained-up factory gates. Where once there had been smoke and noise, there were now empty shells and broken windows. Years later these derelict factory sites would be cleared and turned into retail parks. One, the former F. H. Lloyd steel plant in Wednesbury, became one of IKEA's first British stores, but only after the site had been decontaminated, old mine shafts filled in and the famously polluted River Tame diverted. Later IKEA was joined on the same retail park by B&Q, Currys and furniture retailers. Long before then, another difference in the Black Country was discernible to everybody. Elihu Burritt's 'black by day and red by night' landscape was different. Some disused industrial land was grassed over and planted with trees. The Black Country became quieter, and it also became cleaner. Though clean air legislation had something to do with it, the loss of so much heavy industry was more important. The smogs were gone, and so were many of the smells. You could breathe the air of the Black Country again, though many of its residents had mixed feelings about that.

Never the same again

There is a story to be told about a later manufacturing revival in Britain, of a productivity miracle in the sector and of the country's success in attracting inward investment, particularly from the Far East. Manufacturing in Britain did not come to an end in the ten years from 1973 to 1983, though it would never again play as important a role in the economy as it had done before. The days of 'captains of industry' bestriding the national stage and leading the economic debate were waning fast. Indeed, the plaintive cries of industrialists during the 1980–81 recession, including that of Sir Michael Edwardes, the chief executive of British Leyland in 1980, that if North Sea oil was driving the pound to uncompetitive levels, it would be better to 'leave the bloody stuff in the ground', now look like blasts from a very distant past. Something fundamental changed. The days of British-owned mass manufacturing, of firms small, medium and large making things and profiting from doing so, were over. As with Rubery Owen, and its retreat from manufacturing, those who stayed in business saw better opportunities in other sectors. Those who continued to manufacture opted for strategies that involved moving manufacturing activities to lower-cost locations. Such decisions, made for sound economic reasons, began to have a cumulative effect. Successful manufacturing requires a critical mass of component suppliers and skilled workers. It requires a manufacturing culture. Some would argue that Britain never had a proper manufacturing culture, though that is stretching it too far. Whatever was there, though, was severely eroded, and remarkably quickly.

James Dyson, the engineer and inventor best known for his vacuum cleaners, put it well in his 2004 Richard Dimbleby Lecture. Dyson had attracted criticism for shifting his manufacturing facility from Wiltshire to Malaysia at the cost of more than 500 jobs. The reason, as he put it, was that his manufacturing costs were going up while selling prices were going down. Not only that, but the local council was raising objections to a proposed expansion of the factory. Underlying all this was that, for a variety of reasons, Britain had lost her critical mass in manufacturing, as Dyson recounted in his lecture when describing the development of an earlier product, a barrow with a ball that replaced the customary wheel. As he put it:

> In the 1970s, when I was developing the Ballbarrow, I needed some bent metal tubing. I got in my car and went to Birmingham. In the space of a few streets, I found workshops and suppliers who between them could provide the tubing, cut it, bend it and coat it. It was an extraordinarily vital environment. And it was absolutely essential to the small engineering entrepreneur. You might ask what happened to these British suppliers and subcontractors? Quite simply: we drove them out of existence. Employment and property laws made it difficult for them to take on extra staff and premises. They needed a tax regime that

appreciated the volatile nature of their business. Instead, governments imposed PAYE and hammered them with high interest rates, year after year. By the mid-1980s, most had gone to the wall.

Did Margaret Thatcher destroy manufacturing?

When Margaret Thatcher died, in April 2013, the response was a mixed one. Some detected a north–south divide in the warmth of the tributes and the scale of the criticism, with the Midlands somewhere in between. The Scottish *Daily Record*, quoting lines from the Proclaimers' song 'Letter from America' – 'Bathgate no more, Linwood no more, Methil no more, Irvine no more', citing Scottish industrial plants that had been killed off in the 1980s – put it crisply: 'Thatcher swept like a wrecking ball through the mines, the steel industry, the car factories, shipbuilding and engineering and oversaw the demise of the communities which had built their livelihoods around them', it said. It was a common theme, particularly on the political left. 'Thatcher effectively shut down British manufacturing, much of it forever', said the left-wing magazine *Red Pepper*. 'In its place, she turned to the banks and the City, making their wildest dreams come true with the financial "Big Bang". We know how that ended.' Tony Benn, Thatcher's old political and ideological enemy, told the USA's Public Broadcasting Service that not only had she destroyed British manufacturing but she had also reduced the British people to serfdom, under the control of huge multinational corporations. A line from Morrissey, the former singer in The Smiths, saying simply 'she destroyed the British manufacturing industry', became briefly popular, though it was apparently not written in response to her death.

I used to think that the Thatcher government, in its early days, had much to do with the decline of manufacturing. The figures, showing that industry had recovered much of the lost ground of the mid-1970s before the devastating 1980–81 recession hit, appeared to bear out that interpretation. Unemployment in the West Midlands was still relatively low in the late 1970s, only surging to the highest levels since the 1930s in that grim period of the early 1980s. Mistakes were made in that period of early Thatcher monetarism and the biggest, pointed out by Sir Michael Edwardes and her own personal economic adviser Sir Alan Walters, was the failure to recognise that the strength of sterling, which in four years from late 1976 rose from $1.60 to $2.40, was not only a huge burden for exporters but also represented over-tight monetary policy. In some ways the relative decline of manufacturing, in which many of the country's deep industrial relations had been concentrated, made her union reform agenda easier to push through. Nigel Lawson, her second chancellor of the exchequer, provoked anger when he suggested that the relative decline of manufacturing in Britain was part of a global phenomenon and did not matter as long as the country had successful service exporters. Lord Weinstock, of GEC, in response, evoked a future in which Britain would become 'a curiosity', providing the world with the Beefeaters at the Tower of London and the Changing of the Guard, and little else.

Any complete reading of the 1973–83 decline of British manufacturing has to recognise, however, that the collapse of the early 1980s was the end-result of a very long process. The seeds were sown in industry's failure to modernise and adapt even in the post-war golden age. When times were good, those who ran British manufacturing fell into an easy complacency. Even more than that, the extreme turbulence of the 1970s, with industrial anarchy, a manufacturing sector sent into shock by a quadrupling (and more) of world oil prices and the belated recognition that the world no longer owed British industry a living, spoke of a manufacturing sector in deep trouble.

If Rubery Owen tells the story well, it is notable that its programme of deep job cuts, in an attempt to preserve its manufacturing plant in Darlaston, began many years before Margaret Thatcher was in Downing Street. Manufacturing in Britain was riding for a fall. The recession of the early 1980s may have pushed it over the edge, but the over-manned and unproductive parts of industry would have gone anyway.

When Margaret Thatcher died, the local response in the Black Country was nuanced. The Wolverhampton *Express & Star* recalled a visit by her to the Servis washing-machine factory in Darlaston, where she laughed and joked with trade union officials and workers. Thirty years on, the factory was no more, but it had been, said the newspaper, a victim of globalisation, not Thatcherism. A few years later, the paper recalled, when in the run-up to the 1987 election she was blamed by the Labour leader of Dudley council for the area's high unemployment, her response was that her government had no choice but to tackle restrictive practices and over-manning. The disappointment was that, having tacked these long-standing shortcomings, manufacturing industry's painful adjustment was not followed by a brighter future. Economists like to talk of the process of 'creative destruction', a term coined by Joseph Schumpeter, in which new and vibrant firms emerge, phoenix-like, from the ashes of collapse. During a terrible decade there was plenty of destruction in British manufacturing, but there was not enough of a subsequent revival.

3

Back from the brink

If we can keep our heads – and our nerve – the long-
awaited economic miracle is in our grasp. Britain can
achieve in the Seventies what Germany and France
achieved in the Fifties and Sixties.

Denis Healey, chancellor of the exchequer,
Sunday Telegraph, 4 July 1976

In 2012 the BBC ran a four-part series, written and presented
by the historian Dominic Sandbrook, called simply *The 70s*.
This was not a trip down memory lane by a presenter reliving
his younger days. Sandbrook, as he was quick to point out, was
not born until October 1974, and his personal memories of the
period were sketchy. The programmes, however, including a
lot of news footage accompanied by lavish helpings of the pop
music of the 1970s, were riveting. For me they produced two
reactions. The first was nostalgia, even for the clothing fashions
of the time. The second was a sense of wonderment. How did
we ever live through such chaos and uncertainty? How did we
live through the terrorist bombings? These, mainly by the Irish
Republican Army (IRA), began with a bomb placed in the Post
Office Tower (now the BT Tower) in 1971, and included the

devastating Birmingham pub bombings of 1974. Those bomb-ings, in two pubs, The Mulberry Bush and the Tavern in the Town, killed 21 people and injured 182 others. The Birmingham pub bombings were not the first fatal IRA attack on the main-land. There had been bombings in Aldershot and Guildford, as well as on the M62 motorway. But the Birmingham attacks were the biggest, and their effect was as dramatic as the suicide bombings on the London transport system on 7 July 2005. In some respects their effect was more shocking. The victims were innocent, mainly young, people, with no connection to the armed forces or police. After Birmingham it seemed that everybody was fair game to the terrorists. The fact that in the subsequent crackdown the convictions of those charged over the attacks, the Birmingham Six, were subsequently found to have been unsafe, only compounded the agony of the relatives of the victims.

Britain in the 1970s was less safe and less stable than for many years. The fabric of society was falling apart, and so was the economy. How did we cope with 27 per cent inflation, the rate hit briefly in 1975? How did we cope with strikes, not just in Britain's factories but just about everywhere else? Some did not cope too well. My first job after graduating was with Lloyds Bank, writing economic reports. The head of our small depart-ment, who had spent a lifetime with the bank and actually wore a bowler hat to work, would arrive most days red-faced and fuming about the iniquities of the unions who had disrupted his journey. It took half an hour, sometimes more, to calm him down. Most people, however, did adjust. The abnormal can seem perfectly normal very quickly.

Weird and wonderful

People who lived through the 1970s will have different perspec-tives, but for anybody coming of age in that decade, as I did, the disruption and danger came to seem unremarkable, tragic though that danger was for those caught up in it. When you are young, moreover, disruption adds to the spice of life. Only as you get older does it become a terrible inconvenience. The fact that capitalism in Britain appeared to be teetering on the edge was interesting but not as alarming to the young as it was for many of our elders. Not only that, but the era, like other periods of momentous economic and political change, was one of great creativity. Above all, for young people at least, it was usually fun.

Dominic Sandbrook picked up on this in his book on the first half of the 1970s, *State of Emergency*, quoting from the diary of an Essex teenager, whose obsessions were David Bowie, Suzi Quatro and her (the teenager's) boyfriend, not the fact that the country was falling apart. Nor was she untypical. 'What this teenager's diary reminds us is that, for most people, daily life never approached the extremes often commemorated in histories of the 1970s', Sandbrook wrote.

> Even though the language of British politics was becoming increasingly aggressive, most voters were more interested in the new series of *On the Buses*, the supermarket opening down the road and their forthcoming holiday on the Costa del Sol. And, even during the dreadful economic crisis of 1973–4, most still led relatively comfortable, affluent lives.

People can cope with appalling economic circumstances. Shortly after the 2007–9 financial crisis I went to Riga in Latvia. In the preceding twelve months the country's economy had collapsed, its gross domestic product falling by a fifth. I had expected a scene of devastation but encountered near-normality. There were times in the 1970s when Britain was a long way from normal, but we lived with it. Perhaps, as well as that, we did not quite believe it. It took time, as Sandbrook suggests, before people quite realised that the good times were over. Sir Alan Budd, a former government chief economic adviser, was fond of using the analogy of a famous cartoon to describe the delayed reaction many have to profound economic change. Like Wile E Coyote running off the edge of a cliff and only belatedly realising that there is nothing beneath him, so we did not realise we were facing a big drop in actual and relative living standards.

Unemployment rose a lot in the 1970s, the claimant count climbing above 1 million in early 1976 and not falling below that level again for twenty-five years, but it really rose in the 1980s, reaching more than 3 million. It did not immediately dawn on people that high unemployment was the shape of things to come. Had they realised it, perhaps there would have been less industrial anarchy. The 1970s, the decade when it fell apart for Britain's manufacturers, was a turning point. Until then it was possible to paper over the cracks, to believe that the economy was still fundamentally sound and that the world would always provide us with a good living. It was also possible to believe, even two decades after the Suez crisis of 1956, that Britain was a formidable world power, based on her economic strength. The longer the 1970s went on, the more difficult it was even for optimists to believe that.

Boom

In the early 1970s the world economy boomed. The international monetary framework established at Bretton Woods in 1944 may have been breaking up and an energy crunch looming, but the mood was gloriously upbeat. The post-war golden age ended in a spectacular party. The advanced economies of the Paris-based Organisation for Economic Co-operation and Development (OECD) grew by 6.4 per cent in 1973. Britain went one better, with growth of 7.4 per cent, easily the strongest in modern times. The backdrop was a familiar one: an attempt by the government to prevent a politically damaging rise in unemployment. Anthony Barber, unexpectedly elevated to the role of chancellor in Edward Heath's Conservative government, was an unusual politician by modern standards in that he had a proper post-political career, as chairman of Standard Chartered, the bank. Visitors to the chairman's office were often greeted by John Major, a future chancellor and prime minister but then a bank employee and a senior aide to Barber. Barber's political career is remembered for one thing only: the 'Barber boom'.

During 1971 unemployment began to rise strongly, outweighing concern about rising inflation. Unemployment increased by more than 250,000 in 1971, and the 'headline' total, including school-leavers, rose above 900,000 late in the year, and threatened to break through 1 million, then an unheard-of figure for the post-war period. Inflation also edged up, to more than 9 per cent by the end of 1971. To economists brought up in the tradition of the Phillips curve – a theory which states that rising unemployment tends to be inversely related to (wage) inflation – this was a puzzle. For politicians, with the full employment of the 1950s and 1960s still close at hand, unemployment was a problem that had to be tackled urgently.

The high inflation of the 1970s was partly the result of the big oil price hikes that began in 1973. Much of it was, however, self-inflicted. Changes in the banking system that gave the banks greater freedom to expand credit, known as Competition and Credit Control, were combined with what, at the time, were aggressive reductions in interest rates. Bank Rate was cut to 5 per cent during 1971, alongside rising inflation. The era of negative real interest rates – interest rates below inflation – had begun. It was to last for most of the next decade. Loose monetary policy went hand in hand with a relaxation of fiscal policy, a traditional Keynesian stimulus as used by every previous post-war government. Barber cut personal and company taxes in his 1971 budget, expanded public works programmes and repaid post-war credits – compulsory personal savings for the 1939–45 war effort. The result was a significant injection of demand into the economy.

Nor was this deemed enough by the government. The pound was floated on 23 June 1972, six months after the historic December 1971 agreement at the Smithsonian Institution in Washington DC to suspend the convertibility of the dollar into gold, which effectively signalled the end of the Bretton Woods system. Sterling immediately fell by 7 per cent against the dollar, and commentators said it was not so much floating as sinking. Barber, though, was clear. Preserving sterling's value was a lower priority than achieving faster growth. He was going for growth, and if a weaker pound was a by-product – and helped that process along – so be it. It was a popular move. Many economists had urged the government not to repeat the errors of the Wilson government before the 1967 devaluation but instead to float the pound. If the aim was to produce a boom, it worked.

The money supply, which the International Monetary Fund (IMF) had insisted be targeted and kept under control after the 1967 devaluation, began to expand rapidly. Bank lending, freed from controls, surged. Net bank lending in 1972 was five times its 1970 level. Instead of fretting, Barber abandoned the IMF targets for domestic credit expansion, arguing that inflows of 'hot' money from abroad rendered them redundant. It became a monetary free-for-all. One measure of the money supply, M3, surged by 60 per cent in just two years. Astonishingly, for most economists at the time this was not a particular concern. A few monetarists, including Gordon Pepper in the City of London and the academics David Laidler and Alan Walters – who later became Margaret Thatcher's personal economic adviser

– warned that such a loss of control of the money supply would have severe inflationary consequences but were at first ignored. Eventually the government responded, raising interest rates to 9 per cent by the end of 1972 and 13 per cent by the end of 1973. The high-inflation era was under way, and so was the period of high interest rates.

Booms tend to turn to bust, to end in tears, and in the second half of 1973 the economy began to slide into recession, even before the effect of high oil prices, as a result of the rise in interest rates. The inflationary consequences of the monetary boom, meanwhile, were yet to come through. Britain was about to experience the worst of all worlds.

Nineteen seventy-four, by which time the economy was firmly in recession, was one of only two years in the twentieth century in which there were two general elections (the other being 1910). The first of these, in February 1974 – the 'Who runs Britain?' election – was, on the face of it an act of collective madness by voters, voting in a union-dominated Labour government, albeit a minority one, headed by Harold Wilson, at a time when the damage being done by union militancy was plain to see. If all elections are ultimately decided by the economy, however, the Conservatives deserved to lose. The mismanagement of the economy in the early 1970s was extraordinary. The February 1974 election coincided with the three-day week, energy-saving measures imposed by the government to eke out Britain's power-generation capacity in the face of a miners' strike. Factories were permitted only three days of electricity consumption per week, though there were exemptions for those where continuous production was necessary. Lighting in shops was limited, and at night shop windows were no longer illuminated. One Conservative minister suggested people should share a bath to conserve energy. He probably meant bathwater, but that did not prevent much ribaldry. For me and for many others the most noticeable effect of the three-day week, which lasted from January to March 1974, was that television was required to shut down at 10.30 at night. The reasons may have been known, but it did not smack of competent government. Heath lost. In the second election of 1974, in October, Wilson tried to convert his minority position into a working majority. He won again, but with a barely workable majority of only three.

A banking crisis

During the global financial crisis of 2007–9 commentators often observed that this was the first time in the modern era that Britain's banking system had come under serious threat. Certainly that crisis was the most serious in the modern era. It was far from being the only one, however; there was also a banking crisis in the early 1970s. Its roots lay in two things: easy money and financial reform. The Competition and Credit Control changes allowed mainstream banks to reclaim their traditional markets. In response, 'fringe' or 'secondary' banks, which had expanded during the period when lending by the high street banks was tightly controlled, sought new areas of business. Overwhelmingly they chose property.

Money was easily available in the early 1970s, thanks to the government's cavalier attitude to the money supply. Most of the fringe banks did not need customer deposits; rather, they obtained their funds from the rapidly expanding money markets, and from banks, respectable companies and apparently conservative financial institutions in search of a better return. The search for return, for yield, usually features in the story of most financial crises. The fact that this money was being lent on to property companies and speculators appears to have caused few qualms, as long as it provided a decent return. Pumped up by all this money, the property bubble grew bigger and bigger. Bubbles tend to burst, and this was no exception. When, in the

middle of 1973, the government belatedly reacted to the inflationary explosion of the money supply by raising interest rates,
a commercial property market already reeling from a decision
a few months earlier to freeze business rents went into sharp
reverse. The bubble popped.

The first secondary banking casualty was the publicly
quoted London and County Securities. Unusually for a fringe
bank, it had attracted a high proportion of its deposits from
the general public. In a forewarning of the problems encoun-
tered by Northern Rock which marked the start of Britain's
later banking crisis in 2007, London and County found in
November 1973 that it could no longer obtain funds from the
money markets. The City, which had had its deep suspicions
about London and County for some time, began to look criti-
cally at other fringe banks which, even more than London and
County, were addicted to funds from the money markets.

Though the crisis was concentrated in the fringe banks, the
fear was that it would spread to mainstream institutions. This,
of course, is what happened more than three decades later, in
2007–9, when problems that first emerged in obscure hedge
funds soon affected first the big investment banks and then
the high street banks. As the crisis in 1973–4 spread, at one
stage National Westminster (then an independent bank) had
to issue a public statement to say that it was safe. The fear for
NatWest, and the other banks, was that there would be a run
on all UK banks by foreigners concerned about the stability of
the financial system. The response from the Bank of England
was to call in the big banks, get them to agree on a support
package for their weaker brethren and hope for the best. Over
the Christmas and New Year holiday at the end of 1973 the
Control Committee of the Bank of England and the London
and Scottish Clearing Banks, popularly known as 'the lifeboat', was set up. Its aim was simple: to provide liquidity for
the fringe banks when the markets would not, in order to save

them from collapse. The lifeboat was launched in time for the difficult year of 1974.

It helped, but the crisis did not go away and, indeed, worsened in the summer of 1974, when doubts began to emerge over the First National Finance Corporation and United Dominions Trust, finance companies with large property interests. Not only were these different from the fringe banks but they were also a lot larger, and providing support for them threatened to sink the lifeboat. Alarmed by this, the banks told the Bank of England in August 1974 that they were setting a limit of £1.2 billion on the size of the lifeboat, which was equivalent to 40 per cent of their combined capital and reserves. Any more, they argued, and their own existence would be threatened. As was to be the case three decades later, the Bank stepped in to provide support over the winter of 1974–5 once the £1.2 billion limit was reached. It also undertook two rescues, of Slater Walker Securities at the end of 1975 (the Slater was Jim Slater, a well-known investor, and the Walker was Peter Walker, a senior Conservative politician) and of Edward Bates & Sons in May 1976. But, though there was worse to come for the economy, the crisis abated and the size of the lifeboat shrank from the spring of 1975.

The banking crisis of this period was not confined to Britain. In New York the Franklin National Bank came near to closure in 1974. The Bankhaus Herstatt in West Germany did close, following large foreign exchange losses. There were large losses at the Westdeutsche Landesbank, the Union Bank of Switzerland and the Lugano branch of Lloyds Bank International, though the last of these was due to fraud. As Western economies reeled, their banking systems came under intense strain. The international financial system came within a whisker of collapse. It survived, but only just.

Stagflation

The backdrop to the woes of Britain's manufacturing industry during the 1970s and early 1980s was one of huge economic turbulence. Across the Western world the post-war golden age was swept away in a burst of high inflation, combined with recession. Countries had experienced inflation, and they had experienced stagnation, though neither in recent memory on the scale they suffered in the 1970s. What was new, in the modern era, was to suffer both at the same time: stagnation and inflation or, in what was then a newly coined phrase, 'stagflation'. Though the expression dated back to 1965 – the Conservative politician Iain Macleod used it in a speech in the House of Commons – it came into its own in the 1970s. Macleod, had it not been for his untimely death in 1970, might have had to deal with it. He was appointed chancellor of the exchequer by Sir Edward Heath following the surprise Conservative victory in the June 1970 election but, in a rare modern example of a senior politician dying while in office, was first rushed to hospital with appendicitis just a month after the election and then, thirteen days later, suffered a fatal heart attack following his discharge from hospital. He was chancellor for just six weeks and only fifty-six when he died. He was one of the central figures of the Conservative Party at the time and a huge influence on the design of policy in opposition. One of the great 'what if?' questions is whether things would have turned out differently had he remained chancellor. His successor, as noted above, was Anthony Barber.

In the 1950s and 1960s inflation in the Western world was typically in low single figures. Though growth was strong, sharply rising productivity kept a lid on labour costs. Commodity price pressures were weak, only boosted by episodes such as the Korean War in the early 1950s. Energy was cheap. The price of crude oil varied between $1 and $2.50 a barrel between 1945 and 1972, though it and commodity prices more generally began to move higher in the late 1960s and early 1970s. All this changed in 1973, when, in response to the Yom Kippur War, and American support for Israel, OPEC announced a rise in oil prices, a cut in production and a suspension of oil sales to the USA. The Iranian revolution of 1978–9, which resulted in the overthrow and exile of the Shah of Iran, completed the picture. The world oil price, which averaged $11.58 a barrel in 1974, rose to $36.83 in 1980. The cheap energy era was over, and so, for a time, was the period of low inflation. OECD inflation rose to more than 14 per cent in 1974 (and hit an average of nearly 15 per cent in 1980). In the ten years from 1974 OECD inflation averaged more than 11 per cent.

A fireside chat

This was the period when, for the first time in more than two centuries, the West feared that economic power was drifting away. In 1974, in the wake of the oil crisis, the USA established the Library Group, an informal gathering, or 'fireside chat', involving senior officials from the leading industrial nations: the USA itself, Japan, West Germany, Britain and France. It met in the library of the White House: hence the name. The following year the French president, Valéry Giscard d'Estaing, convened a summit at Rambouillet, near Paris, for the leaders, finance and foreign ministers of the Library Group, plus Italy. It was attended by, among others, Gerald Ford and Henry Kissinger of the USA, Britain's Harold Wilson, James Callaghan and Denis Healey, and Helmut Schmidt and Hans-Dietrich Genscher of West Germany. Italy's delegation was led by its president, Aldo Moro, who three years later was kidnapped and assassinated by the Red Brigades. The six countries, in a communiqué, expressed their joint determination 'to overcome high unemployment, continuing inflation and serious energy problems'. It was to be a long haul, though the Rambouillet summit, which was relatively low-key despite the guest list, set in train a series of increasingly expensive and over-ambitious such summits. The Group of Seven (Canada was soon added to the membership) became the G8 (Russia joined in the 1990s, following the collapse of Communism), but at time of writing had reverted to the G7, in protest at Russia's 2014 actions in Ukraine and annexation of Crimea. The 'fireside chats' were replaced by huge, prestige-building events, costing enormous sums of money. Communiqués were prepared in advance by the summit 'sherpas' – officials who did the preparatory work – and photo opportunities became as important as, if not more important than, any decisions. Gifts were lavished on the participants and, only slightly less impressively, on journalists.

Sometimes, as at Margaret Thatcher's 1984 G7 summit in London, the politicians were well looked after at Lancaster House, while the journalists had to make do with the Connaught Rooms in Holborn, some less than impressive British catering and polyester commemorative ties supplied by Burton. Mostly, however, governments put on the style. The 2000 Okinawa G8 summit in Japan was said to be the most costly in four decades of summitry, with an estimated cost of $750 million – some estimates suggested much more – after which, embarrassment or good taste kicked in and the events were scaled back a little. I particularly remember two. One was the Venice G7 summit of 1987, days before Mrs Thatcher's third general election victory, which became part of her successful campaign. Neil Kinnock, her Labour opponent, could not compete with a prime minister rubbing shoulders with world leaders. The other was the 1997 Denver summit, shortly after Tony Blair's landslide election victory. The prime ministerial entourage, along with accompanying press – including myself – flew to Denver by Concorde; supersonic across the Atlantic and then what seemed like painfully slowly and – inside the plane – noisily, for the rest of the journey. The USA, without its own supersonic passenger plane, did not take kindly to sonic booms. The Blairs, not yet suspicious of the media in the way they would later become, mingled happily with journalists on both legs of the journey. The world was curious to see them as they were warmly welcomed by Bill and Hillary Clinton. The American television networks were fascinated. It may have been their finest hour.

That was all to come. In the 1970s the big question was how the advanced economies would adapt to the end of the cheap energy era. That was the question at Giscard's 1975 summit. The answer was that some adapted better than others. Britain's policymakers, not for the first time, got it seriously wrong. Britain went into the oil crisis in a vulnerable state and then took decisions that added to that vulnerability.

Goodbye, Great Britain

If the West as a whole had problems, brought on or exposed by the end of the cheap energy era, Britain had much bigger ones. When Harold Wilson and his chancellor, Denis Healey, travelled to France in November 1975 for the Rambouillet summit, Britain's inflation rate had hit 26.9 per cent the previous August and was still more than 25 per cent. Though price changes had been much more volatile in the distant past, often reflecting agricultural harvests, official figures show only two years when inflation in Britain was higher than in 1975: 1800 and 1917. Nineteen seventy-five, when inflation appeared to be out of control, was a terrible year for the British economy. In April, in what looks like an unusually well-judged call, the *Wall Street Journal*, then the oracle for American investors, ran the unforgettable headline 'Goodbye, Great Britain' and advised its readers to get out. If 1975 was a bad year, there was worse to come, and it was to come very quickly: 1976 was even worse.

The *Wall Street Journal* had picked up what was happening

to the British economy, and it was not alone. Since the war, Western governments had operated Keynesian demand management policies, adjusting taxation and government spending in a counter-cyclical way, and thus trying to smooth the extent of the cycle; by dampening booms and heading off busts. If that was the strategy during the golden age up until 1973, the policy followed by Wilson and Healey from 1974 to 1976 was Keynesian demand management on steroids. They really believed, it appeared, that you could spend your way out of recession. The numbers are astonishing. In the fiscal year 1974–5 public spending rose 35 per cent in cash terms, or nearly 13.5 per cent in real terms. In 1975–6 there was a further strong rise, of almost 25 per cent, in public spending in cash terms, although most of this was eaten up by the sky-high inflation rate. The strategy was well described by Joel Barnett, the inventor of the Barnett formula for determining government spending in Scotland, Wales and Northern Ireland and chief secretary to the Treasury at the time. Barnett, who had direct responsibility for public expenditure under Healey, wrote in his book *Inside the Treasury* about the surge in public spending:

> The Chancellor had made the fundamental decision to react to the oil crisis in a different way from the Germans and Japanese, and indeed from many other countries. Instead of cutting expenditure to take account of the massive oil price increases of 1973, which in our case cut living standards by some 5 per cent, the Chancellor decided to maintain our expenditure plans and borrow to meet the deficit.

And borrow he did. The public sector borrowing requirement (PSBR) – the amount that the government has to borrow to bridge the gap between expenditure and tax revenues – increased sharply. The PSBR had been eliminated by the previous Labour chancellor, Roy Jenkins, to the point of generating a budget surplus in 1969–70. It had risen under Anthony Barber, reaching £4.5 billion in 1973–4. The first two years of the new Labour government pushed the PSBR up to £8 billion in 1974–5 and £10.6 billion in 1975–6. It was a gamble that failed spectacularly. Other countries, which had adopted more restrictive policies in the wake of the OPEC oil price hike, recovered more quickly and escaped the worst of the inflationary excesses suffered by Britain. West Germany, traditionally the most inflation-averse of countries, held its inflation rate to no more than 7 per cent. In the USA the high was 11 per cent. Other countries also, unsurprisingly, avoided the extreme damage to their public finances of the kind suffered by Britain.

There are certain periods you look back on and wonder how people could have been quite so misguided. In this case the politics of the period contributed. Britain had a rampant trade union movement cock-a-hoop after defeating the Conservatives in the 'Who runs Britain?' election of February 1974. Harold Wilson was a prime minister who, though it was not known at the time, was preparing to stand down before the 1974–9 parliament reached its mid-point. He resigned in March 1976, to be succeeded by James Callaghan (chancellor at the time of the November 1967 sterling devaluation). Wilson left behind a puzzled country and one of the most controversial honours lists in years, sometimes called the 'lavender list' because it was drawn up by one of his advisers on lavender notepaper. It included honours for one businessman, Sir Eric Miller, who committed suicide a year later while under investigation for fraud, and a peerage for another, Lord Kagan, who was convicted for fraud in 1980. It was that kind of period.

One common way for economists to think about economic policy is by reference to the targets of policy and the instruments available to achieve those targets. If four of the main targets were full employment, low inflation, external balance (a sustainable balance of payments position) and internal balance (a manageable budget deficit), this was a time when they were wildly missed. Not only was inflation high, unemployment soaring and public borrowing at record peacetime highs but the current account of the balance of payments was in large deficit. The rise in world oil prices pushed Britain into a current account deficit of 4 per cent of gross domestic product in 1974 and, though it subsequently improved, Britain was dogged by twin deficits – budget and balance of payments – in its efforts to cope with the oil shock. It was no surprise that there was an economic and financial crisis; the surprise would have been if there had not been one.

Nor was the huge increase in public spending in 1974 and 1975 a classic Keynesian response. Men were not set to work digging holes or building roads. Rather, most of the big expansion in spending was on welfare – pensions, social security and unemployment benefit – and soaring public sector pay. The public sector was not alone. In the industrial relations climate of the time employers had only limited success in holding back the tide of rising wages. Average earnings rose by 26.5 per cent in 1975, prompting the adoption of a statutory incomes policy in July of that year. The damage, however, had been done. With the recession hitting output, Britain's unit labour costs – wages and salaries per unit of output – rose by 30 per cent in 1975. This was the reality behind the collapse of British industry.

It was a grim cocktail of appalling industrial relations, sky-high inflation, fast-falling competitiveness and deep problems for both the public finances and the balance of payments. Nor was it obvious how the spiral would end. Some things, and some decisions, look better with hindsight. The economic policy of the 1974–76 period, however, will probably never undergo such a re-evaluation, and quite rightly. Goodbye, Great Britain had it about right.

In the arms of the IMF

Though I did meet him, I never really got to know Denis Healey, Labour chancellor in one of the worst and most humiliating years for Britain in the modern era. A long-standing friend of mine was Derek Scott, a fine economist who worked as his special adviser. He always insisted that Healey was much misunderstood and that other chancellors would have buckled under the kind of pressure he faced, though the fact that much of that pressure was self-inflicted somewhat undermines the claim. I also knew many others who cut their teeth in Downing Street or the Treasury in that period. Healey also made his public and private views well known, not least in his entertaining autobiography, *The Time of My Life*. Healey was the chancellor who had to turn to the IMF to bail out Britain's economy, though he was a surprisingly popular figure, with poll ratings some of his successors could only envy. His good-natured response to being one of the main targets of the comedy impressionist Mike Yarwood, one of Britain's biggest stars in the 1970s, helped.

Britain had been instrumental in the establishment of the IMF at the Bretton Woods conference in 1944, even if the postwar international monetary system was not the design favoured by Lord Keynes, the UK's representative. Few in 1944, or subsequently, could have imagined that its biggest rescue, overseen and heavily influenced by the US Treasury, would be of Britain. Healey, once he saw the light, was a brave but ultimately misguided chancellor who raged against the irresponsibility of many in his party. His attitude to the IMF rescue had three broad strands. The first was that he had been badly advised by Treasury officials from the moment he took over at the Treasury, the second that the IMF rescue was triggered by unreliable official data and even more unreliable official forecasts. The third was that he could not wait for the moment when the IMF would be out of his hair, which he called 'sod off day'.

There was some truth in both of Healey's first two

complaints. The Treasury, alarmed by a government apparently prepared to preside over runaway wage inflation and profligate public spending, had an uneasy relationship with its chancellor, culminating in its advice in March 1976 to secure a gradual depreciation in the value of sterling. A planned gentle depreciation turned into a rout, which made the IMF rescue both inevitable and necessary. As for the numbers: the air of crisis was exacerbated by misleading figures suggesting, wrongly, that public spending had risen to more than 60 per cent of GDP. It did not, though it did reach the equivalent of 49 per cent of GDP in 1975–6, figures now show – a record then and a record now. The public finances were, by any measure, in need of repair, with the budget deficit – public sector net borrowing – reaching a post-war high (at the time) of 7 per cent of GDP. There were to be larger deficits later, in the early 1990s and in the aftermath of the global financial crisis of 2007–9. At the time, however, the impression was of an economy out of control and of a desperate need for a rescue: not just the $3.9 billion IMF loan but also, more importantly, the external discipline that the loan imposed, with deep spending cuts insisted on by the IMF and William Simon, the US Treasury secretary, who acted as a stern midwife during the lengthy negotiations that culminated in the bail-out. The IMF's team was headed by a former Bank of England official, Alan Whittome. His deputy was David Finch, an Australian, and the IMF's managing director, Johannes Witteveen, was also heavily involved. Simon, with the support of his under-secretary, Ed Yeo, and the chairman of the Federal Reserve board, Arthur Burns, was keen to pursue a 'hands-on' approach to British economic policy. Simon, who viewed Britain as something approaching a lost cause, made an unscheduled visit to London in November 1976 to help oversee matters. That demonstrated how far power had shifted from Britain. A country that once dictated terms to the rest of the world now had to accept the conditions insisted on by others.

It could have gone differently. Anybody who wants a glimpse into the battles of the time should look at the Cabinet papers of the period, labelled on every page 'Top Secret' but now released under the thirty-year rule. On 22 November 1976 Healey set out the plan, which included a £3 billion cut in government spending, which he said was necessary. The cut, equivalent to a real-terms drop of 4 per cent, came through in the 1977–8 fiscal year. 'Having considered all the possibilities, I am convinced that we need to make a significant adjustment in fiscal policy, to meet the situation', Healey set out in his memorandum. 'And it is clear from my discussions with them that the IMF team here share that judgment.' Not everybody agreed with Healey, including not everybody in the Cabinet. A week later another memorandum was put up for discussion, this time from Tony Benn, the Energy Secretary, whose death in 2014 produced tributes of the kind normally reserved for former prime ministers. Benn, in his memorandum, headed 'The Real Choices Facing the Cabinet', set out what he described as his alternative economic strategy. The 'IMF road' would be deflationary and would, he said, imply a 'surrender from that moment to any demands that may be made upon us whatever their consequences for the British people'. His strategy involved the imposition of tough import controls to achieve 'a secure home market', a reduction in interest rates and legislation to provide the government with new reserve powers to intervene more heavily in industry. It was not quite a command economy, but it was not far away from it. But Benn's alternative strategy was not adopted. The Cabinet, with some trepidation, stuck with Healey.

1976

Nineteen seventy-six was one of the most important years for the British economy in the modern era, and not just because of the IMF rescue. The year began with hurricane-force winds but is mainly remembered now for the long and relentless summer heatwave. As a newcomer to commuting by Tube in London, I remember the discomfort, and the claustrophobia, to this day. Nineteen seventy-six also saw a mysterious prime ministerial resignation by Harold Wilson, the death of Chairman Mao in China and the election of Jimmy Carter in the USA. The Wurzels, a West Country novelty act, had a big hit with a song about a combine harvester, and *The Muppet Show* was launched on British television. Somewhat bizarrely, given the economic backdrop, some years later the New Economics Foundation declared that 1976 was Britain's best year, measured by what it described as its measure of domestic progress, as distinct from GDP. In reality, it was anything but. In 1976 too, and this was to prove significant, Milton Friedman, the father of modern monetarism, was awarded the Nobel Prize (the Bank of Sweden prize) for economics.

One of the conditions of the IMF loan, as well as deep spending cuts, was that the government had to adopt targets for the growth in the money supply, and what at the time was the sterling M3 measure of it. The money supply, remember, surged during the Barber boom. Three years before the Thatcher government was elected, willingly embracing monetarism, the Labour government under Callaghan adopted a version of monetarism, though somewhat reluctantly. Peter Jay, economics editor of *The Times*, and later the BBC, and for a time British ambassador to the USA, was Callaghan's son-in-law. He was also a convert to monetarism, along with a number of other opinion-formers. Callaghan, in a passage in his speech to the Labour Party conference in September 1976, generally assumed to have been drafted by Jay, signalled one of the most important shifts in economic policy. Remember the attempt to try to avoid the worst effects of the oil crisis by boosting government spending? Remember the high inflation and appalling public finances that had resulted from it? Callaghan did, and he was not going to make the same mistake again. As he told the Labour conference:

> We used to think that you could just spend your way out of a recession, and increase employment, by cutting taxes and boosting government spending. I tell you in all candour that that option no longer exists, and in so far as it ever did exist, it worked by injecting inflation into the economy. And each time that happened, the average level of unemployment has risen. Higher inflation, followed by higher unemployment. That is the history of the last twenty years.

This was tantamount to the burying of post-war Keynesianism. A government that had indeed tried to spend its way out of recession had executed a screeching U-turn. The intellectual battle, of course, did not go away. Monetarists and Keynesians feuded for years. In 1976 Britain's economic policy, having had its walk on the wild side, was being put back on the straight and narrow, under the close supervision of the IMF. Economic policy, and the intellectual basis for it, had undergone a seismic shift.

How much were we aware of it? In 1976 there was a lot going on. In my job at the time, writing economic reports on overseas countries for Lloyds Bank, I did not have a lot to do directly with analysing Britain's economy. But I read the newspapers, and I read economic articles beyond the newspapers. The general sense was more of a country that was getting its comeuppance, and being put on iron rations by a stern bank manager, than of the true nature of the shift that was occurring. Not many people dwelt on prime-ministerial speeches at party conferences. The Labour government was willing to admit that it was pursuing IMF-imposed austerity for a limited period, but not the extent of the shift that had occurred. Its refrain, particularly from Healey, was that the actions the government were taking were mild in comparison with what the true monetarists on the Conservative benches would impose. The true significance of 1976 was only seen later.

The medicine works

Being rescued by the IMF was humiliating for Britain. To this day some Labour supporters believe their government was bounced into unnecessary, unpopular and unacceptable austerity measures. Targets for the money supply became inextricably linked in the public mind with public spending cuts. If you asked a cross-section of British people now what monetarism was, many would say it was all about 'the cuts' – reductions in government spending – rather than control of the money supply to bring down inflation. The IMF insisted on deep spending cuts, and, in order to bring the money supply under control, a Bank of England scheme, the supplementary special deposits scheme, which penalised banks if their lending grew too rapidly (it was popularly known as 'the corset'), was introduced. More dramatically, for most people, the Bank's main interest rate, then known as the minimum lending rate, was pushed up to 15 per cent in October 1976, then a record. With sterling under pressure, not least from a story in the *Sunday Times* by Malcolm Crawford, one of my predecessors as the paper's economics editor – he reported that the IMF wanted a lower exchange rate for the pound – interest rates were pushed up as much to support sterling as to control the money supply.

Whatever the motivation, it worked. Within months the money supply was growing at an even slower rate than the IMF recommended. The pound, having been under pressure, began to strengthen, allowing interest rates to be reduced. A strong recovery in the world economy, by now getting over the shock of sharply higher oil prices, helped propel Britain along. Growth in the advanced economies – the OECD – was 4.9 per cent in 1976, 3.9 per cent in 1977 and 4.4 per cent in 1978. When the world economy does well, so, in general, does Britain.

Britain's particular problems – the greater depth of her post-OPEC recession and the austerity insisted on by the IMF, combined with initially very high interest rates – meant a somewhat slower recovery than the Western world average. It was a recovery nonetheless, with growth of 2.6 per cent in 1976, 2.4 per cent in 1977 and a heady 3.3 per cent in 1978. It was a good example of what was to be a recurring phenomenon: that with a fair wind the economy can grow through austerity. Unemployment took longer to respond. The number of people claiming unemployment benefit rose above a million in January 1976 and was to stay above a million for exactly a quarter of a century. Even so, there were glimmers of light in 1978 and early 1979 when it fell, if only temporarily. Most astonishing of all, perhaps, was what happened to interest rates. Having been raised to a record 15 per cent in October 1976, they were cut to 5 per cent a year later, mainly the result of the government's efforts to keep the now popular pound from rising too rapidly. It was no longer 'Goodbye, Great Britain'. For a while at least, it was 'Hello, new era'. By the end of 1977 Britain's foreign exchange reserves were five times their level at the start of that year.

Britain had come back from the brink, thanks to IMF monetarism but also thanks to the Labour government's ability to strike deals with the unions. The wage-price spiral, Britain's Achilles' heel, was brought under control by an incomes policy which began in 1975 with a flat limit of £6 a week on pay increases. Average earnings growth, more than 26 per cent in 1975, slowed to 10 per cent in 1977. It was a time when governments believed that both prices and incomes could be controlled. For short periods they indeed could be.

It probably could never have lasted, but it is possible to conjure up a scenario in which the Labour government, despite struggling with a barely workable parliamentary position, a new prime minister, James Callaghan, fresh to the job and the humiliation of the IMF rescue uppermost in people's minds, could have remained in power for another term. In a disastrous era for economic policy many people would have found it hard to choose between the mismanagement of the Tories in the early 1970s and that of Labour later. North Sea oil was starting to be seen by international investors as a reason to believe in Britain again and as the potential saviour of the British economy in an era of high energy prices. At this time, more than any, the Labour government needed to demonstrate it could work with the unions. That, unfortunately, proved to be far from the case.

Now is the winter ...

The sequence of events that led to the Labour Party being out of office for nearly a generation – the eighteen years from 1979 to 1997 – is well known. So is the story of the 'winter of discontent' of 1978–9, a pivotal moment for the British economy and for the history of the union movement. The winter of discontent marked the point when most people's patience with union militancy ran out. It did not mark the end of such militancy: the miners' strike of 1984–6 and the Wapping dispute of 1986–7 were still to come. But it was the beginning of the end. The winter of discontent resulted not only in the defeat of Labour but also in the election of a Conservative government which, with public support, brought into law reforms that would permanently curtail the power of the unions. The unions were the architects of their own downfall.

Maybe it is because union disruption was so common in that period that I have no strong memories of the winter of discontent. Strikes had lost their capacity to surprise, though that period was a humdinger. In 1979 alone 29.5 million working days were lost as a result of strikes, more than in any year since the 1926 General Strike. I may have witnessed the piles of uncollected rubbish in the parts of London normally dominated by tourists, but I do not recall them. I do remember the television broadcast by James 'Sunny Jim' Callaghan, the prime minister, on 7 September 1978, in which, against expectations, he told viewers that there would not be an October general election that year. His administration would continue until the following year: 'The government must and will continue to carry out policies that are consistent, determined, that don't chop or change and that brought about the present recovery in our fortunes', he said. 'We can see the way ahead.' Margaret Thatcher, who had told reporters earlier that day, 'I don't imagine he's making a ministerial broadcast just to say he isn't holding a general election', was quickly on the attack, accusing Labour of being 'chicken' and insisting that Callaghan had decided not to hold the election because he feared losing it. There may have been some truth in that. Having been prime minister for just two years, he did not want to risk losing by taking an electoral gamble. Though Labour's position in the polls was improving, Callaghan appears to have been heavily influenced by the private polling carried out for the party by MORI (Market & Opinion Research International) and its energetic head, Bob Worcester. He had the ear of the prime minister and is said to have warned, partly on the basis of polling in marginal constituencies in the spring of 1978, that Labour's position was weaker than it looked. Labour MPs and party activists were as surprised as Thatcher, and many felt let down. An exclusive story in the *Daily Mirror* – the nearest thing to the house newspaper – had told them in August to prepare for an autumn election. When it did not happen, there was some disenchantment, although this was not the main reason for Labour's defeat in May 1979.

David Lipsey, another of my predecessors as economics editor of the *Sunday Times*, was at the time working as an adviser in Downing Street. He lays claim to having come up with the phrase 'winter of discontent' to describe the industrial troubles of 1978–9 which, curiously, Labour's spin doctors rather liked. This was because, as in Shakespeare's *Richard III*, the winter of discontent would be followed by 'glorious summer'. That was the hope anyway. Lipsey, in his autobiography *In the Corridors of Power*, gives Callaghan more noble motives for delaying the election beyond mere political survival.

The Labour prime minister, he suggests, was keen to use his leverage over the unions, trying to get them to play ball on pay – and demonstrate that only a Labour government could secure such a deal – by using the threat of the prospect of an anti-union Thatcher administration to bring them into line. He wanted a 5 per cent pay deal, and thought he could swing it. The unions, however, were in no mood to co-operate, and Callaghan miscalculated his ability to influence them. The incomes policy that accompanied IMF-imposed austerity was already on the wane: in 1977 it only amounted to an agreement with the Trades Union Congress that there should be only one pay rise per twelve-month period, and that percentage pay increases should be kept in single figures. Trying to impose a 5 per cent pay limit at a time of accelerating inflation was always too demanding a task. Callaghan's gamble failed spectacularly. Ford workers, then hugely influential, went on strike in pursuit of a big pay increase, before settling for a 15 per cent rise. There were strikes by dockers, lorry drivers, water workers and even civil servants. Refuse collectors went on strike, halting rubbish collection, as did ancillary workers in hospitals, so many thousands of operations had to be cancelled. Strikes are rarely popular, but these proved hugely unpopular. Labour and the unions suffered the consequences. It was to be a long time before voters would again trust Labour to manage the economy. The unions, meanwhile, would never again occupy such a key role in Britain. After the winter of discontent they were frozen out.

Lipsey dismisses the argument that the industrial disruption of that grim winter of 1978–9 was exaggerated by the Conservative press, or that it has acquired a bigger status that it deserves with the passage of time. As he writes:

> There is a revisionist school among historians of the period which states that the 'winter of discontent' never happened, or at any rate was much exaggerated. It was, these historians argue, got up by the press to discredit the Labour government. It did not feel like that in Number 10 ... There was no mistaking the atmosphere inside Number 10, nor was there much mistaking what was happening outside. In Liverpool the dead lay unburied as municipal workers struck. In Leicester Square, a few hundred yards from the centre of government, stinking rubbish was piled high in the streets. We felt we had lost control. Indeed we had lost control. And the British public is not charitably opposed to governments who lose control.

Though inflation was climbing and strikes became the norm, the economy was growing. Indeed, in the year to the spring of 1979, the economy grew by more than 5 per cent. Governments usually aim to boost growth in the run-up to an election. In this respect, despite a weak parliamentary position, Labour succeeded. It was not enough. On 28 March 1979 Callaghan lost a vote of confidence in the House of Commons and was forced into the election he had had the luxury of delaying a few months earlier. In theory he could have soldiered on until the autumn of 1979. Instead, there was to be an election on 3 May, and the Labour Party, suffering the first throes of the deep divisions that were to tear it apart in the early 1980s, was not well placed to fight it. Helped by the iconic 'Labour Isn't Working' poster created by Saatchi & Saatchi, Thatcher won against a tired, divided and apparently incompetent Labour Party. Nor was it as close as people expected. The Conservatives gained more than sixty seats, Labour lost fifty, and the swing was the biggest, but in the opposite direction, since Labour's 1945 landslide. Mrs Thatcher's majority was more than forty.

Britain had come back from the brink of the IMF rescue – the nearest thing an economy can come to bankruptcy – but the problems had not gone away. The 'sick man of Europe', with chronically high inflation and persistently disruptive industrial relations, still needed treatment. Margaret Thatcher aimed to provide it. Her victory on 3 May 1979 was not a cause of great national celebration, as I recall, and her victory message, loosely adapted from St Francis of Assisi – 'Where there is discord, may we bring harmony' – jarred rather than reassured. She was to bring many things. Harmony was not one of them.

4

A close-run thing again

To those waiting with bated breath for that favourite
media catchphrase, the 'U' turn, I have only one thing to
say. You turn if you want to. The lady's not for turning. I
say that not only to you but to our friends overseas and
also to those who are not our friends.

Margaret Thatcher, Conservative Party conference
speech, Brighton, 10 October 1980

The 1970s, fascinating, turbulent and dangerous, must rank
as the most disastrous decade for UK economic policy of the
modern era, under both Conservative and Labour governments. For a time, with the election of another Conservative
government in May 1979, it appeared that nothing much had
changed. Margaret Thatcher took office with a clear idea of
what she wanted her government to do. The Conservatives, in
opposition, had thought a lot about economic policy. Not for
them the malaise that has affected many new governments in
Britain: having devoted so much effort to getting elected, they
have no very clear idea of what to do when they come to power.
Unfortunately for Thatcher's Tories in 1979, governments also
often discover that the best-laid plans can be blown off course

by events. What looks straightforward in theory can be a lot more complicated in practice.

For Thatcher, determined to bring harmony to a fractured country – and to convince the many voters unconvinced that Britain's first female prime minister was the right woman for the job – there were three particular problems. The first was that, while winter had given way to spring by the time she took office, this did not mark the end of industrial disruption: far from it. September 1979, four months after her victory, was the worst single month of the year for days lost due to labour disputes. In fact, with nearly 12 million working days lost, it was the worst month for strikes since the 1920s. It included a strike by ITV – then Britain's only commercial television broadcaster – which resulted in it being off the air for nearly three months from August to October 1979. Like the three-day week in 1974, this was a dispute that few people could have been unaware of. The entire ITV network was down for weeks, and there were withdrawal symptoms. Legend has it that the system designed to record the number of viewers for programmes found that some households kept their sets tuned to the test-card and background music. This, of course, was in an era long before satellite and cable television. Video recorders and players were a novelty, having only been introduced to Britain in 1978.

ITV was not the only strike-prone media organisation. *The Times* and *Sunday Times*, then owned by the Thomson Organization, were not published for a year from November 1978 to November 1979, as a result of a dispute between management and unions over the introduction of new technology. For *The Times* it marked the first sustained production shutdown in nearly two centuries of existence. The papers missed out on the May 1979 election, as well as many other important events. The strike cost the Thomson Organization tens of millions of pounds, and, more importantly, the Canadian-owned business lost patience with the British national newspaper industry. *The*

Times and *Sunday Times* had been acquired by Roy Thomson, first Baron Thomson of Fleet, in 1966. He died in 1976, two years before the year-long strike. Ken Thomson, the second Baron Thomson, had less of an emotional attachment to the titles, and in Rupert Murdoch he found a willing buyer. As with the winter of discontent and Thatcher's election, the unions shot themselves in the foot. Had *The Times* and *Sunday Times* remained under Thomson's ownership, the later and bitter Wapping dispute might still have happened for Murdoch's other titles. Printers at the two prestige titles might, however, have enjoyed a more comfortable existence, despite appalling industrial relations. It was not to be.

Strikes were not the only issue for the new government. Task number one of the Conservatives' 1979 manifesto was 'to restore the health of our economic and social life, by controlling inflation'. It quickly became clear, however, that inflation was going to get a lot worse before it got better. The other two factors that made the new government's life difficult, one of which was self-inflicted, both related to inflation. For a while, as in the mid-1970s, the fear was that the government, this time a different government, had lost control of it.

20 per cent inflation again

The Callaghan government, in an attempt to calm the rapidly deteriorating industrial relations climate in the run-up to the 1979 election, established a Commission on Pay Comparability, under the chairmanship of Hugh Clegg, professor of industrial relations at Warwick University. The establishment of the commission in March 1979 was aimed at public sector workers, generally the most disenchanted group, with a view to producing pay recommendations for them which the government would honour. The Conservatives, perhaps surprisingly, did not dismiss the Clegg commission as the last desperate attempt of Labour to remain in power, or even challenge the idea of pay comparability. Such interference in setting pay would have smacked, it might have been thought, of socialism. Rather, they said they too would honour its recommendations. One theory of why they did so was that, with the outcome of the election uncertain – polls showed that Thatcher was a less popular leader than Callaghan – the Conservatives could not afford to risk alienating such an important group of voters. In 1979, 30 per cent of employment was in the public sector, including the nationalised industries. A lot of households were dependent on public sector pay packets, and they carried with them a lot of votes. The other possibility is that some of Thatcher's advisers were so convinced that their brand of monetarism would work its magic on inflation that changes in relative prices – the pay of public versus private sector workers – would not affect overall inflation. The Clegg recommendations were for public sector pay rises of between 15 and 25 per cent. Conservatives were soon regretting their decision to honour the Clegg commission's recommendations. By 1980, with average earnings up by nearly 21 per cent and the pressures on public spending growing, Thatcher may have realised her mistake.

The second big problem for the new government was a re-run of the one that had helped defeat the Conservatives last time: a sharp rise in world oil prices. After the 1973–4 oil crisis, the first prompted by OPEC, oil prices had crept a little higher over the next few years, though not significantly. Then, at the end of 1978 came 'OPEC II', which, if it had been a film sequel, would have had the subtitle 'The Nightmare Returns'. OPEC II was triggered by the Iranian revolution. Islamic fundamentalists, under the leadership of Ayatollah Khomeini, overthrew the Western-supporting Shah of Iran. The new regime in Tehran was the opposite of Western-supporting. In November 1979 fifty-two American diplomats and citizens were seized and held hostage for 444 days by student supporters of the new regime. The immediate practical effect of the overthrow of the Shah was that Iran, OPEC's second-largest oil producer, reduced output sharply. Oil production, 5 million barrels a day, was suspended for ten weeks from 27 December 1978, before being resumed at a new lower level of 2 million barrels a day.

The world was not ready for a second oil crisis, and neither was Britain. While the high oil prices established in 1973–4 had some permanent effects on consumption – it resulted in the introduction of the 55 m.p.h. speed limit on American roads – it was still the case that a recovering world economy meant higher demand for oil. Add in the harshness of the winter of 1978–9, in both Europe and the USA, and there was still a huge amount of vulnerability to higher oil prices. The Iranian revolution, in combination with these other factors, led to a sharp rise in the price of oil. Saudi Light crude rose from $12.98 a barrel in October 1978 to $35.40 in June 1979. Some crude, including that produced in Britain's North Sea, touched $40 a barrel, more than twenty times its level less than a decade earlier.

Had Labour held on to power in May 1979, it would have had to deal with the consequences of OPEC II, but that task fell to the new Conservative government. A big rise in oil prices is both inflationary – it pushes up the rate of inflation – and deflationary, reducing demand in the economy. The effect of a big rise in oil prices is equivalent to a significant increase in taxes, except that the 'tax collectors' are oil producers in other countries, particularly the Middle East, although thanks to North Sea oil there was also a tax boost for Britain. The most noticeable impact, however, was on inflation. A perfect storm of higher public sector pay, a surge in world oil prices and an increase in valued-added tax (VAT) by the new government pushed inflation to within a whisker of 22 per cent in May 1980. This was below the peak of almost 27 per cent reached in August 1975, but not that much below it. Every country was affected by the oil price hikes, but Britain was particularly affected. The old inflation vulnerability remained. The new government had started off on the wrong foot.

A rush to reform

It is often said that Margaret Thatcher was elected in May 1979 on a bland manifesto which concealed most of the radical ideas it would introduce when in office. It is often said, but it is not true. The 1979 Conservative manifesto included most of what we later came to associate with Thatcherism, including the control of inflation by monetary means, trade union reform, denationalisation (the word 'privatisation' had yet to be invented) and the sale of council houses to their tenants. It also pledged to revitalise the private rented sector. Union reform, including restricting the closed shop (under which all employees had to belong to a union), banning secondary picketing (when workers not directly involved in a dispute picketed the place of work) and secret ballots, was set out in some detail. There was a promise to denationalise some recently nationalised aerospace and shipbuilding firms. What is sometimes forgotten is that in 1979 nationalisation had not come to an end. The Conservative manifesto cited Labour plans to nationalise 'yet more firms and industries such as building, banking, insurance, pharmaceuticals and road haulage'.

Perhaps most explicit was the promise to reduce income tax. The manifesto said:

> We shall cut income tax at all levels to reward hard work, responsibility and success; tackle the poverty trap; encourage saving and the wider ownership of property; simplify taxes – like VAT; and reduce tax bureaucracy. It is especially important to cut the absurdly high marginal rates of tax both at the bottom and top of the income scale. It must

pay a man or woman significantly more to be in rather than out of work.

The top rate of tax, then 83 per cent (or up to 98 per cent when earned and unearned income was taken into account) would be cut to the European average. This looked like a programme for a parliament. Indeed, tax pledges by opposition parties have a tendency to slip into the distance once they are elected and have had a chance to examine the books. How would a newly elected government determined to cut public borrowing be able to afford to implement big income tax cuts?

The answer, just six weeks after the election, came with Sir Geoffrey Howe's first budget, on 12 June 1979. The clue was in the manifesto words about simplifying taxes 'like VAT'. In the language of politicians, 'simplify' often means 'increase', and this was the case this time. There had been newspaper stories before the election about Conservative plans for a big increase in VAT (value-added tax), but nobody was sure. David Lipsey, from his ringside seat in 10 Downing Street towards the end of the Callaghan premiership, recalls how the prime minister was being pushed by Gavyn Davies, later a distinguished City economist and BBC chairman, then a special adviser, to say in a speech in the run-up to the election that the Conservatives planned to double VAT. Callaghan was reluctant to do so. 'I can't do it', he said. 'Of course they aren't going to double VAT. If I say they are, I will just lose all credibility.' He did say it, reluctantly, though it was not enough to frighten enough voters away from the Conservatives.

The Conservatives did indeed almost double VAT, Howe announcing it in that first budget in June 1979. Before the election there had been two rates of VAT: 8 per cent for most products eligible for the tax and 12.5 per cent for luxuries. Many products, including food, books, children's clothing and shoes and newspapers were and are zero-rated. But for those previously subject to the 8 and 12.5 per cent rates there was, from the Monday after the budget, to be a 'new unified rate' of 15 per cent. Howe's increase in VAT gave him room to achieve a manifesto pledge almost before the ink was dry on it. So the top rate of income tax was cut from 83 to 60 per cent, with a range of higher rate bands below that level. As eye-catching was the cut in the basic rate of income tax from 33 to 30 per cent, with a pledge to reduce it over time to 25 per cent. Not only did the budget achieve an earlier and bolder cut in income tax than most expected, but it was also the practical application of an important piece of Conservative economic philosophy. Given the choice between direct taxes such as income tax and indirect taxes such as VAT, it is always best to reduce the former, even if the latter have to be increased. Direct taxes affect incentives, and people's willingness to work. Allow them to keep more of their earnings, and they will work harder. Income tax cuts did that. As for the hike in VAT, many essentials, including food and, at the time, household energy bills would be VAT-free.

The 1979 budget was big and bold. Rarely has a government set out its stall, and its philosophy, so clearly. The argument was that if these big changes were delayed, they might never happen, once events intervened. As significant as the income tax cuts and the big shift from direct to indirect tax was another section in Howe's speech. Exchange controls had been the cross that British individuals and businesses had had to bear through sterling's long period of vulnerability. During the worst of the country's 'sick man of Europe' period in the 1960s, before and after the 1967 devaluation, a £50 'foreign travel allowance' operated, this being the limit on the amount of money British travellers could take abroad. That was probably the least important though most visible aspect of exchange controls. Partly to hold the Bretton Woods system together, most countries operated controls on the amount of capital that could flow in and out. For countries with vulnerable balance of payments positions, which could be exposed by flows of 'hot' or short-term money, such controls had come to be seen as very important. All that changed for Britain in the space of just a few months in 1979. In his budget speech Howe said it was now 'an appropriate time to start dismantling our apparatus of controls on outward capital flows'.

In the budget, Howe suggested that his approach to the removal of exchange controls would be a cautious one. It would be a 'progressive dismantling', he said, and determined by the strength of sterling, among other factors. In the event, the chancellor was able to proceed a lot more rapidly than he thought. Just four months after his budget he announced to a surprised House of Commons that all the remaining exchange controls were to be abolished. This was quite a moment. Nothing better illustrated the commitment of the Thatcher government to free markets than this bold move to allow people and businesses to decide for themselves how to move money across Britain's borders. It set the standard for the rest of Europe, which eventually followed suit by removing national exchange controls, though in some cases not for a decade or more. The Labour Party complained that the move would cost British jobs, as firms used their new freedoms to invest overseas, although in subsequent years Britain was a net beneficiary of such flows, as inward investment increased sharply, particularly from the Far East. It also signalled to the world that the Thatcher government meant it when it said it would be radical and reforming.

The removal of exchange controls was one of the most important reforms of the Thatcher era, alongside other financial liberalisation, including freeing the banks to enter the home loan market, the removal of hire purchase controls and the Big Bang reforms of 1986, which opened the City up to foreign ownership and brought the phenomenon of investment banks to Britain. A controlled financial system became a liberalised one, with both good and bad consequences.

But a dive into recession

When Margaret Thatcher was elected, in May 1979, the economy appeared to be enjoying a boom. In the second quarter of 1979 alone, GDP jumped more than 4 per cent. Was this the 'glorious summer' dreamed of by Labour after the winter of discontent? To a certain extent it was, though mainly for statistical reasons. The return to work after some of the strikes were settled produced a temporary boost to economic activity that was never going to last. Even so, there was no general expectation that the economy was about to enter a deep and damaging recession. In his budget speech in June 1979 Howe offered the prospect of 'no growth in the period immediately ahead', not a warning of recession. Perhaps there should have been such a warning. High oil prices had been a harbinger of recession only a few years earlier; why should the sharp OPEC II price hikes be any different? Not only that but, while busy reforming the economy, the new chancellor was also pushing interest rates up sharply. From 12 per cent at the time of the election (itself a big rise from the low point of just 5 per cent in October 1977), interest rates were pushed up to 14 per cent in June and 17 per cent in November, a record. The Conservatives were determined to squeeze inflation out of the economy, even if it meant squeezing the life out of it too.

The recession did not come immediately. The strikes, alongside fast-rising pay settlements and a big increase in inflation, appeared to confirm that the economy needed harsh medicine, which the government was happy to supply. By the start of 1980, however, the writing was on the wall. The first Thatcher recession, the great manufacturing recession of the early 1980s, began. It was a manufacturing recession because much of it was concentrated in industry. A peak-to-trough fall in GDP of 4.6 per cent meant it was, at the time, the worst recession in the post-war period, a record it held until the global financial crisis hit in 2008–9. The Thatcher government did not

single-handedly bring about the destruction of British manufacturing, as noted earlier. The seeds of decline had already been
sown. It did, however, preside over a time when owners of many
marginal businesses, who had hung on through the turbulence
of the 1970s, decided it was time to throw in the towel. This
was a period of factory closures, which persisted for years after
the recession itself ended. Across large swaths of the country
the abiding image was the chained and padlocked factory gates.
Manufacturing output dropped by a fifth during the recession,
and took nearly a decade to get back to pre-recession levels.
During 1980, its worst year, factory output fell 17 per cent.
Manufacturing employment would never again reach the levels
of the 1970s. There was, however, some relief in sight.

Walters and the pound

I did not get to know Alan (later Sir Alan) Walters during
his first or second spells advising Conservative governments,
although I did get to know him well during his explosive third
spell in Downing Street, in the late 1980s. Following his death
in 2009, after talking to his friends, family and colleagues, I
wrote his entry for the *Dictionary of National Biography*.
Walters was a straight-talking East Midlander from Leicester
whose common-sense approach appealed to the Grantham-
born Thatcher. Though robust in his views, which he always
set out clearly, he verged on shyness in expressing them. He
was distinguished in two fields, transport economics and
monetary economics, and was one of Britain's most prominent
monetarists. The son of a Leicester grocery clerk and born, on
his own admission, in a slum, he was Mrs Thatcher's personal
economic adviser from 1981 to 1984, having come to know her
through the free-market Institute of Economic Affairs. He was
a striking figure, with a shock of white hair and a somewhat
cadaverous appearance. Having failed his eleven-plus exam, he

struggled through to become accepted as an external student at the University of Leicester. A plain speaker, with a gift for cutting through complex arguments, he was one economist whom Thatcher could listen to. His first spell in government, as a part-time adviser to Edward Heath, ended in tears when he wrote an internal paper with the title 'Inflation and More Inflation and then ... Devaluation'. Heath received a copy and, as Walters said later, 'everything then hit the fan'. The two parted company.

His contribution in the early 1980s was no less challenging but altogether more constructive. Having been summoned to advise Thatcher from his US academic position at Johns Hopkins University in Baltimore, he had something of the outsider's perspective when he took up his Downing Street post in January 1981. The issue was the strength of the pound and its effect on industry. Sterling, a basket case five years earlier, was now flavour of the month. A newly elected Conservative government, determined to control the money supply, was hiking interest rates. Not only that but, thanks to North Sea oil, sterling was now a petrocurrency. The sharp rise in oil prices that followed the Iranian revolution had an equally sharp effect on the pound, leading to justifiable squeals from British industry. For a government determined to bring inflation down, a strong currency, which would push down import prices, was helpful. The fact that it appeared on the surface to be due to factors outside the government's control – political developments in the Middle East – diverted some of the criticism. It did, however, produce the memorable quote from Sir Michael Edwardes, the chairman of British Leyland, in 1980, when he said at the CBI conference: 'If the Cabinet do not have the wit and imagination to reconcile our industrial needs with the fact of North Sea oil they would do better to leave the bloody stuff in the ground.'

Sterling was indeed strong. Towards the end of 1980 it was

trading at $2.45, nearly a dollar above its level a few years earlier. Walters, however, was sceptical of the extent to which oil was the cause. His own view, expressed in seminars in the USA, was that the strength of the pound meant that monetary policy in Britain, far from being too loose as the money supply figures suggested, was in fact too tight. Aware that this would be a highly controversial verdict, particularly for Treasury ministers committed to controlling the money supply, before taking up his post he recommended that the Centre for Policy Studies, the body set up in the mid-1970s by Thatcher and Sir Keith Joseph, should commission Jürg Niehans, the monetarist professor of economics from Bern University in Switzerland, to conduct an investigation into monetary conditions in Britain and, in particular, the strength of sterling. This was clever. Walters knew that, even if Thatcher was not convinced by him, she would believe a Swiss monetarist economist. Not only did the prime minister love to spend time in Switzerland but she had the greatest of respect for its sound money tradition.

The conclusion Niehans came to chimed in with Walters's own. The policy of very high interest rates to control an apparently uncontrollable sterling M3 money supply measure amounted to monetary shock treatment for the economy, of which the soaring pound was a powerful symptom. 'UK monetary policy not only seems to have rejected any concession to gradualism, but also refused to make any allowance for real growth', Niehans concluded. The challenge was to convince the Treasury. The biggest obstacle to change proved to be not Howe but his junior minister at the time, Nigel Lawson, then financial secretary to the Treasury. In a foretaste of the battles between Walters and Lawson that were to come later, when the latter succeeded Howe as chancellor, Lawson set out his objections to a change of course in a speech in Zurich in January 1981.

Who won? The pound reached its high point of more than $2.45 in November 1980, stayed around that level for a couple of months and then began to fall, not least because the government began to reduce interest rates. Old feuds take a long time to pass, and Lawson could not let this one pass. In his book *The View from No.11* he dismissed Walters's attempt to drive down the pound by reducing interest rates as 'not a great success'. But the pound never got back to those highs. The squeeze, from this quarter at least, was at an end.

Mild-mannered austerity

Sir Geoffrey Howe, Margaret Thatcher's first chancellor, was also the first chancellor I got to know on a personal basis. I was working for *Financial Weekly*, a now defunct City newspaper. It had been launched, in 1979, by the then owners of the *Daily Express* and *Sunday Express*, with something of a fanfare. Money was spent on it, and high-profile columnists hired at considerable cost, including Harold Wilson, the former Labour prime minister. Later I was deputed, with a colleague, to take Wilson to lunch in Westminster and tell him that we could no longer afford to carry his column – news he was able to avoid, on that occasion at least, through the simple expedient of not turning up. *Financial Weekly* had failed to live up to its founders' expectations. When I joined, in the spring of 1981, it was already clear that neither circulation nor advertising made it a viable proposition. A year later the original owners closed it, and everybody received a redundancy cheque. It was a short-lived period of idleness. Two weeks later the title was bought by Robert Maxwell, the flamboyant Czech-born businessman and one-time Labour MP, today remembered for appropriating funds from his companies' pension funds and dying, in 1991, after apparently falling overboard after a heart attack from his yacht, the *Lady Ghislaine*, which was cruising off the Canary Islands. That was much later. I remember him as a huge presence, literally, with a domineering manner. Anybody on the receiving end of Maxwell's bullying, which I fortunately never was, did not forget about it in a hurry. As almost a comic-character magnate, he was also the subject of a lot of gentle mockery. One story about him, which I do not think was apocryphal, was of him coming across a man he thought was an employee in one of the corridors in Maxwell House (yes, it was called that) north of the City, smoking a cigarette while reading a notice-board. Maxwell, for some reason, took an instant dislike to the person, called him into his office and in his booming voice asked what his annual salary was. He then wrote out a cheque for the amount and told him never to appear in the office again. The man, it turned out, was not a member of staff but a visiting sales representative from another company, who had just enjoyed a large and unexpected bonus. In the meantime a new proprietor meant a relaunch for the newspaper. We asked the Treasury if Sir Geoffrey Howe would agree to an interview, and he did.

Over the years Howe has acquired a reputation as one of the most downtrodden political figures of recent times. In 1978, when he was shadow chancellor, he was famously the subject of one of the cruellest House of Commons putdowns of all time. Following an assault on his economic policies by Howe, Denis Healey, the chancellor, said that being attacked by his opponent was like being 'savaged by a dead sheep'. Once in government, stories began to emerge of Howe being humiliated by Thatcher in Cabinet meetings, and later some of those humiliations came out in some of her public utterances. It was no secret that she used her personal economic adviser, Alan Walters, and Sir John Hoskyns, head of the Downing Street policy unit, to bolster her chancellor's resolve. At a time when the Treasury was resistant to the new government's policies, she always feared that Howe would 'go native'. One explanation of Howe's devastating Commons resignation speech in 1990, which triggered the leadership contest that brought down Thatcher, was that it was his revenge for years of humiliation. He later denied this strongly, saying his speech was a matter of conscience. When I met him in 1982, it struck me that people had perhaps sometimes mistaken his courteousness for weakness. He was certainly courteous. When I said we were very pleased to have the interview for our relaunch, he said: 'Do you think it will get on the front page?' There was of course never any doubt that it would. The story, a variation on the theme that the economy was decisively on the up, fitted perfectly. That he was able to say that in 1982 was far from guaranteed.

This was a year after Howe's most dramatic moment as chancellor, his 1981 austerity budget. In the depths of the 1980–81 recession he had turned the conventions of post-war economic policy on their head. Unemployment had risen above 2 million and was increasing by 100,000 a month. Though there was some tentative evidence that the pace of decline was easing, nobody could be sure that the economy was near a turning point. It was a moment when most governments would have trodden carefully, for fear of making a bad situation worse. Instead Howe, egged on by Thatcher and her advisers, unveiled a budget that even with the passage of time looks bold, to the point of foolhardiness. Had it gone wrong, it could have been the end of the Thatcher government.

Howe and the 364

Though Keynesian economic policies had been abandoned by the Callaghan government in 1976, they were buried by Howe in 1981. His budget raised taxes, mainly by freezing personal tax allowances at a time of high inflation, raising employee National Insurance contributions and announcing big increases in excise duties on petrol, alcohol and tobacco. Popular it was not, even though there was a one-year windfall levy on the banks, which were benefiting from the very high interest rates that were part and parcel of the government's monetarist experiment. Most notoriously, the budget produced a response from 364 economists, a round-robin letter circulated around university departments that was published in *The Times*, which condemned the government's approach. The letter, initiated by Frank Hahn and Robert Neild of Cambridge University, two of Britain's most distinguished professors of economics, attracted the signature of four former chief economic advisers to the government and one future governor of the Bank of England, Mervyn (later Lord) King. 'There is no basis in economic theory or supporting evidence for the Government's belief that by deflating demand they will bring inflation permanently under control and thereby induce an automatic recovery in output and employment', it warned. 'Present policies will deepen the depression, erode the industrial base of our economy and threaten its social and political stability.'

The letter could have been an epitaph for the Thatcher government's economic experiment. The story goes that when Michael Foot, the Labour leader, asked her in prime minister's question time to name two economists who agreed with her policies, Mrs Thatcher was able to say, quick as a flash, Walters and Patrick Minford. But in the car back to Downing Street she turned to an aide and said: 'It's a good job he didn't ask me to name three.' Nineteen eighty-one was certainly the government's toughest year. Just a month after the austerity budget the first of the inner-city riots broke out. The riots – in Brixton in London, Toxteth in Liverpool, Chapeltown in Leeds and Handsworth in Birmingham – appeared to be a direct response to high and fast-rising unemployment, though subsequent investigations showed that the causes were more complex. For several months the austerity budget appeared to be a gamble that had failed. Though it is now seen as one of the episodes that were the making of the Thatcher government, it did not look like that for some time. Figures now show that the 1981 budget did mark the low point of the recession, and that the 364 economists were wrong. By focusing on fiscal policy – the budget measures – they had failed to spot that the purpose of the budget was to make space for a relaxation of monetary policy. Howe was able to announce a two-point cut in interest rates in the budget, and in subsequent months it became clear that the government had moved away from its initial very tough monetarist approach, which Denis Healey had christened 'punk monetarism'. The pound came down in response, easing some of the pressure on industry. Inflation also began to fall sharply, easing the pressure on living standards. Monetary policy revealed itself to be more powerful than fiscal policy, establishing a pattern for economic policy that was to become the norm.

The effect of the letter from the 364 within Thatcher's inner circle was interesting. It reinforced her suspicion for, even contempt of, mainstream economic opinion in Britain. Years later she scripted (or had scripted for her) a short episode of the television comedy *Yes, Minister*, in which she appeared. The theme was the abolition of economists. The attack, according to Alan Walters, merely strengthened the resolve of the government. 'The statement probably had an effect which was the opposite of what its signatories intended', he wrote in his book *Britain's Economic Renaissance*.

> If anything, it reaffirmed the government's resolve and frightened only the fearful. Academic economists had sunk so low in both ministerial and, I believe, popular esteem that the conjunction of so much academic opposition was taken as some faint confirmation that the policy must be right – or at least not obviously wrong. The confounding of the 364 came quickly. At almost the precise time that the 364 were signing the letter, the decline was not only arrested but there was a decisive upturn in output.

It is easy with the benefit of hindsight to mock the 364. Their timing was poor, and their letter has come to symbolise how, when economists agree on anything, they are usually wrong. I often wonder whether, if I had been an academic economist at that time, I would have signed it. I think not, because of an aversion to round-robin letters and because the wording of the letter was a little odd. It is easy, however, to see why many did. There were some university economics departments where signing the letter was clearly the thing to do. Perhaps because of this, many of the signatories were, maybe foolishly, signing up to sentiments they did not understand very well, macroeconomic policy not being their area of expertise. It should also be remembered that it was a long time after the letter before there was any real confidence that Britain was through the worst. As far as economic policy was concerned, the government still had its back to the wall.

The economy's climb out of that recession was initially very slow, and convincing the public that things were getting better when unemployment was still rising sharply was not easy. Labour Force Survey statistics show that unemployment rose above 2 million in October 1980. It hit 3 million in April 1983, two months before the general election. It did not peak until 1986, allowing some of the 364 to claim they were right all along, though demographic factors – a bulge of young people entering the labour market – were the key source of the problem. Unemployment, on a scale that would have seemed barely believable in the golden age of the 1950s and 1960s, was the scourge of the 1980s. It stayed above 3 million for more than four years, until June 1987.

Once growth got going, however, it was strong, averaging more than 3 per cent a year until the mid-1980s, from which point it accelerated into an unsustainable boom, of which more later. Politically, the Tories benefited from a divided opposition, with the new Social Democratic Party (SDP) badly weakening

Labour. The creation of the SDP, formed in March 1981 by four senior Labour moderates – Roy Jenkins, David Owen, Bill Rodgers and Shirley Williams – otherwise known as the 'Gang of Four', coincided almost to the day with the publication of the letter from the 364. The SDP has come and gone, merging with the Liberals in 1988.

There is a view you often hear expressed which is that, had it not been for the victory in the Falklands War of 1982, itself much less guaranteed than it looks with the benefit of hindsight, Thatcher would have been a one-term prime minister, and not a particularly successful one. It is more complicated than that. The liberalisation of the financial system, including the removal of many of the controls on mortgage and consumer borrowing (hire purchase controls were abolished in 1982) – the domestic counterpart to the abolition of exchange controls in 1979 – may have stored up some problems for the future, but they helped bring about a sharp improvement in household confidence. The economic optimism index produced by MORI showed a 35-point rise between July 1980 and March 1982. In March 1982, a month before the Falklands War, more people thought the government's economic policies were good for the country than thought they were bad. Howe, in fact, enjoyed consistently good ratings on this measure. A united opposition, or a stronger Labour leader than Michael Foot, might have given the Conservatives more of a run for their money, but even that is not certain.

The rise in economic optimism measured by MORI reflected the fact that the country was on the mend, and the public were becoming aware of it. It had been a close-run thing, but in the space of a few years Britain had come back from the brink twice. It was to be more than a decade before it had to do so again.

Monetary mumbo-jumbo

One of the effects of looking back over decades of British economic performance and policy is that it provides a reminder of the things that are sometimes better forgotten. Governments bring to prominence different targets for policy, and different ways of measuring success. Economic policy is, perhaps, more prone to these fashion shifts than other areas. For a time, while the policy is in place, every journalist, commentator and analyst is required to become an expert, or at least claim some expertise, on the most esoteric of concepts. Then, when the fashion changes, they are quietly forgotten. So it was with the 'high monetarism' of the first Thatcher term, a period when no self-respecting commentator or parliamentarian could afford to be unaware of the various measures of the money supply – M0, M1, sterling M3 and so on – the differences between them and their significance for economic policy. (M0 and M1 were the 'narrowest' definitions of money, mainly consisting of notes and coins. The larger 'M' numbers – M3, M4 and even, at one time, M5 – were 'broad' measures, including bank, building society and other deposits.)

The high point for this high monetarism was March 1980, and the government's launch of its medium-term financial strategy (MTFS). It was presented by Howe, but its architects were Lawson, an enthusiastic monetarist, working with Terry Burns, the affable, newly appointed government chief economic adviser (who had attracted attention while at the monetarist London Business School), and Peter Middleton, then deputy secretary but later permanent secretary to the Treasury, its top civil servant. The strategy, launched on 26 March 1980, had a clearly stated intention:

> Control of the money supply will over a period of years reduce the rate of inflation. The speed with which inflation falls will depend crucially on expectations both within the

United Kingdom and overseas. It is to provide a firm basis for those expectations that the Government has announced its firm commitment to a progressive reduction in money supply growth. Public expenditure plans and tax policies and interest rates will be adjusted as necessary in order to achieve the objective.

The official forecasts accompanying the launch of the MTFS in March 1980 made clear that the immediate economic outlook was poor. Through it all, however, one thing was non-negotiable. The guiding star would be the money supply. 'There would be no question', it was said, 'of departing from the money supply policy, which is essential to the success of any anti-inflationary strategy'. It turned out, in fact, that there was every question of departing from the money supply policy. The monetary targets were badly missed, for a variety of reasons, for the first three years, only coming back to the original target by 1983–4. One reason was a direct consequence of the abolition of exchange controls. Throughout the 1970s the supplementary special deposits scheme, popularly known as 'the corset', had been used to keep a lid on the growth in bank lending. When exchange controls were abolished, and people and businesses could borrow from abroad, including from the foreign subsidiaries of British banks, the corset became redundant. The effect of its abolition was a large and, it seems, unexpected jump in the money supply. The Bank of England had warned of a temporary boost of perhaps 3 per cent to sterling M3 from the corset's abolition. In the event, there was an increase of 8 per cent in the course of two months. There were red faces in the Treasury, and even redder ones at the Bank. Thatcher's reaction, according to Lawson, was to 'blow her top'. 'These strains were as nothing compared to Margaret Thatcher's fury at the overshoot of the monetary target following the abolition of the corset', he wrote later. 'She was not appeased by the practical evidence of the severity of the squeeze, as she felt the Government was being brought into ridicule.' These were not the only strains. Milton Friedman, the renowned American monetarist economist, could be expected to lend support to the Thatcher government's monetarist approach. But, brought over to testify to a committee of MPs, he castigated the method chosen by the Thatcher government, with its emphasis on controlling the budget deficit. 'Only a Rip Van Winkle' who had ignored all recent research could have chosen it, he said.

This is all now ancient history and lost in the mists of monetary time. The Treasury said it would stick with sterling M3 but promised to examine changes consistent with 'the eventual adoption of a monetary base system', but different 'Ms' – M0, M1, M4 and M5 – came to be given greater prominence. Through it all the search went on for a simple monetary rule, a measure of the money supply that could be easily controlled and which had predictable results. It was a search in vain, if you believed Goodhart's Law, the economic policy version of Murphy's Law devised by Charles Goodhart, a long-term adviser to the Bank of England. His law was that any measure of the money supply adopted as a target would automatically be subject to distortion. Monetarism in practice proved to be a lot harder than monetarism in theory.

The best chancellor?

Howe, chancellor from 1979 to 1983, after which he became foreign secretary, was a much more important figure than he is often given credit for. When the Conservatives were in opposition from 1974 to 1979, he chaired the group which came up with the document 'The Right Approach to the Economy', an economic manifesto for the government. His mild-mannered image was useful, indeed necessary in tough times, taking the hard edges off what could have been an even more hard-edged

Thatcher government. Political opponents found him easy to mock but hard to dislike. Many years later in the *Sunday Times* I did a league table of post-war chancellors based on five tests (such tests were popular at the time because the Blair government was using them to determine whether Britain was ready to join the euro). In my case the five tests for a chancellor were: the state of the economy when they took over; their economic record; whether they made the economy more productive and entrepreneurial; whether they left the tax system in better shape than they found it; and the legacy they passed on to their successor. Howe's inheritance had been awful, an economy on the verge of very high inflation and beset with strikes. His record, particularly on inflation, was very good, despite the vagaries of money supply control described above. He reformed and simplified the tax system. When he passed the baton on to Nigel Lawson in 1983 (Lawson had helped Howe's chancellorship considerably as one of his junior ministers), it was in remarkably good shape. Though it may not have been his choice, he timed his move to the Foreign Office (where he was to remain foreign secretary for six years) rather well. So in 2004 I put him at the top of my table of chancellors, ahead of his flashier but usually flawed rivals. By this time he was rather infirm and had withdrawn from public life, but his friends told me how pleased he was. He was what the economy needed in those very turbulent times: a safe pair of hands.

5

A renaissance of sorts

I can't bear Britain in decline. I just can't.

Margaret Thatcher, BBC interview, 27 April 1979

From France to the Philippines, from Jamaica to Japan,
from Malaysia to Mexico, from Sri Lanka to Singapore,
privatisation is on the move ... The policies we have
pioneered are catching on in country after country. We
Conservatives believe in popular capitalism – believe
in a property-owning democracy. And it works! ... The
great political reform of the last century was to enable
more and more people to have a vote. Now the great Tory
reform of this century is to enable more and more people
to own property. Popular capitalism is nothing less than
a crusade to enfranchise the many in the economic life of
the nation. We Conservatives are returning power to the
people. That is the way to one nation, one people.

Margaret Thatcher, Conservative Party conference,
Bournemouth, 10 October 1986

In 2013 the London School of Economics published the find-
ings of its Growth Commission. The LSE commission, a group

of academics and others set up to seek ways of achieving healthy and sustained long-term growth for Britain, was chaired by two LSE economics professors, Tim Besley and John Van Reenen. Its membership included economists, business people and former policymakers, including Philippe Aghion, Lord John Browne, Francesco Caselli, Richard Lambert, Rachel Lomax, Christopher Pissarides and Lord Nicholas Stern. The LSE Growth Commission had recommendations for what a twenty-first-century Britain needs to do to raise its economic game. Its relevance to the past, however, came in one striking finding.

The LSE Growth Commission noted that Britain's long-term growth rate, taking the period from 1830 to 2008, was a reasonably impressive 2 per cent a year. Though 2 per cent a year average growth does not sound that much, the effect of compounding means that such a trend delivers a doubling of living standards every thirty-five years. In 2008, in other words, living standards were more than five times higher than in 1830, when the duke of Wellington was prime minister. For much of that period, however, Britain's relative performance, in comparison with other industrial countries, was second-best. 'Although the UK has enjoyed significant improvements in material well-being for well over two centuries, UK GDP per capita was in relative decline compared with other leading countries, such as France, Germany and the US, from around 1870', it pointed out. The effect of this was that, by the late 1970s, the USA's per capita GDP was 40 per cent higher than Britain's, while per capita GDP in the big European economies was 10 to 15 per cent higher.

Then things changed, and they changed around 1980. After a century in which Britain's relative performance had been poor, and competitors had done much better, a trend particularly pronounced in the period since 1950, Britain threw off the shackles. As the LSE authors wrote, of the experience since 1980: 'The subsequent three decades, in contrast, saw the UK's relative performance improve substantially so that by the eve of the crisis in 2007, UK GDP per capita had overtaken both France and Germany and reduced significantly the gap with the US.' There was a British economic renaissance, at least in part, from around 1980 onwards, and it was no flash in the pan. Though there were macroeconomic ups and downs, some of them significant and damaging, Britain's underlying performance improved. For the first time in a very long time, there was something to envy about the economy, something to be learned from the UK experience. If it was possible to build a lasting revival from the wreckage of a humiliating IMF rescue, and a deep manufacturing recession, Britain was demonstrating how.

Of course, as those who remember the period will recall, it was never plain sailing. The decade of the 1970s was turbulent, and that turbulence did not come to an abrupt end in the 1980s. If there was a miracle, it kept itself pretty well hidden for quite a long time. Neither, however, was the revival built on sand, or the narrow contribution of the City, the financial services sector. The LSE Growth Commission found that the improvement was not 'a finance-driven statistical mirage'. Of its estimate of 2.8 per cent annual market-sector productivity growth, or increase in output per employee, over the period 1980 to 2007, only a small proportion came from financial services: 0.2 percentage points in the period from 1979 to 1997 and 0.4 percentage points in the immediate pre-crisis decade, 1997–2007. Other parts of the service sector, including business and professional services, made a sustained contribution, as did manufacturing and information and communications. It was a broad-based revival. The question is why it happened.

Part of the union

Though the 1979 general election could be seen as a vote against the industrial relations chaos and trade union extremes of the winter of discontent – a collective cry of 'enough is enough' – it was still the case that many people belonged to a union. I certainly did. Most journalists belonged to the National Union of Journalists (NUJ), not least because to work on many titles, and certainly on Fleet Street, it was a requirement. In some cases the Institute of Journalists was also recognised but, just as the print unions ruled the roost in the physical production of newspapers, so the NUJ was a dominant force in the nation's newsrooms. The union controlled entry into journalism, insisting that most reporters had first to serve an apprenticeship by working for a regional or local newspaper, usually for three years. One way round that, which I exploited, was the so-called specialist route into journalism. But that route did not preclude union membership. Though many grumbled, union membership was unremarkable. For a brief period when I was working at *Financial Weekly*, I was the NUJ 'father of chapel', the equivalent of a shop steward, which was strange, and thus had to negotiate with management. Though the paper never went on strike, another of the titles based at Robert Maxwell's Maxwell House did, and staff occupied their floor of the building for several days. Maxwell, despite being a former Labour MP, presided over pretty poor industrial relations.

To belong to a union was common, in both the public and private sectors. Union membership peaked at 13.2 million in 1979, more than half of the number of people in employment, though a small minority of those who were union members were unemployed or retired. Even in 1983, after a deep industrial recession and four years of Margaret Thatcher there were 11.3 million union members, just under half of the employed workforce. Some belonged to a union because they wanted to and because they believed it brought better pay and conditions. Some remained in a union because of inertia, or because it was the natural and expected thing in the sector in which they worked. Many were in a union because it was a condition of their employment; they were in a 'closed shop'. It was this closed shop – not giving people the right to choose whether they wanted to be unionised or not – which was the first target of a Thatcher government determined to reduce the power, and what it saw as the malign influence, of the unions.

Step-by-step reform

Trade union reform was central to the Conservative Party's manifesto promise to voters in 1979, and union reform was the centrepiece of the 'supply-side' changes that provided the basis for the improvement in Britain's long-run economic performance. There were four major pieces of trade union legislation under Thatcher, beginning almost from the start of her eleven years in power. So the 1980 Employment Act gave employers the right to take legal action against unions engaged in secondary picketing (union members not directly involved in a dispute picketing a workplace). It removed the right of unions to claim – and expect – recognition from employers, and allowed employees to opt out of union membership on conscientious grounds, even in closed shops. Before that, even people with the most fundamental objection to union membership had to belong, if they were in a closed shop and it was a condition of their employment. The 1980 Act also introduced something that was later to become increasingly important: funding for postal ballots. It was the beginning of a shift away from 'show of hands' votes for strike action, which were not only under the control of the shop stewards but also saw workers often intimidated into supporting industrial disputes.

A second Employment Act followed in 1982, further strengthening the rights of employers to take legal action against unions engaged in industrial action, rather than just the local organisers of disputes. It also made it more difficult for the

unions to bring workers out for 'political' strikes: strikes uncon-
nected with pay, conditions or other direct grievances. The aim
was to outlaw so-called days of action (which in practice meant
inaction), which were common in the period. One example was
over union recognition at the Government Communications
Headquarters (GCHQ). It became a *cause célèbre* for the union
movement. The 1982 Act made unions liable for the costs of
such days of action, if employers decided to pursue them for
such costs. This Act also continued the process of squeezing out
the closed shop, offering employers and employees protection
against closed shops that had not been approved by an over-
whelming majority of workers and prohibiting 'union labour
only' contracts.

There were two more significant pieces of legislation in
the 1980s. The 1984 Trade Union Act required secret ballots,
usually by post, for the election of senior union officials. It
also gave unions a powerful incentive to hold secret ballots
ahead of strikes. Unless there was such a ballot, the unions
would lose their legal immunity against the costs of a strike.
Unions would also be required to ballot their members every
ten years on whether they wished to continue their political
funds (overwhelmingly donations to the Labour Party). The
aim, apart from taking the politics out of union membership,
was to weaken Labour's funding base. Finally, the Employment
Act of 1988 consolidated many of the themes from the earlier
legislation. It ended legal protection for closed shops and out-
lawed industrial action to enforce them. It also, among other
things, protected union members from disciplinary action by
their unions if they refused to take part in strikes.

This was an impressive legislative barrage against the unions,
deliberately done in a step-by-step way, and was important. The
legal and other privileges that the unions had built up over
eighty years were dismantled over the course of a decade. But
laws are one thing. What the Conservatives also needed were

some big victories against the unions. After all, governments – Conservative and Labour – had introduced laws before to restrict the power of the unions, only to lose their nerve in the face of concerted industrial action. As well as legislating, the government had to show it had the stomach for the battle. Fortunately, those opportunities soon arrived, with two big industrial disputes. And, fortunately, the government did its homework, and prepared the ground.

The energetic Nigel Lawson

One of the genuine major figures – so-called big beasts – of the Thatcher era, and beyond, was Nigel Lawson. Until Gordon Brown (chancellor from 1997 to 2007) beat his record, Lawson's six and a half years at the Treasury helm – from 1983 to 1989 – were the longest chancellorship in the modern era. Before then, he helped win one of the Thatcher government's most important battles. Lawson was a big figure in more ways than one. Until he went on a self-imposed diet many years later, albeit on his doctor's advice, and enjoyed brief success with *The Nigel Lawson Diet Book*, the best way to describe him was round. Not exactly fat, and more than merely stocky, he was what tailors used to describe as portly. He was also a big figure in other respects. Having been a journalist himself, on the *Financial Times*, as editor of *The Spectator* and City editor of the *Sunday Telegraph* (his son Dominic followed a similar path, though he went one better and became editor of the *Sunday Telegraph*), the elder Lawson did not have too much time for most journalists. He retained friends from his *Financial Times* days, most notably Samuel Brittan, but with most in the economics press pack and the political journalists in the lobby his general approach was aloof and superior. He gave the impression that he thought most of us, as he later said of City economists, were 'teenage scribblers'. Press conferences or briefings with Lawson were occasions where he handed down tablets of wisdom. Rarely was there a dialogue, and often his reaction to a question was to feign bemusement at its naivety, though that did not stop him being a fascinating character.

In 1981, having helped lay the groundwork of the government's economic strategy as financial secretary to the Treasury, Lawson was appointed energy secretary. He succeeded David Howell (later to be George Osborne's father-in-law), who had just endured a humiliating climbdown in the face of pressure from the National Union of Mineworkers (NUM). Though economically dry, Howell was too gentle a figure for politics – he is said to have once committed the mortal sin of 'blubbing', or crying, in front of Thatcher – and she probably did not trust his resolve in any battle with the miners. In any case, the one thing she did not want in February 1981 was a battle with the miners, which she feared the government would lose. You did not need to be a Conservative Party historian to know the antecedents. The episode, like the honouring of the Clegg commission's recommendations on public sector pay described in the last chapter, was a reminder that in the early 1980s the unions still had considerable power, and that it was far from one-way traffic in the government's favour.

It is often thought that Thatcher was merely biding her time in waiting for the right moment to defeat the miners. But, though that may have been how it turned out later, it was not her intention when Lawson was given the job of energy secretary. When he was appointed to the post in September 1981, Lawson's brief, as Thatcher told him directly, was to avoid a coal strike. So he did, and there was no such strike during his period in charge at energy: Thatcher's first term in office. Lawson knew, however, that it was only a matter of time before the NUM, under its militant leader Arthur Scargill, and the government locked horns. So, as he put it: 'I subordinated almost everything to the overriding need to prepare for and win a strike. It was not that I was seeking one. But it was clear that Arthur Scargill was, and I was determined that he should lose it when it came.'

There were three elements to Lawson's planning for a confrontation with the miners he believed was inevitable. The first was to ensure that the right people were at the helm of both the National Coal Board (NCB) and the Central Electricity Generating Board (CEGB), both nationalised industries. This was a period when much of British industry was still under state ownership; the great wave of privatisation was to come later. A tough NCB chairman was needed to take on the union, the NUM, which was accustomed to winning its industrial disputes. Lawson found such a chairman in Ian MacGregor, an American given to occasionally eccentric bouts of behaviour, then running British Steel. At the CEGB, meanwhile, the need was for somebody who would willingly comply with the second element of the plan, which was to build up coal stocks at the power stations to a sufficient level to allow the lights to stay on during a long miners' strike. The débâcle of 1974, when a three-day week as a result of power shortages caused by a miners' strike hit the government harder than the unions, was not one to be repeated. Walter Marshall, a scientist who was running the UK Atomic Energy Authority, and who had fallen out some years earlier with Tony Benn, was happy to take on the role. Finally, and more subtly, Lawson hoped to be able to exploit differences within the NUM, knowing that miners in some of the coalfields did not back Scargill's militancy. Those miners had to be offered a carrot. The proposed development of a new coalfield in the Vale of Belvoir in Leicestershire had raised hopes of future jobs among East Midlands miners, but it had been rejected on environmental grounds by Michael Heseltine, the environment secretary. Lawson managed to persuade Thatcher to get Heseltine to reconsider his decision. This was easier said than done, because the environment secretary was acting, as in all such decisions, on a quasi-judicial basis. Heseltine did, however, partly reverse his decision. The East Midlands miners had their carrot.

A man and a woman

By the time of the miners' strike of 1984–5, Thatcher had been re-elected with a huge majority of 144 – effectively a landslide – the economy was recovering and the opposition was still split between Labour and the SDP. There is probably never a perfect time for a major industrial dispute – the miners' strike was expensive and temporarily pushed the economic recovery into reverse – but this was about as good as it could be for the government. This is not to say that the government was very popular and the miners unpopular – polls showed a lot of sympathy for rank-and-file miners, if not for their leadership. Even more fortunately for Thatcher and her ministers, Scargill and his vice-president, Mick McGahey, made two fundamental blunders. The first, in response to what it regarded as provocation by the NCB's Ian MacGregor – the announcement in early March 1984 of the closure of the Cortonwood colliery in Yorkshire because it was 'uneconomic' – was to call a strike without first holding a national ballot. This not only broke with NUM tradition, such ballots having been carried out before previous strikes, but also allowed the government to dismiss the strike as undemocratic. Opinion polls carried out among NUM members, interestingly, suggested there would have been a comfortable majority in favour of strike action – one MORI poll in March 1984 suggested 62 per cent support – but the leadership's blood was up. The second fundamental error was the timing of the strike. The reason the miners had won in 1974 was because they had made life difficult for industry and the public during the winter. A strike starting in spring was, almost by definition, bound to be less effective. Many months would go by, months in which miners would be without pay, before such a strike could be expected to seriously bite. It was a long time from March 1984 to the following autumn and winter.

The year-long miners' strike was bitter and bloody, and this is not the place for a detailed account of it. The bitterness will take many years to go away. In April 2013, when Margaret Thatcher died, the former mining village of Goldthorpe in South Yorkshire held a celebration to coincide with her official ceremonial funeral at St Paul's Cathedral. There were many such celebrations in mining areas. At Goldthorpe, where the pit had closed in 1994, a decade after the strike, a horse-drawn carriage carrying a coffin containing an effigy of the former prime minister was paraded through the streets past (mainly) cheering residents. At the end of its journey the effigy was burned alongside a fireworks display. One prominently displayed poster said: 'The Lady's not for turning but tonight she'll be for burning.' Some residents, to be fair, said that, though they disagreed with Thatcher and everything she stood for, the celebration of her death was disrespectful. Apart from the closure of the village pit two decades earlier, there was another reason for local anger. During the miners' strike, in an episode that could have been taken from the pages of George Orwell's *The Road to Wigan Pier*, two teenage brothers died while picking coal when the embankment they were on collapsed beneath them.

While the preparatory work was done by others, including Lawson, his successor at the Department of Energy, Peter Walker, and the heads of the relevant nationalised industries, the miners' strike came down to a battle of wills between Thatcher and Scargill. Lawson's three-part strategy worked, so that by the time of the strike the power stations were replete with coal: almost 50 million tons of it. The CEGB also had the flexibility to be able to switch to nuclear and gas to generate electricity. Ian MacGregor, the NCB chairman, was up for the fight. The strike was not unanimous, which again was part of the plan. Miners in Nottinghamshire and North Derbyshire did not come out on strike, and neither did those in Lancashire. The NUM's tactics played into the government's hands. Thatcher, however, left nothing to chance. She insisted on a national policing strategy for the strike, co-ordinated by Scotland Yard, to ensure that the miners were defeated whenever and wherever they gathered in numbers. Thousands of miners regularly did battle with similar numbers of police, in what became a fight to the finish. Fresh from her victory in the Falklands two years earlier, she decided that the war with the miners had to be run like a military campaign. Sometimes it was too close to open warfare for comfort. The 'Battle of Orgreave' – the fight over the picketing of a coking plant near Rotherham in Yorkshire – has become part of the legend of this bitter dispute and, for the miners, a case study in police brutality. It was not just a battle between the police and the miners but it also pitched North against South. Many of the officers on duty were from the Metropolitan Police in London.

About half-way through the miners' strike I moved to *The Times* as economics correspondent. The paper, then based in Gray's Inn Road, near Holborn, was just about to celebrate its bicentenary. For that we were given, by the editor Charles Douglas-Home, a print of the painting *Waiting for The Times* by Benjamin Robert Haydon, which I still have on my wall, as well as commemorative mugs and other gifts. There was also a visit by the queen, early in 1985, to mark the bicentenary. As one of the few people who knew how it worked, I was given the task of demonstrating the Datastream machine, a now ancient piece of technology which we used to generate economic and financial charts, to the duke of Edinburgh, though for some reason it never happened. Something else did, however. The queen was introduced to Paul Routledge, the paper's formidable labour editor. Such was the prevalence of strikes in those days that every newspaper had a team of labour or industrial relations editors and correspondents. *The Times* had a team of three. The queen got to talking with Routledge about the miners' strike, and she said words to the effect: 'I suppose it is all down to one man now.' News buzzed around the office that Routledge, quick as a flash, had said: 'And one woman.' The truth, sadly, was a little more prosaic. His own account later was that he said it was rather unlikely that one man could single-handedly get 100,000 miners out on strike. At the time he was sympathetic to Scargill. Later he blamed the NUM leader for mishandling the strike.

The miners returned to work in March 1985, with only miners in the Kent coalfield remaining on strike. It was a bitter defeat. The pit closure programme would continue, and there would be no amnesty for sacked miners. For Thatcher this was the domestic victory that complemented her success in the Falklands and, more than anything, established her reputation as the iron lady. There was another big industrial dispute to come – Wapping, of which more later – but the 1984–5 miners' strike, in combination with the government's legislative reforms, broke the back of the unions. There were bitter recriminations over the failure of the Labour Party and the Trades Union Congress to do more to support the NUM. But divisions within the union and the rise of the rival – and peaceful – Union of Democratic Mineworkers complicated the issue. But after the strike, the union movement would never be the same again. In less than six years in office Thatcher had achieved one of her central aims.

Was it a good outcome for Britain? In terms of bringing industrial peace, however hard won, undoubtedly yes; the miners' strike was a pivotal moment. The strike, however, also marked the beginning of the end of large-scale coal production in Britain. An industry that had provided the basis for two and a half centuries of industrial strength would be wound down dramatically. At the start of the strike there were 195,000 people employed in coal-mining in Britain, and output was 105 million tonnes a year (itself less than half the peak in the 1950s). By 2013 there were fewer than 6,000 working in the industry, and output was just 13 million tonnes. This did not mean that Britain was not using coal, just that most of it was imported: between 45 and 50 million tonnes a year. Britain's mining industry had been run down because it was regarded as expensive and prone to difficult industrial relations. It may not have been the best thing to do in the country's long-term interests.

Industrial peace brings its rewards

Industrial peace did not come to Britain immediately after the collapse of the miners' strike, but it soon did. During the period 1891 to 1990, an average of 9 million working days were lost a year as a result of industrial disputes. That average was bumped up by the General Strike, when 162 million working days were lost, and by 1921, when the total was nearly 86 million. The 1921 national coal strike, in response to proposed wage cuts when the mines were returned to private ownership after the First World War, was accompanied by strikes in other industries and was a rehearsal for the General Strike. But in the hundred years from 1891 there were only two years, 1934 and 1940, when fewer than a million days were lost to strikes. In contrast, in two decades and more from 1991 there were only four years when strikes led to the loss of more than a million working days. The average was just over 600,000, a fraction of what had been regarded as the norm.

Industrial peace as a result of the decline in union membership and militancy was not the only factor in the improvement in Britain's long-run performance that began in the 1980s. It was, however, certainly a significant factor. So the LSE Growth Commission noted the improvements in Britain's labour market, its improved flexibility, 'through reform of the public employment service in improving job search for those on benefits, reducing replacement rates, increasing in-work benefits and restricting union power'. Professor Stephen Nickell, the labour market expert, who served on both the Bank of England's monetary policy committee and at the independent Office for Budget Responsibility, has been more explicit about the role of union reform. In a speech in 2001 he observed that in most European countries wages were still mainly determined by collective bargaining between employers and unions. This had been very much the case in Britain; in 1980, 70 per cent of employees were covered by such trade union collective agreements. In the following two decades the proportion covered by such agreements halved.

There were three factors behind the decline in union membership, as described by Nickell. One was the legislation itself. A second was the decline in employment in some of the heavily unionised sectors of the economy. A third, partly as a result of the legislation and partly the change in the structure of the economy (more services, relatively less manufacturing), was that newer businesses were much less likely to be unionised. Only 14 per cent of manufacturing plants set up since 1980 were unionised, compared with 50 per cent before, while in services the figures were less dramatic but also down: 18 per cent versus 28 per cent. The effect of these changes, the shift to a more flexible labour market, was to improve the trade-off between inflation and unemployment.

The decline in the power and influence of the unions was one of the key changes of the 1980s, and one of the lasting legacies of the Thatcher era. By 2013 there were still around 6.5 million trade union members in Britain, less than half their peak in the late 1970s. Just over a quarter (25.6 per cent) of employees were union members, though this varied significantly between the public sector, in which 55.4 per cent of workers belonged to a union, and the private sector, where just 14.4 per cent – one in seven – were.

The unions were not yet an endangered species, particularly in the public sector, but their role was seriously circumscribed.

Supply-side revolution

Though it is common now to talk about supply-side economics – reforms that increase flexibility, incentives, productivity and thus long-run economic growth – the phrase is a relatively recent one. It came from the political right in the USA, with opinions varying about whether it should be attributed to Jude Wanniski, a *Wall Street Journal* columnist, or Herbert Stein, an American Enterprise Institute fellow who chaired the Council of Economic Advisers under two US presidents: Nixon and Ford. All are agreed that it came into use in the mid-1970s in the USA and took a couple of years after that to make its way across the Atlantic. One big set of supply-side reforms was located firmly in the labour market. Employers were given more freedom to hire and fire with the abolition of employment protection legislation. They were also given more freedom to set wages with the scrapping of most wages councils, which had set industry norms.

In contrast to most of the rest of Europe, where labour markets were and are tightly regulated, Britain had a powerful blast of liberalisation. The fact that these changes were, for much of the Thatcher era, associated with high unemployment did not make them easy to sell politically. Unemployment averaged just over 2.8 million during Thatcher's time in office. The fact that it was swelled by the bulge of the large numbers of young people born in the 1960s entering the workforce meant that leaving things entirely to the market was never an option. The government introduced the Youth Training Scheme (YTS), for which the record was mixed, and which prompted accusations of using a 'make work' programme to massage down unemployment. The Manpower Services Commission, which operated the YTS, was created by the Heath government in the early 1970s and lasted until the late 1980s. As always, Thatcher's radicalism was accompanied by a large dose of pragmatism.

The other supply-side reforms of the era had the virtue of being generally popular. It took time before the Thatcher government could genuinely be said to have delivered low taxes. Following the first Geoffrey Howe budget of June 1979, when the top rate of income tax was cut from 83 to 60 per cent and the basic rate from 33 to 30 per cent, there was a long wait for further action. Howe partly reversed the effects of his 1981 austerity budget in his pre-election budget of 1983, raising the personal tax allowance by more than inflation. And for a time raising the personal allowance appeared to be the Conservatives' preferred mechanism for reducing income tax, as it did for the Conservative–Liberal Democrat coalition government elected in 2010. When, in 1986, Nigel Lawson, by then chancellor, announced a modest cut in the basic rate of income tax from 30 to 29 per cent, the 1979 target of achieving a basic rate of 25 per cent had been almost forgotten. That was followed by a reduction to 27 per cent in 1987, in time for the election of that year. Lawson's biggest and boldest move, cutting the basic rate to 25 per cent and the top rate to 40 per cent, came in March 1988. In terms of sending out a signal to the world that Britain was a low-tax country, particularly for high earners but also for those on average earnings, it could not have been more powerful. As an example of sensible macroeconomic management, as we shall see, it was about as badly timed as it was possible to be.

Low taxes and a flexible labour market were two key elements of the supply-side revolution, but there were others. Before he was radical on income tax, Lawson reformed corporation tax in his first budget in 1984, in a way that encouraged existing businesses to invest and new ones, particularly from other countries, to set up here. This, it may be recalled, was part of the rationalisation for the abolition of exchange controls in 1979.

His reform abolished many of the tax reliefs that businesses had previously enjoyed and used the proceeds to announce a big cut in corporation tax. It was cut, in three stages, from 52 to 35 per cent. Before Britain became a low income-tax country, it achieved one of the lowest rates of business tax in the industrialised world. This was popular, and business-friendly, though it was accompanied by another slice of pragmatism. Nissan, which was in negotiation to establish what became its successful car plant in the north-east – the chosen site was Washington, Tyne and Wear – had been attracted by the promise of generous tax reliefs: being able to offset some of their investment against tax. Special arrangements were put in place to allow it to do so. The Nissan plant, along with plants established by Toyota at Burnaston in Derbyshire and by Honda in Swindon, represented a rebuilding of Britain's motor industry out of the ashes of the failure of the indigenous firms. I remember Lord Young of Graffham, when he was running the Department of Trade and Industry (though he took the title Secretary of State for Enterprise), telling a group of sceptical journalists that these Japanese-owned 'transplants', which had their eyes on the European as well as the UK market, would return Britain to a trade surplus in cars. He was right, though it took a lot longer than he thought. Some twenty-five years after he made the prediction, Britain ran such a surplus: in 2013.

Scaling back the state

When, in November 1985, the earl of Stockton, the former Conservative prime minister Harold Macmillan, made a speech to the Tory Reform Group which touched on the theme of privatisation, nothing better illustrated the gulf between the old, Eton-educated high Tory of the 1950s and his brash state-school successor. He described what families, or governments, do when strapped for cash. 'First of all the Georgian silver goes', he said.

'And then all that nice furniture that used to be in the salon. Then the Canalettos go.' The implication was clear, and quickly and widely reported. The Thatcher government's privatisation programme was akin to selling the family silver, squandering precious assets for a fast buck. Not only would Thatcher and her loyal ministers never have used analogies about Georgian silver and the salon, but what came naturally to the grouse-shooting Tory grandee would never have occurred to them. Moreover, there could have been nothing more fitting for a modern Conservative than reversing the scourge of nationalisation. Most of the industries that the post-war Attlee government had taken into public ownership in the 1945–51 period were still there, plus one or two more besides. Privatisation not only fitted the Tory ideology of scaling back the state but it also reversed one of the key policies of their political opponents (a policy that, had Labour been re-elected in 1979, it wanted to take further).

A few days after making his remarks, Lord Stockton sought to clarify what he had said. He had been, he said, misunderstood. 'As a Conservative, I am naturally in favour of returning into private ownership and private management all those means of production and distribution which are now controlled by state capitalism', he said in the House of Lords. What he was worried about was the idea of the proceeds of these sell-offs being used as just another source of government revenue, rather being put to more productive use by being reinvested. He was a wily old fox, and knew what he was doing. Just as he had expressed his concern over the impact of the recession of the early 1980s on Britain's industrial heartlands, and the effects of the miners' strike on coalfield communities, so he was demonstrating that there was also a caring Conservatism, possibly one that would re-emerge when Thatcher was gone. If his 'selling the family silver' speech was misunderstood, part of that misunderstanding was his own doing.

Privatisation was one of the defining policies of the Thatcher era. In her first two terms Mrs Thatcher was not particularly successful at reducing the size of the state as conventionally measured. Public sector current spending (wages, salaries and public services) was equivalent to 39.7 per cent of GDP in 1986–7, compared with 38.3 per cent in 1978–9, though the booming economy and falling unemployment helped push it down to just over 35 per cent of GDP by the time she left office in 1990. Privatisation, however, addressed an equally relevant measure of the state's role: its direct involvement in areas which had once been the preserve of the private sector, and could be again. Under Thatcher around forty businesses employing more than 600,000 were moved from the public to the private sector, some in a blaze of publicity and 'Tell Sid' (the British Gas sale) small shareholder campaigns, some more quietly. Privatisation saw not only traditional industries such as steel back in the private sector but also the utilities – gas, electricity, water – the ports and telecommunications (and eventually, though much later, Royal Mail). Privatisation, at first ideological – with Labour pledging to reverse it – became permanent, on pragmatic grounds. When Tony Blair was elected in 1997, he was under pressure to reverse the complex railway privatisation that had just occurred – initially one of the least successful sell-offs – but successfully persuaded his party that there were bigger priorities than compensating the new private owners of the railways.

The list of privatisations included the sale of government stakes (some of them partial, some 100 per cent) in British Petroleum, British Aerospace, Cable & Wireless, Associated British Ports, British Telecom, BAA (the former British Airports Authority), British Gas (nationalised by the Attlee government when over a thousand local gas companies were brought into public ownership), British Airways (formed out of BOAC – the British Overseas Airways Corporation – and British European Airways), Rolls-Royce, British Steel and the water industry, when ten publicly owned water and sewerage companies were privatised in 1989. After she left office, there were four other significant privatisations. They included British Rail, perhaps one of the most controversial sell-offs, and British Energy, which operated eight nuclear power stations, both in the 1990s. Perhaps most symbolic of all was the privatisation of the coal industry roughly a decade after the bitter strike which divided the nation. In 2013, the Conservative–Liberal Democrat coalition government privatised Royal Mail, something regarded even by Thatcher as a bit daring.

Privatisation stuck, and it was copied around the world. It is perhaps the most enduring legacy of the Thatcher era. When Tony Blair successfully persuaded the Labour Party in 1994 to abandon its commitment (under Clause IV of its constitution) to common ownership of the means of production, distribution and exchange, the success of the privatisation had much to do with it, as did Blair's rejection – despite pressure from within the party – of re-nationalisation. There was an arc of privatisation. It started tentatively in the early 1980s, with the sale of part of the government's stake in British Petroleum, before giving way to the mass 'popular capitalism' sales of the rest of the decade, including British Telecom and British Gas. These sales were criticised for giving too much to investors and, in particular, giving an instant profit to professional investors who engaged in so-called 'stagging': buying a large stake on the day of issue with a view to making an instant profit by selling immediately. Not everybody did so, however. When two of my aunts died, I inherited, along with my cousins, small stakes in British Telecom and the successor company to British Gas. The privatisation model changed in the 1990s with British Rail, and its break-up into three constituent parts: the owners of the track, the rolling stock and the franchised train operators. Though the privatised rail industry has been successful, it is far from clear that the chosen model was the right one.

Interestingly, when the coalition privatised Royal Mail in 2013, it went back to the original 1980s' model and was criticised for selling a national asset off too cheaply, allowing investors to make a fat profit.

So comfortable do the former nationalised industries seem in the private sector that it is hard to remember they were state-owned. Certainly if you asked many young people whether British Airways or British Telecom were once state-owned, they would look askance. Privatisation changed the culture. It fostered a belief, which has also stuck (though it was a little battered during the financial crisis), that businesses are better if they are privately owned, and run by managers rather than public servants.

A fast track to home ownership

Britain did not become a nation of home-owners during Margaret Thatcher's time in office, but she provided a significant boost to owner-occupation. At the end of the First World War, just 23 per cent of UK households were owner-occupiers, compared with 76 per cent in private rented accommodation and only 1 per cent in social housing. By 1939 home-ownership had risen slightly, to 32 per cent, where it was to remain until the 1950s. Two things then happened: rising home-ownership and an increase in social (mainly council) housing provision. By 1971, just over half of all housing was owner-occupied, while nearly a third was council housing. The private rented sector declined to just a fifth of the housing stock, and it was to fall further, dropping to just 9 per cent in the early 1990s. By the time the Conservatives were elected in 1979, there was just over 55 per cent owner-occupation, while just under 32 per cent of households were in social housing. The boom in such housing was remarkable. In the thirty years from 1948, council house building never fell below 100,000. In some years it approached

250,000. Nineteen seventy-eight was the last year of 100,000-plus council house building.

This was the context in which the Thatcher government launched what was to be the hugely popular 'Right to Buy' programme. It resulted in millions of council houses being sold to their tenants, though little thought was given to replacing the lost social housing with new properties. For the Thatcher government, allowing people to own their own homes, particularly homes that had been previously owned by the state, was an achievement in itself. The scheme, introduced in 1980, offering tenants huge discounts to buy their council house, had by the mid-1990s resulted in 2.2 million such homes being sold.

Council estates, which at least for a time during the building boom of the 1950s had verged on the classless, with people from many walks of life taking up council tenancies, if only temporarily, became very different. The new owners would declare their independence from council ownership by quickly changing their front door – that decision having been previously the preserve of the local authority – before embarking on other improvements. Those that remained in council ownership, in contrast, often suffered from neglect: either council neglect or neglect by their tenants. It was not a hard-and-fast rule, but anybody walking around a council estate could usually spot the 'Right to Buy' homes by their doors and well-tended gardens. Tory councillors and candidates knew which doors to knock on if they wanted a good reception during election campaigns.

Social housing provision went out of fashion, even though the need for it did not. In 1979–80 local authorities built 85,000 new homes, itself a big drop from the situation a decade earlier, in 1969–70, when 185,000 new council homes (houses and flats) were built. But by the end of the 1980s, fewer than 20,000 council homes were being built (19,380 in 1989–90). By the 1990s local authorities had virtually stopped building new homes. Many of them had transferred their remaining stock to housing associations, and they took up some of the strain of social housing provision. They did not, however, come close to compensating for the drop in council building. At the start of the 1980s housing associations built just over 18,000 new homes, but this declined to under 15,000 by the end of the decade. There was then a rise to more than 38,000 in the mid-1990s (under a Conservative government). Again, however, this was a pale shadow of previous social house-building. Owner-occupation – the private sector – was the thing.

'Right-to-Buy' council house sales helped push owner-occupation up from just over 55 per cent to more than 66 per cent under Thatcher. Two-thirds of housing was owner-occupied by the time Thatcher left office, a proportion that was to creep to an all-time high of just over 70 per cent in the early 2000s. This was a big change. The answer to the question of why the council houses sold to their tenants were not replaced with new housing for the next generation of tenants is a simple one: it barely occurred to ministers. Just as Thatcher is supposed to have said that any man using a bus over the age of thirty was a failure, so it was with social housing. Everybody, surely, would want to own. Why would any government want to maintain a failed tenure model by replacing the council housing sold off to tenants? That was the view, if only slightly caricatured. It was a mistake, but it was one that was to endure. The lowest level of building for new social housing in the post-war era occurred in 2003, under Tony Blair's Labour government.

The Battle of Wapping

There was one more major union dispute to come in the 1980s, and it was one I was intimately involved in. I joined *The Times* as economics correspondent in September 1984, as noted. There have been many benefits to having studied economics at university, which I did at both undergraduate and post-graduate level. This was the most obvious. The job came down to a choice between me and an internal rival. He, unfortunately for him, had done a history degree. The editor believed his economics correspondent should have an economics degree. I had two, so the job was mine. As an aside, this was a more successful interview process than I went through at the end of my first degree in Cardiff in the 1970s. Cardiff had a highly successful postgraduate school of journalism, and, given my interest, I went along to explore the possibility of studying there. After a very pleasant afternoon visiting the various heads of department, my final interview was with the school's director. I remember to this day him leaning well back in his chair, and saying: 'Mr Smith, there are many things you will do well in life but I can assure you that journalism will not be one of them.'

Working at *The Times*, and conscious, if only in the back of my mind, of proving that director wrong, was wonderful. All of us, working in trade papers, the specialist press or magazines, wanted to work for a national paper, to work on Fleet Street, though *The Times* was a couple of long streets away from the traditional home of newspapers. My journey into journalism had been a haphazard one. My second job as an economist, working for the Henley Centre for Forecasting, involved contributing to a regular forecast article for the *Sunday Telegraph*. It was trying to compete with the *Sunday Times*, which since the mid-1960s had had a similar relationship with the London Business School. When the City editor of the *Sunday Telegraph*, Patrick Hutber, let it be known that he wanted an economist to work with him on a new publication, a weekly glossy (and right-wing) news magazine being launched by the flamboyant billionaire Sir James Goldsmith, the job came my way, though only after a colleague had turned it down. The early death of Hutber in a car crash meant I was thrust into more by-lined writing than I had expected. The magazine, *Now!*, lasted nineteen months (I still have a full set of copies) before it folded under the burden of huge losses, despite a pledge from Goldsmith to keep it going for at least five years. Fortunately, this was a time of expansion for publishing. Armed with a redundancy cheque, I was able to walk straight into another job, with *Financial Weekly*, after just over three years of which I got the job on *The Times*.

On *The Times* I was economics correspondent and Sarah Hogg was economics editor. Kenneth Fleet was the City editor, in charge of the business section. He, like Patrick Hutber, was among the last of the breed of big and hugely influential City editors. There were opportunities to meet senior officials and politicians when working at *Financial Weekly* and *Now!* Such access increased hugely, however, at *The Times*. Suddenly politicians, including ministers, were very keen to meet. Suddenly too, you were expected to lunch and talk regularly to senior officials at the Treasury and the Bank of England, and elsewhere. There were times when such relationships did not run smoothly. At one stage I did an interview with Eddie George, later the governor of the Bank of England, and later still Lord George. There was a dispute, after publication, over whether some of his quotes were on or off the record, and a furious George banned me from the offices of the Bank of England, which also prohibited any contact with the Bank's press office, or any of its officials. Fortunately, Kenneth Fleet stood by his journalist and said that if there was to be no contact between me and the Bank, there would be no contact between the Bank and any *Times* journalist. The ban was quickly lifted.

Though working for *The Times* was great, there was a cloud hanging over it. The dispute that had closed it and the *Sunday Times* in 1978–9 had never been properly resolved. The print unions continued to resist changes in working practices and, in particular, the introduction of new technology. Newspapers were overmanned and, thanks to the resistance of the unions, stuck with very old 'hot metal' technology. They were also increasingly unreliable bearers of news. There were too many days, at Gray's Inn Road, when production was disrupted by an industrial dispute, in some cases with the loss of the entire print run. When you have worked all day to produce a newspaper, hearing at a late stage that your efforts were wasted did not endear the printers to you. Despite this, the sudden announcement in January 1986 that, under Rupert Murdoch's direction, members of the print unions were to be dismissed was a shock. So was the fact that his four titles, *The Times*, the *Sunday Times*, *The Sun* and the *News of the World*, were to be transferred immediately to a new site at Wapping. The fact that hundreds of journalists were unaware of the move showed how successful the secret operation was, which included the recruitment of replacement printers, a smaller number of them, from members of the moderate electricians' trade union.

At *The Times* journalists had a weekend of meetings at a nearby Holborn hotel, to decide whether we wanted to go along with the move to Wapping. My memory is that those who spoke out most strongly in favour did not stay long at the new plant, which came to be called Fortress Wapping because it was surrounded by barbed wire and razor wire, and heavily guarded. Some decided not to go, to become 'refuseniks' (the name given to Soviet dissidents), and for a short time I was one of them. I turned up at the headquarters of the NUJ, near King's Cross, on the Monday morning we were supposed to report for duty at Wapping, along with around fifteen others from *The Times*. We were then given the bad news that the company was perfectly within its rights to move our place of employment within a three-mile radius, which was all it was. This was leavened by the fact that our friends on Fleet Street were pulling together to provide opportunities, and that there were sub-editing shifts available on the *Daily Express*. Having never done such a shift in my life, I made my excuses and, with one or two others, left for Wapping.

The Wapping dispute was bitter and often violent. Travelling into work through picket lines was never less than uncomfortable. You did not broadcast who you worked for. One *Times* journalist who returned to an old Gray's Inn Road haunt, a pub, was attacked with a glass. Plenty of others were subjected to lower-level threats. It was a nasty time. Many of the journalists who worked in Wapping did so less than willingly, though as the dispute went on most fell out of any sympathy they had had with the print unions. The Wapping dispute ended in February 1987, less than two years after the collapse of the miners' strike. The print unions ended up as neutered as the National Union of Mineworkers. Two big defeats left the unions irrevocably weakened. They would never be the same again. Through a combination of legislation and big tactical victories the Thatcher era signalled the end of the unions as a powerful force in Britain.

As I write this, the Wapping site, over which so much blood was spilt and emotion generated, is being demolished. News International moved its printing operations away from the site to a new purpose-built facility in Broxbourne in 2005. The journalists, advertising teams and others followed in 2010 and, when a plan for the company to redevelop the site was abandoned, it was sold for £150 million. When the dust settles on the demolition, Wapping will become an urban village, developed by the Berkeley Group's St George subsidiary, with luxury housing, including what it describes as 'stunning apartments and penthouses, beautifully landscaped open spaces, water and market gardens, central squares and promenades, lined with shops, bars and restaurants'. It is not known whether there will be a plaque there, to commemorate its more notorious past.

From renaissance to boom and bust

The Thatcher era began with the economy on the brink of a nasty recession, and it ended with Britain back in recession. Inflation, which had been tamed in the middle of the decade, was back above 10 per cent by the time a tearful Thatcher left Downing Street on 28 November 1990. For all the achievements on the supply-side – the microeconomic improvements – the macro record was decidedly mixed. For Thatcher, who had made sound money, as well as free markets, the cornerstone of her political philosophy, to leave office against a backdrop of high inflation – and an economy sliding into recession – was mortifying, perhaps even more than what she saw as the treachery of her Cabinet, most of whom had offered her little support in her hour of need. The woman who had saved Britain, as Conservative loyalists saw it, was regarded as an electoral liability by most of the party's professional politicians. Even her closest advisers acknowledged that it was an inglorious end. Though he did not blame her for it, as we shall see, Sir Alan Walters, her erstwhile personal economic adviser, once told me that perhaps a third of the economic gains achieved during her time as prime minister had been squandered in the period after the 1987 general election, her final victory.

Part of the story of how it happened is best kept for a little later, to set the context for 'Black Wednesday' in September 1992, another of those national humiliations that pepper Britain's modern economic history. The Lawson boom and subsequent bust is, however, easily understood without reference to the pound. It begins in 1986, when despite five years of pretty good economic growth, averaging more than 3 per cent a year, unemployment was still above 3 million and panic was starting to build at senior levels in the Conservative Party about the government's chances of winning another election with the jobless total so high. Frequent changes to the calculation of the figures for the numbers claiming unemployment benefit had aroused suspicion, and the government was vulnerable to the charge that a recovery that did not reduce unemployment was not a real recovery at all.

The panic was unnecessary. Figures now show that the

economy was growing by more than 4 per cent in 1986. Unemployment, swollen by a bulge of young people entering the job market, was about to start falling of its own accord, without the need to apply the economic boosters. Apply them, however, Lawson did, under pressure from Thatcher and other members of the Cabinet. It was said that the one thing she would never object to was a cut in interest rates, which reduced mortgage payments for her new generation of home-owners and was always welcomed by the business community. High interest rates were the norm for the Thatcher era. The official interest rate, now known as Bank Rate, averaged 12 per cent over the 1979–90 period. A rate in single figures was unusual, even daring. But this was what Lawson did, reducing the rate below 10 per cent in the run-up to the 1987 election and further – after a very temporary rise brought to an abrupt end by the October 1987 stock market crash – to just above 7 per cent in the spring of 1988.

An interest rate of 7 per cent or so now seems absurdly high. As I write this, Bank Rate has been at 0.5 per cent for more than six years, with the expectation that, when it rises, it will do so only gradually, to perhaps 2.5 or 3 per cent. In the late 1980s, however, 7 per cent was high-risk, the lowest rate for a decade, and fuel for a booming economy and a runaway housing market. Add to the mix three tax-cutting budgets, 1986, 1987 and 1988, which between them reduced the basic rate of income tax from 30 to 25 per cent and the top rate from 60 to 40 per cent, coupled with other measures that clumsily boosted an already overheated housing market, and these were the conditions for the mother of all booms. Lawson did not break Anthony Barber's 1973 record, when the economy grew by 7.4 per cent, but he did achieve growth averaging 5.5 per cent a year in 1987 and 1988. It was enough to get Thatcher comfortably re-elected in June 1987. It was, in almost every other respect, too much. Inflation, it was soon discovered, had not been tamed after all, and from the spring of 1988 began to rise inexorably. House price inflation rose even more spectacularly, reaching more than 30 per cent nationally in late 1988 and early 1989. The added push inadvertently given to house prices by Lawson in his March 1988 budget – abolishing the system whereby multiple buyers of a property (including unmarried couples) could each claim tax relief on mortgage interest – produced even more extraordinary results. Lawson's move, abolishing what one minister described as a 'mortgage racket', was right. The mistake was allowing five months of grace before it was scrapped, leading to a mad scramble to take advantage of the tax relief prior to its abolition (for those taking out new mortgages).

The Treasury was worried, fearing that it had created a monster it could not control. I remember taking Sir Terry Burns to lunch in Westminster around this time, at the Royal Horseguards hotel. Short of writing it down on the napkin, the government's chief economic adviser, later Treasury permanent secretary, could not have been clearer about his worries about the housing boom that had been unleashed. Something had to change, to put a lid on the rise in general inflation and in house prices. Having run interest rates down to what were then very low levels, Lawson had to reach for the only weapon at hand to slow the economy, halt the rise in inflation and prick the housing bubble. The turnaround was sudden, swift and, for both businesses and, more particularly, the home-owners who had rushed into the housing market at the top, very painful. By late November 1988, just six months after their low point, interest rates had almost doubled to 13 per cent. That was not the end of it. In early October 1989 Lawson was forced to raise interest rates to 15 per cent, on the eve of the Tory autumn party conference. The chancellor, under extreme pressure, was particularly troubled by a story in the *Sunday Times* about the interest rate rise. The story, which I wrote, said that Alan Walters, now back in Downing Street as Thatcher's personal economic adviser – and thorn in Lawson's side – had opposed the interest rate hike, fearing correctly that, as in the early 1980s, it would drive the economy into recession. Thatcher had reluctantly sided with her chancellor in agreeing to the rate hike, it said.

Lawson, as he recounts in his autobiography, got to know about the story on the Saturday evening and, via the legendary Downing Street switchboard – said to be able to locate anybody at any time – got hold of Walters. He insisted he had not spoken to the *Sunday Times* but, despite pressure from Lawson, refused to deny the story, as did Downing Street. 'Any dissociation was so feeble that the markets were left to draw their own conclusions', Lawson wrote in his autobiography, *The View from No. 11*. He was badly bruised by the episode, under pressure from within the Tory party, and nearing the end of his long chancellorship. On 26 October he resigned, after first warning Thatcher that either Walters must go or he would have to. The pound, and membership of the European exchange rate mechanism (ERM), were the key points of difference, but what Lawson saw as Walters's malign influence on other aspects of policy, including interest rates, was also a big factor.

'To this day, I do not know how the paper came by their story', he wrote later. With the passage of time, and Walters no longer alive, I should perhaps solve the mystery, and put him out of his misery. Walters was telling the truth when he said that he had not spoken to the *Sunday Times*. I did not talk to him directly over that story. He did, however, have some close and trusted confidants, whom he spoke to regularly, and who were among my best contacts. Whether he knew that, by talking to them, his views would find their way to the front page of a Sunday newspaper I cannot say for certain, but he was a canny operator. The reason no denial could be issued was, of course, that the story was entirely accurate.

6

Another fine mess

Mr President, exactly a week ago, John Major dropped
one of his quiet surprises on an unsuspecting press. Well,
they surprise us sometimes too. He announced that
interest rates would be cut by 1 per cent and that Britain
would enter the Exchange Rate Mechanism. Of course,
we have long been committed to joining the ERM, but
only when our own policies of firm financial discipline
were seen to be working.

Margaret Thatcher, speech to the Conservative Party
conference, Bournemouth, 12 October 1990

Any long-term account of the British economy sooner or later
comes back to the pound. Sterling and sterling crises have punc-
tuated the country's economic progress. This has happened
throughout my lifetime, and indeed long before it. The pound
has been a headache for chancellors and prime ministers through
the decades, usually because it is worryingly weak – and there is
no easier indicator for financial journalists of the country's woes
than a tumbling pound – and occasionally because it has been
too strong. Generations of foreign exchange dealers have grown
up with the idea that the default position for sterling is for it

to be falling. This goes back a long time. After the devaluations of 1949 and 1967, and the IMF crisis of 1976, assuming sterling would continue to fall was the least risky option.

In the late 1970s, in my second full-time job, I was an economist at the Henley Centre for Forecasting responsible for its exchange rate projections. I say responsible for them, but I had to work within the parameters set by James Morrell, the Henley Centre's founder and director. He left me to my own devices when it came to forecasting what might happen to other currencies, but he laid down the rule that the pound would always fall by a few cents a year against the dollar. Sometimes that assumption was contradicted by events, such as the pound's unwelcome strength during the early 1980s. Mostly, it worked. The old adage in the City of London that you rarely lost money betting against the pound was a pretty good one.

Not only was sterling's general record one of frequent turbulence, devaluations and depreciations, but its relationship with currency arrangements in Europe was also a chequered one. In 1972, in the aftermath of the collapse of the Bretton Woods system of fixed but adjustable exchange rates, Edward Heath's Conservative government put sterling into the 'snake in the tunnel', a forerunner of the ERM, intended to maintain currency stability in Europe. The pound lasted for just six weeks in the snake, before the government was forced to allow it to float freely. In the grand scheme of things it was not one of Britain's great currency humiliations, but it told us something. Sterling does not fit happily into fixed currency arrangements, particularly those involving Europe. It was a lesson that had been forgotten in the mists of time.

A surprising convert

Nigel Lawson, as previously noted, was one of the intellectual forces behind the Thatcher government's monetarist experiment. When Alan Walters suggested that the strength of the pound in the early 1980s pointed to monetary policy being too tight, he was dismissive. For the monetarists and for Lawson then, if the money supply was kept under control, the pound could look after itself. All this changed in 1985, just a few months after he had publicly rejected the idea of an exchange rate target in a key speech (his Mais lecture at City University) in October 1984. The commitment to monetary targets – the core of monetarism – had gradually been weakened.

Most of all, Lawson had seen for himself what many of his predecessors as chancellor had experienced. Twice in six months, in July 1984 and January 1985, Lawson had had to respond to a sharply weakening pound. The January 1985 sterling crisis, the more serious of the two, was the death blow to the Thatcher government's monetarist experiment. As sterling tumbled towards one-for-one parity with the dollar, interest rates were increased from 9.5 to 14 per cent in the space of seventeen days. This, a few months after I had joined *The Times* as economics correspondent, was high drama, as well as being a re-run of past episodes in which the government had to respond desperately to a falling pound. Even the Conservatives were not prepared to leave it to the markets. While I was watching and reporting on this at *The Times*, there was even more excitement on another floor of the building at the *Sunday Times*. In January 1985 sterling was falling fast towards one-for-one parity with the dollar. A $1 pound had never happened before, and was a far cry from sterling's heady $2.40-plus heights of just a few years earlier.

After interest rates had first been increased in response to the pound's slide, Margaret Thatcher's press secretary, Bernard Ingham, briefed Sunday newspaper journalists. The government, he said, would not authorise heavy currency intervention to prop it up. Ingham, in a typically robust briefing, appeared to sum up Thatcher's view, which was that you could not artificially support currencies, or, as she later put it, 'you can't buck the market'. This was duly reported by Michael Jones, the *Sunday Times*'s political editor, later a colleague, as the government's willingness to let the pound fall further. Ingham, a great bear of a Yorkshireman, with an impressive set of bushy eyebrows, was careful not to preclude further interest rate increases to support the pound, but the damage was done. The impact was to require an even bigger interest rate response to sterling's decline, to convince dealers that the Treasury, at least, was determined to arrest its fall. Ingham later recounted how he was summoned to the Treasury on 14 January, the Monday after his fateful press briefing; Lawson, Sir Peter Middleton, the permanent secretary to the Treasury, and other senior Treasury officials were gathered, apparently intent on giving him a dressing down. But Ingham's opening line, 'I come to you directly from the Prime Minister', headed off the Treasury attack. He also told the chancellor and his Treasury officials, in a highly provocative comment: 'One thing to come out of this is that at least we will get a policy.' It was a foretaste of the tensions to come.

Lawson's new enthusiasm was for tying sterling, and Britain's monetary policy, to the low-inflation Deutschmark by joining the ERM, and he was not alone. Sir Geoffrey Howe, the foreign secretary, and Sir Leon Brittan, the trade and industry secretary, were powerful allies. Robin Leigh-Pemberton, appointed governor of the Bank of England in 1983, was also in favour, as were a number of senior Treasury officials. This was a period when much of the British establishment, and the business community, collectively decided that its future lay in closer ties with Europe. To oppose ERM entry, as some did inside and outside the Treasury, was to be out of step with the fashion of the day. There was a collective lurch in favour of joining. Such lurches are not unusual in the UK economic policy debate. There is a lesson there somewhere.

An immovable object

Lawson did not get to announce ERM entry in his March 1985 budget speech, but he managed to get it on the Cabinet agenda for a discussion in July 1985. In the meantime his officials had put together a dossier of Treasury evidence, putting the case for entry. The task, it said among other things, was to lock in the government's success in reducing inflation, which sterling's volatility (and particularly its falls) put at risk. Though journalists did not get to see that dossier, the change of Treasury approach, and in Lawson's stance, was clearly visible from private briefings and public hints. Changing Thatcher's view, it seemed, would not be that difficult. She trusted Lawson, and she trusted the Treasury officials who had come round to favouring entry, in contrast to the officials hostile to her policies whom she had inherited in 1979.

Thatcher, however, was not easily persuaded. Her instinctive belief in free markets meant that she was inherently opposed to the idea of putting sterling into an artificial currency arrangement, and a European one at that. Would her great intellectual heroes, Friedrich Hayek and Milton Friedman, have favoured ERM entry? No. Would it be seen as a U-turn and an admission that monetarism had failed? Yes. Would Europe's other political leaders, with whom she had had frosty relations, be quietly rubbing their hands at her capitulation? Yes, too. Apart from all this, she also had Alan Walters, always available on the phone, if not on one of his regular visits to Britain, to stiffen her resolve.

Walters was back in the USA when the ERM debate first began to rage in 1985, but he made clear his view that entry was a thoroughly bad idea. Not only did Walters think Britain should shun the system but he also advanced what became known as the Walters critique of the ERM. As long as the markets were sure that currencies would stick at their agreed exchange rates, in other words no devaluations, currency markets would favour those currencies which offered the highest interest rates, such as high-inflation Italy. Low-inflation economies such as Germany would, paradoxically, suffer weak currencies. The result was that Italy would be under pressure to reduce interest rates to make the lira less attractive, while for Germany the pressure would work in the opposite direction. Left to work through, the level of interest rates in high-inflation Italy and low-inflation Germany would converge, meaning, according to Walters, 'there will be great pressure to expand money and credit in Italy, whereas in Germany there will be a substantial financial squeeze'. So, far from bringing inflation rates in different member countries closer together, the ERM would have the opposite effect. There was a strong echo of this later in what happened when the ERM evolved into the euro.

Thatcher did not need any further persuading. While agreeing on a form of words that committed the government to entry 'when the time is ripe', she made it clear that she did not expect it to be ripe soon. After the March 1985 budget, the next available slot for announcing entry was the Treasury's autumn statement in November of that year. Ahead of that, at a key meeting of ministers and officials, she asked for their views on entry. Her summing up, on being told everybody else around the table favoured it, echoed Abraham Lincoln. 'Yes', she said. 'Ayes seven, noes one, the noes have it.'

Given what happened later, Thatcher's opposition to ERM membership can be seen as heroic. At the time, however, conventional wisdom was that her dogged refusal to contemplate entry was holding Britain back. Even in a business community generally supportive of her reforms her stance was seen as anti-European dogma. While she was sticking to her views, the world was moving on. That, I have to say, was also what I thought at the time. With the benefit of hindsight, that was a significant misjudgement. In the same vein, I was no great admirer of Thatcher the prime minister. Though her governments succeeded in breaking the cycle of decline, she herself was abrasive and appeared to court unpopularity, and her approach often seemed anti-intellectual. Along with most other economic journalists, if we took sides in the Treasury–Downing Street debate, it was on the Treasury's side. Walters, who I did not get to know until later, seemed to be a throwback to an earlier age of monetarist purism.

Shadowing the D-mark

The Group of Five, or G5, later to draw in Italy and Canada and become the Group of Seven (G7), burst into prominence in the mid-1980s. At the end of February 1985, a month after sterling's slump against the dollar had forced a sharp rise in interest rates in Britain, a programme of large-scale dollar sales was instituted by the major central banks. It was driven not by pressures on Britain, though it led to a welcome rise for the pound, but by what was seen by the leading Western economies as the urgent need to get the dollar down to help resolve the problem of the so-called twin deficits (the budget and balance of payments deficits) of Ronald Reagan's USA.

This was a fascinating time. For a while, what the G5 and G7 said and did was the biggest preoccupation of the financial markets. Any snippet of what it might be planning made for a good story. As an economic journalist, you had to be on hand at all the international gatherings: in Washington, New York, Paris, London and occasionally more obscure locations. Finance ministers and central bankers acquired the status of film stars, ferried around in large limousines, their every move followed by journalists, photographers, TV reporters and cameramen. They were the movers and shakers of the world economy. The big central banks, directed by their finance ministries, showed their willingness to back up their talk with action, intervening heavily in the currency markets. The G5's most important action against the dollar came on 22

September 1985 at a meeting at the Plaza Hotel, New York. It issued a statement calling for a 'further orderly appreciation of the main non-dollar currencies against the dollar', or a dollar fall, and spent more than $10 billion to achieve it. The Plaza agreement, or accord, probably represented the high-water mark of such co-operation. However, it was followed seventeen months later by a meeting at the Louvre in Paris. This time, on 22 February 1987, the agreement was that, having achieved the initial aim of getting the dollar lower, it was now necessary to stabilise it at its new lower level.

All this was manna from heaven for Lawson. Having been snubbed by Thatcher in his quest to manage the pound by taking it into the ERM, he had signed up to a deal to manage, or stabilise, all the leading currencies. More importantly, so had the Reagan administration, as ideologically committed to free markets as the Tory government. Currency management was in vogue. Indeed, it was in the ascendancy. For Lawson, with a formal link to the German mark – ERM membership – ruled out by his prime minister, the Louvre accord provided an opening for the next best thing, an informal link: 'shadowing the D-mark'. For him the appeal was twofold. If it worked, it would free him of the sterling instability that had blighted his chancellorship. It would also give him an opportunity to demonstrate that exchange rate targeting worked, as a preparatory exercise for ERM entry, to take place soon after the June 1987 general election.

So the secret strategy was embarked upon, controlled and implemented by Lawson and a small group of senior officials in the Treasury. Thatcher was not told, and was furious when she found out, and the Bank of England was not explicitly involved, though its officials quickly worked out what was going on. The aim was to keep the pound from falling below DM2.80 and, as soon became more relevant, stop it from rising above DM3, mainly by adjusting interest rates, or hinting at doing so. Leaving the Bank out of the inner circle allowed it to distance itself later.

For Lawson the beauty of the new arrangement was that the markets, deterred from attacking the pound by the fear of being caught on the wrong side of central bank intervention, decided instead to start pushing it higher. This produced, for the Tories, the pre-election ideal, by making room for interest rate cuts in the run-up to the June 1987 election, giving Lawson room to reduce rates in stages from 11 to 9 per cent. As was often the case, the only fault Thatcher could find with Lawson at the time was that he did not get his hair cut more often.

It all goes badly wrong

Lawson may have helped win the 1987 election and, unknown to Thatcher, his policy of shadowing the D-mark had helped him to do so. He was, however, about to enter the period of both his greatest success – reducing income tax and in the case of the top rate of tax giving Britain one of the lowest rates in the world – and his greatest failure: losing control of the economy. Within months of the June 1987 election he was faced with the challenge of responding to the October 1987 stock market crash. This was important in its own right, but it was also particularly important to the government because at the time it was in the middle of finalising the sale of the government's stake in British Petroleum: nearly a third of the company, with a market value to the Exchequer of £6 billion. On 19 October 1987, on what immediately became known as Black Monday, shares on Wall Street fell by more than one-fifth, driving down prices elsewhere. The London market dropped by £50 billion, and this was followed by a further £40 billion fall the following day. Around the world markets plunged, but there was a particular eeriness to what happened in Britain. On Friday 16 October a freak hurricane had blown across southern England, ripping centuries-old trees from the ground throughout the London commuter belt of Kent, Surrey, Sussex, Hampshire and East Anglia, and causing extensive damage to buildings. Six of the seven ancient oaks of Sevenoaks in Kent were blown down. I recall a tree-lined suburban street near my home. Against each semi-detached house a tree lay at a 45° angle, having crashed through a roof or bedroom window. That Friday, with transport severely disrupted, the Stock Exchange suspended share trading. On Monday, after a weekend of clearing up, dealers returned to their desks to find a financial hurricane blowing. It felt like the end of an era.

In fact it was. Markets had begun to doubt the Louvre accord agreed the previous February, and so had some of its signatories. The famously independent German Bundesbank, later the model for the European Central Bank, was worried about inflation, as it often was, and wanted to raise interest rates to head off the danger. The problem was that, if it did so then, to keep their currencies stable, others would need to follow. A fierce row erupted between James Baker, the US Treasury secretary, and Karl Otto Pöhl, the Bundesbank president. Baker was reluctant to see US interest rates rise in the run-up to the following year's presidential election. But the Bundesbank would not be deterred. The cosy era of low interest rates (by the standards of the day) and stable currencies was nearing its end, and the markets responded. Even before Black Monday, Wall Street had fallen by 16 per cent in the first half of October 1987.

Lawson, having sprung a surprise by raising interest rates in August 1987, two months after the election, was soon cutting them again. The first cuts were in an attempt to steady the ship in the wake of the stock market crash. Later reductions were in an effort to stop the pound rising too rapidly – and breaching the DM3 ceiling – as the cracks emerged in the Louvre accord. The financial markets decided that Britain was the place to be. Thatcher was apparently politically unsinkable, and her government was turning the country into an oasis of enterprise in a moribund Europe. Money flooded into London, and into sterling, pushing it up against the unofficial ceiling. Lawson ordered the Bank of England to intervene in the markets, selling sterling to hold it down.

This was where the chancellor paid the price for not involving the Bank more closely in his 'shadowing' policy. In early March, two weeks before the budget, the Bank's governor, Robin Leigh-Pemberton, warned Lawson and Thatcher that the policy of holding down the pound could not be sustained, except at the cost of a serious bout of inflation. For the prime minister this was a red rag to a bull. Lord Griffiths, the head of her policy unit, was another distinguished monetarist economist. He recommended abandoning the D-mark target, in line with the Bank's advice, and she needed little persuading. Lawson was summoned to 10 Downing Street and, before he had a chance to argue his case, was told by her: 'I haven't got much time. I've only time to explode and get my way.'

The pound duly rose, as the Bank stopped intervening to hold it down. The DM3 ceiling was breached without any resistance. Lawson, however, had not entirely given up the fight. Too rapid a rise in the pound would hit industry hard, he warned Thatcher. He also played on her weakness for lower interest rates. Even if currency intervention was not desirable, surely there could be nothing wrong with lowering interest rates to reduce sterling's appeal? So in the weeks after his 15 March 1988 budget he again embarked on a policy of cutting interest rates in order to restrain the pound. It was, said one adviser, 'an obsession'. It was also a dangerous one. By May 1988 interest rates had been cut three times since the budget, from 9 to 7.5 per cent – a ten-year low – and this at a time when the economy was booming, income tax had been cut dramatically and the inflation clouds were starting to gather. It was a time of madness which, even at the time, seemed destined to end in tears. The sterling obsession had, once again, led a chancellor astray. The pound's strength gave way to weakness. That and the inflationary pressures the Bank had warned about forced interest rates sharply higher. Within eighteen months they had doubled to 15 per cent. Lawson's strategy backfired badly, and his chancellorship, which for so long had been so promising, ended in failure, with his resignation in October 1989.

The remarkable rise of John Major

Of all the politicians I have come across, the one with the most extraordinary back-story, and the most remarkable rise, was John Major. He was born in Brixton, the son of a former music-hall performer, Tom Major-Ball, who was sixty-four when Major was born. Major left school at sixteen, in 1959, with three O-levels and, having failed to get the job of bus conductor that he applied for, worked as a clerk for the London Electricity Board. He was also a youthful member of the Conservative Party, perhaps slightly eccentrically giving speeches from his soap-box in the unpromising territory of Brixton. He then embarked on a long career in banking, with Standard Chartered, including long spells abroad. Later he worked as an assistant to Anthony (Lord) Barber, the former Conservative chancellor known for the Barber boom, who became chairman of Standard Chartered. Ivan Fallon, one of my former *Sunday Times* colleagues, deputy editor for some years, remembered Major as the man who took your coat when you went to visit Barber, although this did not prevent Fallon from being highly impressed with him when he was challenging for the Conservative leadership in 1990.

Major's relatively humble beginnings, and the fact that he had had a life before politics, set him apart from the generation of career politicians that followed him. So did his meteoric rise. His first ministerial appointment, as a junior minister in the Department of Social Security, was in September 1986. Just over four years later he was prime minister, having held two of the other great offices of state, chancellor and foreign secretary, if only briefly. Only Harold Macmillan and James Callaghan in the modern era have held the posts of prime minister, chancellor and foreign secretary. Major did so in the space of eighteen months in 1989–90, eventually serving as prime minister for a creditable six and a half years: longer in the post-war period than Clement Attlee, Anthony Eden, Harold Macmillan, Alec Douglas-Home, Edward Heath, Jim Callaghan and Gordon Brown.

I first met Major in late 1987, when I was working at *The Times* and he was chief secretary to the Treasury under Lawson, a Cabinet post he had been promoted to after the June 1987 election victory. In those days, getting to know the ministers in the Treasury was an essential part of the job of covering economics. Later, in Gordon Brown's period as chancellor, this became rather less important, because the ministers were often not part of the inner circle, and in many cases knew less about what was going on than we did. There was an element of that when Lawson was chancellor, but his ministers were worth knowing, and, while nobody could have predicted how far or how dramatically his star would rise, Major certainly was. So I met him in the Treasury for a sofa chat. The convention then was not to take a notebook, and certainly not a tape-recorder, to such background meetings. This puzzled him. After spending an hour telling me in great detail how he saw the economy, and what he intended to do about government spending, his brief, he turned to me and said, in a voice that was later to become very familiar: 'Now, you've listened very carefully to everything I've had to say but you haven't written any of it down. How on earth will you remember it?'

Into the ERM

It was on the issue of the ERM that, freshly arrived at the *Sunday Times*, I had one of my best stories, a long-forgotten scoop. The question was whether Thatcher would ever agree to membership of the system. The answer, provided on the morning of Sunday 25 June, was that, subject to what later became known as the Madrid conditions (after the European summit at which she publicly revealed them), she would agree to entry. The conditions, which seemed very important at the time, boiled down to two main things. First, inflation, then running at around 8 per cent – roughly twice the average for ERM member countries – had to be reduced to that average. Second, France and Italy had to remove their remaining capital controls, just as Britain had done in 1979, soon after her first election victory. She was not interested in joining a system that only worked because of controls over capital movements. The hand of Sir Alan Walters, her adviser, could be seen all over these conditions. In particular, his own critique of the ERM meant that joining with a high inflation rate would have the perverse effect of putting the pressure on to reduce interest rates more rapidly than was justified.

Unbeknown to me at the time, on the Sunday morning my front page 'splash' appeared, Lawson and Sir Geoffrey Howe (by then foreign secretary), having earlier requested an urgent meeting with Thatcher in her Downing Street study, pressured her to agree to something like the conditions set out in the newspaper. Whether they had not read it, did not believe it or thought that only by getting her to promise it face to face would it happen is hard to say, even with the passage of time. Lawson and Howe both came away believing they had swung her towards agreeing membership, though she was already clear in her own mind on accepting it subject to her conditions. The ambush, in fact, almost backfired. It took two days for Thatcher to give voice to the Madrid conditions, during which time Downing Street refused to confirm or deny that my story was right. That was a nervous couple of days. Thatcher, meanwhile, was furious about the Downing Street ambush. A month later Howe was demoted to Leader of the House of Commons, though with the fig leaf of the title deputy prime minister. Four months later Lawson was no longer chancellor.

Major succeeded them both, initially taking over from Howe as foreign secretary in July 1989, to almost universal surprise, and then three months later succeeding Lawson as chancellor. Though Major's views on the ERM were not well known, which may have helped his rapid elevation, it quickly became clear that he was an enthusiast, who saw it as his mission to take Britain in. His achievement in doing that should not be understated. Lawson's experiment in shadowing the D-mark, a dress rehearsal for ERM membership, had gone badly wrong. Thatcher, having clipped the wings of Howe and with Lawson no longer in the government, may have thought that the pressure was off to join. Major, however, had two advantages. Thatcher, having lost Lawson, could not afford to risk losing another chancellor, even an inexperienced one, so quickly. He was backed by Douglas Hurd, the new foreign secretary. As one Treasury adviser put it: 'She had lost one chancellor and foreign secretary, so she could hardly afford to do so again.' He also had a strong economic argument. Sterling was weak, partly hit by Britain's political turbulence, even with interest rates at 15 per cent, and there was talk of the need to raise them even further to steady the pound and bear down on inflation. Major argued that by holding out the promise of early ERM entry he could provide a prop for sterling and prevent a politically and economically devastating interest rate rise.

Major and Hurd worked on persuading Britain's European partners that the government was serious about ERM entry. The message was got out to the markets, often via the newspapers. In the *Sunday Times* we consistently predicted that entry would occur in the autumn of 1990. We ran a story describing a 'golden scenario' for the Conservatives in which the ERM would provide the pound with the support needed to cut interest rates dramatically in the run-up to the next election: music to Thatcher's ears. Occasionally in the months leading up to membership there would be speculation that entry would be deferred. But, like clockwork, there would always be a call from the Treasury saying that it was still very much on track.

There were occasional comic moments. On a car journey to a political meeting, Major asked one of his advisers to write on a piece of paper the best time to take the pound into the ERM. He did the same. Both had precisely the same timing, the weekend before the Conservative party conference in October. There was then some consternation when Major's suit jacket, containing both pieces of paper, was lost for a few anxious minutes, having been hung up by a helpful party official.

Though Major wanted to take sterling into the ERM, there was one obvious hurdle. Though Alan Walters was no longer at Thatcher's side, there were still the Madrid conditions. How could Thatcher agree to membership while Britain's inflation rate was so far above the European average? Major, however, was nothing if not inventive. He and his Treasury team devised a reformulation of the inflation condition, so that as long as the Treasury's official forecast predicted a closing of the gap between UK and European inflation, which it did, there was no barrier to early membership. Thatcher and Major met on 3 October 1990, at which point she gave the formal go-ahead for ERM entry, though subject to the condition that it be combined with a confidence-boosting cut in interest rates. Though the Treasury and Bank of England were unhappy with this, because it smacked of counting chickens before they were hatched, Major agreed. And so, two days later, at 4 p.m. on Friday 5 October, a small group of economic journalists, including me, were summoned to the Treasury. The announcement of

ERM entry came not in a grand press conference but in a small conference room, at a briefing by Sir Terry Burns and Sir Peter Middleton, chief economic adviser and Treasury permanent secretary respectively. Everybody knew ERM membership was coming, but it was still one of those historic moments that send a slight shiver down the spine. We were handed a piece of paper, which I wish I still had, the first paragraph of which was that interest rates were to be cut from 15 to 14 per cent. The second, and more important, paragraph announced that Britain would join the ERM the following Monday at a challengingly high central rate of DM2.95, though with wide 6 per cent bands on either side of that to allow for the pound's volatility. So the pound was expected to be at DM2.95, but it was allowed to fall as far as just under DM2.78, and to rise to almost DM3.13.

A few days later Major was given a hero's reception at the Conservative Party conference in Bournemouth when introduced by Thatcher, approvingly, as 'the man who took us into the ERM'. Britain had thrown in her lot with Europe, and the Tory faithful were happy. So, it seemed, was the country, and so was the business community, though in every case not for too long.

Terrible timing

ERM entry had been debated for so long that it was perhaps inevitable that it should happen at the wrong time. Major was determined to bring inflation down and coined a phrase for the high interest rate regime he had inherited: 'If it isn't hurting, it isn't working.' For most of 1990 the concern in the Treasury was that the economy was too strong, not too weak, and failing to respond to the harsh interest rate medicine. Major's only budget, in March 1990, was a 'budget for savings', specifically designed to entice people away from excessive spending by offering them tax inducements, one of which was in the form of TESSAs (tax-exempt special savings accounts), to get them to save more. The storm clouds were, though, gathering. For me the strongest sign of trouble came in July 1990, when the Confederation of British Industry (now known simply as the CBI) published its quarterly industrial trends survey, which showed a sharp dive in business confidence. I remember writing the story before getting one of those phone calls you dread: my father had had a heart attack and was dangerously ill. I raced up the motorway and got there in time, but sadly he did not survive. As far as the economy was concerned, from then on it was clear, to me at least, that the country was heading into recession, even as the government was planning to join a new currency arrangement.

The recession of the early 1990s, which began in the middle of 1990 and ended in the autumn of 1991, was not particularly severe. Figures now, after many years of official revisions, show that the peak-to-trough decline in gross domestic product (GDP) was a mere 2.2 per cent, spread over more than a year. In the later recession of 2008–9 there were single quarters when GDP fell as much. It did not feel like a mild recession, however. For one thing, the figures of the time pointed to a drop in GDP roughly twice the size of what the statistics now show. For another, unemployment rose sharply. The struggle in the 1980s to get unemployment down had been a long and difficult one. By early 1990 it appeared to be succeeding, with the claimant count unemployment level down to 1.6 million. The recession pushed it back up to almost 3 million, and almost doubled the unemployment rate. There were other big effects. The housing market, which had boomed during the late 1980s, went into sharp reverse. Not only did prices fall sharply – nationally by one-fifth and in the south-east of England by more than 35 per cent – but as a result of high interest rates there was a sharp rise in the number of repossessions: people forced out of their homes because they could not keep up their mortgage payments.

There was also another phenomenon, partly related to the weakness of the housing market. In 1991, a colleague and I wrote an article in the *Sunday Times* suggesting that the banks were taking a harsh attitude to some of their small business customers. There was evidence, it said, of banks raising interest rates to such customers and removing overdraft facilities at short notice. With many small business owners having put their house as security against business loans, there was a nasty interaction between falling house prices and failing businesses. After the article appeared, we were astonished to receive, in the following days, hundreds and eventually thousands of letters. Small firms all over the country were, it seemed, being badly treated by their banks, and in many cases being forced into closure. We turned it into a campaign which eventually resulted in a Treasury inquiry and a code of practice for the banks on how they treated their small firms.

The recession of the early 1990s felt brutal because in many ways it was; the much deeper recession of 2008–9 had less of a direct impact on most people and, in fact, a smaller rise in unemployment, and barely any increase in mortgage repossessions. Lessons had been learned. The 1990–91 recession was also much more of a shock because, rightly or wrongly, people had come to believe that, after the pain of the early 1980s, sudden lurches into recession were a thing of the past.

By the first anniversary of ERM entry, Major's remarkable rise had continued. Within two months of taking sterling into the system, in fact, he had succeeded Thatcher as prime minister. When he looked back on the first year of membership at the Conservative conference in Blackpool in the autumn of 1991, he maintained that it had been a considerable success. Interest rates had been cut to 10.5 per cent, and inflation was down to just over 4 per cent. Critics of the decision to join were 'selling Britain short', Major said. It was, however, becoming an increasingly tough policy to sell to voters. It is hard to say whether the recession would have been any worse had Britain stayed out of the ERM; it was already well under way by the time of entry, the product of the earlier very high interest rates.

The problem with membership was that it appeared to offer no way out of the morass in which the economy found itself. The data we now have shows that in the autumn of 1991, when Major was lauding the benefits of ERM membership, the economy was beginning to recover. Norman Lamont, who became chancellor after running Major's successful leadership campaign, talked of the 'green shoots of recovery'. At the time, though, the statistics made his claims look foolish, as did the national mood. Lamont was roundly mocked for his optimism. I had a frosty relationship with him when he was chancellor, not least because as a newspaper we were highly critical of him – 'Lamentable' is one single-word editorial headline I remember from the period – though we later got on well. Lamont was determined to leave his mark on the Treasury, although it did not work out in quite the way he intended. Lamont was no great fan of ERM membership, though his task was to try and make it work. He also had to try and make other things work, including getting the Conservative government off the hook over the poll tax. The poll tax, or community charge, a per-person levy to pay for local services, had been introduced as one of Thatcher's last acts. It was hugely unpopular, prompting riots in April 1990. Indeed, its introduction almost certainly hastened her departure from office. To reduce its effect, Lamont announced a £140 reduction in the tax in his March 1991 budget, in preparation for its eventual abolition. To pay for it, however, he announced an almost equally unpopular increase in VAT from 15 to 17.5 per cent. This was not quite a re-run of Geoffrey Howe's 1981 budget, given that the reduction in the poll tax and the increase in VAT broadly cancelled one another out, but a big increase in VAT when the economy was in recession was a bold move, if not foolhardy.

The pressures build

The recession had changed the dynamics of ERM membership. Entering the system was a way of putting a floor beneath the pound and allowing interest rates to be reduced from sky-high levels. That it did. Soon, however, it became a strait-jacket, preventing the interest rate cuts that the economy needed to get out of recession. It allowed the government to reduce rates from 15 to 10 per cent. But when 10 per cent became too high for an economy experiencing sharply falling inflation and mired in recession and a housing slump, life outside the ERM suddenly began to look a lot more palatable. Economists, some of whom had argued that ERM entry had been at the wrong time, at the wrong rate and for the wrong reasons (to secure a politically popular interest rate cut) began to publish assessments which pointed to a grim future if Britain remained within the system. The National Institute of Economic and Social Research projected an average unemployment level of 2.8 million from 1992 until the end of the century. Others argued for devaluation, or exit from the system. Sir Alan Walters, now free of the constraints of government, argued for leaving the system and aggressively cutting interest rates. Andrew Neil, my editor at the *Sunday Times* at the time, had been an advocate of ERM entry. Soon the newspaper was arguing for devaluation, as were others, and he was asking why I had not told him about the risks. Public and business opinion was turning against the ERM.

This did not prevent Major securing an unexpected victory in the April 1992 general election, winning more than 14 million votes, a record, in an election that Labour, under Neil Kinnock, thought it had in the bag. Labour also supported ERM membership. The election victory took the pressure off the pound for a while. In late July 1992 Major was even telling a dinner of *Sunday Times* journalists at Andrew Neil's flat that the pound could become the strongest currency in Europe. 'Look, I want sterling to replace the D-mark as Europe's benchmark currency', he said. 'I want Europe's currencies to revolve around the pound rather than the D-mark.' His comments, said quietly but firmly, were sincere. He believed them, and they were duly reported at some length in the newspaper the following Sunday.

Major and his ministers did their best to make the ERM work. In August, Lamont announced the issue of a foreign currency bond to demonstrate the government's commitment not to devalue or leave the ERM (because its cost would increase sharply). On the weekend of 5–6 September economic journalists, including me, travelled down to Bath for an informal 'Ecofin' meeting of European finance ministers and central bankers. The meeting, held in the Pump Room, was fiery. Indeed, standing outside while waiting for it to conclude, we had little idea how fiery it was. Outside, all was calm; it was a pleasant Saturday afternoon in Bath. I remember Will Hutton telling me that he was going to write a book, not on the ERM but on the state of Britain: a project that turned into the very successful *The State We're In*. Inside the meeting Lamont wanted a commitment from the president of the Bundesbank, Germany's central bank, not to raise interest rates and preferably to cut them, to take the pressure off the pound and the Italian lira, which was also in trouble. Not only did the Bundesbank president, Helmut Schlesinger, refuse to do so, four times, but he also made it clear that he regarded the request as an impertinence, if not a serious breach of protocol. No German politician would ever expect such a commitment from him, and he was certainly not going to provide one to a British politician. The Bundesbank closely guarded its independence. As I say, from outside the meeting it was hard to gauge how bad things were going, though one sign was that Sir Terry Burns, by then the permanent secretary to the Treasury, its senior civil servant, was summoned from the golf course to be driven at speed down the M4 to try to smooth things over. He was unsuccessful.

This was one of many occasions when I wished that my language skills were better. Those who got the best stories and most details out of the meeting were the German-speakers who listened in to the hushed briefings of the German delegation. But it was clear to all of us that something had gone badly wrong, and as I drove back to London on the Saturday evening the BBC was reporting it. Britain had lost an important ally. Indeed, Schlesinger got his revenge a few days later with an interview that many saw as the final nail in sterling's coffin. In the meantime, however, the government went on as if it were business as usual. France was due to vote in a referendum on the Maastricht treaty on Sunday 20 September. The view in the Treasury was that the pressure in the markets to force some currencies out of the ERM was directly related to the political uncertainties resulting from this referendum. If it was possible to hang on until then – and French voters did in the event narrowly approve the Maastricht treaty – then the storm would be soon over.

Major certainly thought so. In a speech to the Scottish CBI on 10 September 1992 the prime minister dismissed 'the quack doctors peddling their remedies' of a brighter future outside the ERM. Quoting Keynes, something he conceded he did rarely, he reminded his audience of the great economist's words, that there was no surer way of overturning the basis of society than 'debauching' the currency. Then he said, to loud applause:

Let me say this to you, Chairman, for it is something that I believe passionately – all my adult life I've seen British governments driven off their virtuous pursuit of low inflation, by market problems or political pressures. I was under no illusions when I took Britain into the Exchange Rate Mechanism. I said at the time, that membership was no soft option. The soft option, the devaluer's option, the inflationary option, in my judgement that would be a betrayal of our future at this moment, and I tell you categorically that is not the government's policy.

Black and white Wednesday

The story of 16 September 1992 has been often told. It was one of those occasions when the economy was centre-stage and when the world appeared to be crumbling beneath our feet. As with the 1976 and the IMF crisis and the autumn of 2008 and the worst phase of the banking crisis, it was a time of massive uncertainty and national humiliation. The fact that most of the action was concentrated in a single day made it seem rather worse.

On the evening of Tuesday 15 September the German financial newspaper *Handelsblatt* released part of an interview it had conducted with Helmut Schlesinger, the Bundesbank president. Though there was later a dispute over whether he had said exactly what was attributed to him, his reported words were dynamite. One or two currencies would come under pressure, he said, even beyond the French referendum, and he had doubts about whether the ERM could hold together. Since nobody needed any help identifying who those one or two were – sterling and the lira – they were immediately under intense pressure. The selling wave, famously led by the hedge fund billionaire George Soros, began overnight in Asia and intensified when the European markets opened. A hike in Britain's interest rates from 10 to 12 per cent failed to prop the pound up; the markets did not believe it would be enough to keep the pound in the ERM. Neither was heavy Bank of England intervention, involving pretty well all Britain's foreign currency reserves. The Bank's ammunition was insufficient when faced with the markets' heavy artillery. The last throw of the dice, agreed by Lamont, Major and a small group of senior ministers gathered at Admiralty House (10 Downing Street was undergoing repairs after an IRA mortar attack the previous winter), was to authorise a rise in interest rates to 15 per cent the following day.

That may have given the game away. Had the hike to 15 per cent taken immediate effect, the markets might have been convinced of the government's determination to keep sterling in the ERM. Delaying it until the following day, by which time membership of the ERM had been suspended – never to be resumed – meant that it never happened. Since that day I have spoken to many people for whom that announcement of a 15 per cent interest rate was a dagger to the heart, only to be followed by relief when it did not happen. At 7.30 on the evening of 16 September, Lamont, flanked by Gus O'Donnell, then Major's press secretary, and a young David Cameron, the chancellor's special adviser, announced that as a result of 'a difficult day' in the markets the pound was no longer in the ERM. Some saw this as the economy's long-awaited liberation from the yoke of the ERM; the following day Anatole Kaletsky in *The Times* was writing of 'white' Wednesday, and a few months later Lamont made clear that he was not unhappy with developments (an admission which helped cost him his job the following May). It was a liberation, as the economy's subsequent performance showed. But it was also a humiliation, and for some months the country appeared to be in crisis, despite the aggressive interest rate cuts the economy needed and which we at the *Sunday Times*, to Major's irritation, had been calling for. Though Lamont disputes this, insisting that the Conservatives recovered their opinion poll position once the dust from Black Wednesday had settled, I firmly believe it contributed to Labour's landslide victory in 1997. The Conservatives lost their reputation for economic competence on Black Wednesday, and took a long time to get it back. There were rumours that the events of Black Wednesday had hit Major so hard that he suffered some kind of breakdown, but that was not true. I remember him calling Andrew Neil on the following Saturday, with half a dozen of us listening in on speaker-phone. Slightly strangely, he thought ERM exit would pose more problems for Labour, depriving them of an economic policy, than it did for the Conservatives. He was wrong about that.

In subsequent years some, not all, of the official documents on the events surrounding Black Wednesday have been released. Thirteen years after the event the Treasury put a figure of £3.3 billion on the cost of the day, mainly the net losses on Bank of England intervention. This is probably the lowest estimate of the true cost of ERM membership, which made life more difficult during the two years that sterling was in the system than it needed to be. On the other hand, Major continues to insist that without the discipline of membership inflation would never have fallen as much as it did. A policy that ended in fiasco and embarrassment, however, was a big price to pay for lower inflation.

The papers released by the Treasury under Freedom of Information in February 2005 showed that, if ERM membership looked like a shambles from the outside, it was scarcely any better when seen from the inside. The forecasts produced by the Treasury's economists were, as was later conceded, 'spectacularly wrong'. So convinced was the Treasury that entering the ERM was a political rather than an economic decision that it had taken a 'blinkered' attitude to the economics, doing far too little preparatory work. Major had conceded an interest rate cut to Thatcher as a condition for taking sterling into the system in October 1990, but Sir Nigel Wicks, one of its senior officials, revealed that he and others were 'extremely unhappy' with that. Even as Major was denying that the government would ever contemplate devaluation, a Treasury official, Chris Riley, was preparing a paper arguing just that. Lamont, some said, was quietly in favour of devaluation, though not of exit from the system, though he could never say so in public. Riley's paper, ironically, was circulated the day after Black Wednesday, with a comment attached that it could be a 'blessing in disguise'. The Treasury was also revealed to be dissatisfied with the way the Bank of England had gone about fighting the speculators in September 1992, echoing a Bundesbank criticism of the time, which was that the Bank did not act 'until the ball was on the goal-line'. Another Treasury official, Paul Gray, writing in 1994, was worried that the economy had had a temporary fillip, a 'purple patch', after leaving the ERM, which would not last. He was too pessimistic, as we shall see in the next chapter.

It is interesting to speculate on what might have happened if the government and the Bank of England had been successful in fighting off the speculators. Would it have been one sterling crisis after another, or could it have worked? We will never really know. Would it have put Britain at the 'heart of Europe', which Major insisted he always wanted to do? Probably not, but it might have, even to the point where a successful period of ERM membership could easily have been followed by Britain being in the first wave of countries forming the single currency, the euro. The Bank of England might still have been made independent, but only as a requirement for monetary union, after which interest rate decisions would have rested with the European Central Bank. It did not happen, but it could have done. My view is that Britain would have struggled and that ERM exit, while entirely unintentional, was a very lucky escape. Some will disagree.

7

No return to boom and bust

The government will pursue the long-term strategy that
is necessary to achieve stability. We will not return to
the stop-go, boom-bust years which we saw under the
Conservatives.

Gordon Brown, House of Commons, 23 April 1998

After decades of Tory boom and bust, it is New Labour
which is the party of economic competence today.

Tony Blair, Labour Party conference speech,
Bournemouth, 28 September 1999

Between the autumn of 1991 and the first quarter of 2008 –
after which it was plunged into recession by the global financial crisis – something remarkable happened to the British
economy. It grew and grew, with barely a pause for breath. Over
that period the UK's gross domestic product rose for more than
sixteen years, uninterrupted by even a mild recession. Even
more remarkably it did so, quarter in quarter out, without even
a temporary dip. Growth persisted, with clockwork regular-
ity. Britain's accident-prone economy had, it seemed, turned
into a perpetual motion machine. This was unprecedented:

sixty-six consecutive quarters of growth compared with a previous record expansion of just nineteen in the 1980s. Quarterly GDP records only go back to the 1950s, but it is unlikely that there has been anything to compare with this run of growth even going back to an earlier age, where the trade or business cycle was ever-present and – even further back – where the state of the harvest was an important determinant of economic performance. As I sometimes say to people, I hope they file away in their memories that record run of growth from the early 1990s to the global financial crisis, for we are unlikely to see it happen again.

There is a legitimate debate about whether this record run of growth was in the end healthy or whether it bred a mood of complacency and encouraged excessive risk-taking. Certainly a reminder along the way that there was still a downside might have tempered some of the irrational exuberance before the crisis. A couple of small recessions, in other words, could have prevented the big one from being quite so big. Mostly, however, the politicians were glad for what they had. The seeds of the long upturn were sown by Norman Lamont and his remaking of economic policy in the aftermath of Britain's embarrassing exit from the ERM. They were tended by Kenneth Clarke – always one of my favourite politicians – in the period from 1993 to 1997. In that period the concern was not that people were taking the recovery for granted but that they were not taking enough notice of it. I remember a mildly despairing Clarke, whom we took to dinner at the Conservative conference in 1996, in the days when he could still smoke his beloved small cigars at the table, bemoaning the fact that voters were curmudgeonly about the economic improvement that was clearly taking place, and seemed determined not to give the government any credit for it. The Labour landslide the following year showed that his fears were justified. Just ahead of that election Michael Heseltine, then the deputy prime minister, assured a small group of us from the newspaper that governments presiding over a strong rise in real incomes never lost elections. I pointed him towards examples, such as the 1979 election, when that was not the case, but he was breezily confident. Maybe that was his default position, but the scale of the Tory defeat in May 1997 proved that, while rising prosperity is usually a necessary condition for re-election, it can never be a sufficient one.

Though the Conservatives set the ball rolling for this record run of apparently untroubled expansion, and in many respects did most of the hard work, most of it was presided over by Gordon Brown. While even Kenneth Clarke at his most ebullient would never have been bold enough to claim that there would be no return to boom and bust, this became the mantra of Brown, and of Tony Blair. Brown was a modern-day phenomenon. Though he would have preferred an earlier move from 11 to 10 Downing Street, and the job of prime minister he had long coveted, he made up for it by setting a record – in the period when the job was one of the most pressured in politics – for tenure as chancellor. When he finally persuaded Blair to step aside at the end of June 2007, he had served ten years and fifty-six days as chancellor. Not since Nicholas Vansittart, who was in the role from May 1812 to January 1823, in very different conditions, had a chancellor stayed in the job continuously for more than ten years. Also in the nineteenth century William Gladstone did a cumulative twelve years in the post, though that was achieved over a thirty-year period in four separate spells. Brown was a modern-day record-breaker.

The son of the manse

I first met Gordon Brown in 1989. He was the rising star of the Labour Party, widely regarded by colleagues as a better prospect than his friend and subsequent rival Tony Blair, with whom he once shared a House of Commons office. At the time he was shadow trade and industry secretary. We had arranged lunch at L'Amico, a favourite haunt of MPs which once hosted a meal for Mikhail Gorbachev, just before he became Soviet leader, and Spaghetti Gorbachev became a staple on the restaurant's menu. On this occasion Brown arrived late, not untypically, slightly bedraggled and very apologetic. He exchanged greetings with the Italian restaurant manager, and compared notes over their respective games of tennis. Sport was often a conversational opener for Brown, both because he was genuinely interested and because he thought it made him come across as a more rounded character. Many years later a newspaper editor with no interest in football complained to a colleague that before getting on to discussing politics he had to spend twenty minutes feigning interest in Brown's beloved Raith Rovers. Brown was, on this occasion, charming, flattering and self-deprecating. The legend, even then, was of the son of the manse (his father was Presbyterian minister in his native Kirkcaldy) who was fiercely intelligent – he attended Edinburgh University at the age of sixteen – and an intellectual livewire. Brown certainly was very intelligent, though he combined it with a formidable work ethic. He was, then and later, always well read, excited about the latest book he had laid his hands on, usually from the USA – he would buy several copies to hand out to friends – and up to speed with news and gossip.

At that time Brown, in his late thirties, had just been promoted to an important shadow Cabinet job, trade and industry, but could not have expected as rapid an ascent as soon occurred. Neil Kinnock was Labour leader and had every expectation of soon winning power. John Smith, like Brown a Scot, was Labour's avuncular and popular shadow chancellor. While Brown was a fast-rising star, and Blair was another, Kinnock and Smith were the senior figures. Things changed quickly. Kinnock resigned after losing the April 1992 election, which Labour was widely expected to win. The party itself was confident, perhaps over-confident, of victory. After the defeat, the wind went out of Labour's sails, with some pundits declaring that if it could not win power in the circumstances of April 1992, with the economy widely believed to be still in recession, it could never win. As noted above, subsequent figures showed that recovery had begun in the autumn of 1991, so by the time of the election the country was several months into it. It did not, however, feel like much of a recovery.

The ill wind of the election defeat blew Brown into the job of shadow chancellor, once Smith had been elected leader. In that job Brown set about the task of rebuilding Labour's credibility on economic policy, with considerable success. We were in close contact. I remember him telling me that he had recruited a young adviser from the *Financial Times* and was interested in my views on a paper the new adviser – Ed Balls – had written. Unusually for a shadow chancellor, he generated intense interest among journalists in the policies he was developing. This was because, for economic journalists at least, they appealed because they had a strong basis in economic evidence and theory – his speeches were more grown-up than most – and because of the expectation that, once the Conservative Party began to self-destruct by the mid-1990s, it was possible that there might indeed be another Labour government. Labour's 1992 defeat, it appeared, was not the death knell for the party it seemed in its immediate aftermath. Sometimes those economic speeches went a little awry. A passage penned by the Oxford- and Harvard-educated Balls which included the phrase 'post-neoclassical endogenous growth theory' was famously lampooned by Michael Heseltine in a memorable Conservative conference speech. But Brown was getting noticed, and that was what mattered most. His close-knit team, which included Charlie Whelan and, in 1994, Ed Miliband, the future Labour leader, was a wonderful source of stories. Some of these were about his policy plans; he gave the *Sunday Times* the story of his planned New Deal for the young unemployed. Perhaps the best, however, were those that caused maximum discomfort for the government and exasperation for Kenneth Clarke, the chancellor. There were times when Brown and his team appeared to know more about what was going on in the Treasury than its minister, probably feeding off disgruntled civil servants desperate for a change of government.

Brown loved a debate. I recall one occasion when he and Andrew Neil, the then editor of the *Sunday Times*, argued late into the night at the Labour Party conference in Brighton over his position on the ERM. They were like two fencers; point and counterpoint as the argument went backwards and forwards. At the heart of it was whether Labour had missed the boat by not abandoning its commitment to ERM membership ahead of the government's Black Wednesday embarrassment. Later some of those debates could become a little wearing. Breakfasts at 11 Downing Street became a regular diary feature after Brown became chancellor and Neil was succeeded at the *Sunday Times* by John Witherow. I cannot say that any of us particularly looked forward to those occasions. Though always courteous, in contrast to his reputation for throwing around pieces of office equipment when angry, I do not recall Brown ever conceding a point. Chewing on a banana, he would argue until the cows came home. That was all for later, as was our falling out. The last time I saw him, for an interview at his house in Scotland just before the 2010 election, he wanted nothing to do with our newspaper or me but had clearly been persuaded by his advisers to give the interview. It was grim. As I say, that was for later. Brown's chancellorship, as well as being very long, began with one of the most important changes in the management of the British economy.

As safe as the Bank of England

On Tuesday 6 May 1997, five days after Labour's landslide election victory, journalists were invited to a press conference to be given by the new chancellor. The post-election weekend had been followed by a bank holiday, and expectations for the press conference were fairly low. What could Brown possibly have to announce of note after just a few days in the job? Most of the interesting policy announcements were expected in his inaugural budget a few weeks later. One thing we did expect was the announcement of a rise in interest rates, because this was the way the electoral cycle worked. Governments delayed unpopular rate hikes until after the vote. The City was also braced for an announcement of higher interest rates, which Brown duly delivered. That, however, was the least of it. Yes, interest rates would rise immediately, from 6 to 6.25 per cent, but this, Brown said, would be the last such decision by a chancellor. In future, interest rate decisions would be taken by an independent Bank of England. Britain was to have an independent central bank, as had long been advocated by many economists and, though it only came out later, unsuccessfully battled for by Conservative chancellors, including Nigel Lawson. Norman Lamont, Conservative chancellor from 1990 to 1993, also strongly supported it, though it was criticised by Kenneth Clarke, Brown's immediate predecessor. To be fair to Lamont and Clarke, they had laid the groundwork for Bank independence. Lamont had established an inflation target in the aftermath of sterling's embarrassing slide out of the ERM, and given the Bank an enhanced role in publicly advising on interest rate changes and monitoring and predicting inflation. The 'Ken and Eddie' show, monthly chancellor–governor meetings between Clarke and Eddie George, became a feature of this quasi independence.

Brown's announcement was, though, still a big surprise. It was a bombshell, which in Brown's words would 'set in place a long-term framework for economic prosperity' and 'break from the boom-bust economics of previous years'. It took a while to sink in. One of the first questions at the press conference was from a television journalist who asked about the new Bank of England committee which would set interest rates. He asked: 'You will sit on it, of course, and presumably the chief secretary, but who else?' Brown let him down gently, explaining that the whole idea of independence was to take interest rate decisions out of the hands of politicians. It is easy to mock because it is fair to say that nobody in the room was prepared for it. The number of occasions when I have been present for genuinely big game-changing announcements is quite small, at least for those which had not been briefed beforehand. This was one of them. Before the election Brown had expressed support in general terms for Bank independence, though he indicated that he would monitor the existing system of quasi independence, in which the Bank gave public advice on interest rates to the chancellor but did not make the decisions, before making any move. The immediate switch to Bank independence was as much a surprise to journalists as it was to senior Treasury officials, who had spent a frantic holiday weekend putting the new framework in place, having only been told about it the previous Friday.

The decision was heavily influenced by Brown's enthusiastic following of events in the USA, and in particular an important meeting with Alan Greenspan, the then chairman of the Federal Reserve, the US central bank. Greenspan, in fact, became something of a hero for Brown. When the Treasury moved to a new, or rather an extensively refurbished, building, he invited Greenspan to open it, and also arranged for him to receive an honorary knighthood. In February 1997, three months before the election, Gordon Brown and Ed Balls travelled to the USA. There was a Labour fundraising party in New York organised by Tina Brown and Harold Evans, and some high-profile meetings for the chancellor-to-be. Among them were meetings with

Alan Greenspan and Robert Rubin, the then US Treasury secretary. As Brown and Balls were driven back to Washington's
Dulles Airport after their meetings, they realised that all the
talk at 'the Fed' had been about monetary policy: interest rates
and the control of inflation. At the US Treasury, in contrast,
the discussion had been about long-run economic issues such
as productivity. Brown knew that previous Labour chancellors (and plenty of Conservative ones) had been faced with
repeated sterling crises and agonising decisions about when
and by how much to raise interest rates. Rarely did they get it
right. On his return from Washington, Brown set out his plans
of establishing a monetary committee of insiders and outsiders
at the Bank of England, as well as a US-style Council of Economic Advisers. Bank independence was, however, somewhere
down the track. The decision to do it immediately, in fact, was
only taken on 28 April, three days before the 1 May election, by
which time it was clear that nothing could stand in the way of
a Labour victory. The secret was kept until the announcement
on 6 May.

Managing the 'great stability'

The announcement of Bank of England independence had
huge ramifications. For Brown, the drama of his own first act
proved impossible to replicate. When he became prime minister a decade later, political journalists were promised a series of
announcements of comparable importance. None was forth-
coming. Some Conservatives, having done much of the preparatory work by giving the Bank a greatly enhanced role, kicked
themselves for allowing Brown an easy opportunity to show
himself to be a radical chancellor. Even then, things nearly went
wrong. When we were told on 6 May about the independence
decision, it was assumed the Bank's new responsibilities would
be in addition to its existing role. It would, in other words,

continue to be responsible for supervising the banks and the financial system more generally. Brown had other ideas. Two weeks after he had told a delighted Eddie George, the Bank governor, about the independence decision, he summoned him back to tell him that he had decided to take banking supervision away from the Bank, hiving it off to a new financial regulator, the Financial Services Authority (FSA). George, having assured Bank staff a fortnight earlier that this would not be the case, was mortified. Legend has it that he decided on resignation on the Jaguar journey back along London's Embankment from the Treasury to the Bank, because of what he saw as a breach of trust. Had he done so, it would have been the worst possible start for the Bank's independence era, and he was persuaded not to do it. Though George later made clear that he did not disagree with the substance of the announcement, the impression was that it had been steamrollered through against Bank objections. Brown, in fact, had intended to keep the establishment of the FSA back for a later announcement but was persuaded that, to guarantee space in the parliamentary timetable, it was sensible to move quickly. The episode did, however, give Brown's critics plenty of ammunition later, when the FSA was seen to have fallen down on the job of supervising the banks in the run-up to the financial crisis that broke out so devastatingly just after the tenth anniversary of independence.

For now, however, the independence of the Bank was generally seen as embedding a new stability in the economy that Britain had lacked before. By the time it happened, the economy was nearly six years into the long upturn. Initial fears that heavy-handed central bankers would scupper the recovery by being too quick to raise interest rates – one Labour MP, Diane Abbott, questioned whether they would become, as she put it, 'inflation nutters' – gave way to the view that this was a decisive improvement in the management of the British economy. Mervyn King, who succeeded George as Bank governor in

2003 and was the principal architect of the inflation-targeting regime that had formed the basis of monetary policy since the early 1990s, is not an impartial witness. His description of the benefits of independence, in a 2007 speech looking back at the ten-year record, however, put it well. As he said:

> Although the announcement in 1997 of independence for the Bank of England was a bolt from the blue, it was a long time in the making. During the 1970s inflation in the United Kingdom averaged 13 per cent a year and peaked at 27 per cent. Only towards the end of that decade, with first a Labour and then a Conservative Government recognising that the control of inflation was the first step towards any semblance of a coherent macroeconomic policy, did the transition from the Great Inflation to the Great Stability begin. But the first steps were faltering. It took two painful recessions and sterling's exit from the exchange rate mechanism in September 1992 to reach the goal of low inflation. Even then, the long-term commitment of the United Kingdom to low inflation was not fully believed by financial markets. Granting independence to the Bank of England was the dramatic constitutional change that convinced financial markets of the United Kingdom's conversion to stability as the basis of macroeconomic policy.

Bank independence and the 'Great Stability' went hand in hand. For policymakers, the combination of growth – prolonged growth – and low inflation was the Holy Grail. While it was not confined to Britain during the 1990s and 2000s (though the length of the upturn was), it was much more of a novelty. Such was Britain's record of instability and policy experiments, followed by embarrassing reversals, that the change in economic performance was not just novel: it was remarkable. Most astonishing of all, Britain went from being the least stable of the big economies to being, it appeared, the most stable. In his tenth anniversary assessment King was able to cite statistics showing average growth of 2.8 per cent a year in the first ten years of independence, with inflation on average a tiny 0.08 percentage points away from the official target. In the decades before independence, 1950–96, Britain's performance on growth and inflation had been the worst in the G7. From 1997 to 2006, by contrast, it was the best. Growth became smooth and predictable, rather than jerky and uncertain. Brown, it seemed, had finally cured the British economy of its volatile boom-bust tendencies, and mainly by the simple expedient of making the Bank of England independent. When boom later turned to spectacular bust, much of the gloss rubbed off. Nobody, however, seriously talked about reversing Brown's 1997 decision.

The new monetary masters

The independent Bank of England changed things in many ways. For the first time interest rate decisions were taken – on a vote – by a committee of nine men and women. Those votes were made public, after a brief delay, as were the minutes of the monetary policy committee (MPC) meetings. Not only was this an unprecedented level of transparency, but it also brought a new certainty to policy. Except for in extreme circumstances, interest rate changes would be announced in line with a pre-set timetable – at noon on the first or second Thursday of each month – and explained. The old system, whereby interest rates could change at a chancellor's whim, and at any time, was consigned to the history books. This had a direct effect on economic journalists. Before Bank independence we could happily speculate on the timing and direction of interest rate changes without fear of serious contradiction. Readers, and the financial markets, believed that we were tipped off by the Treasury about the chancellor's intentions. Sometimes, indeed, we did find something out. The result was often bizarre. In pre-independence days rumours would often circulate in the City on Friday afternoons, to the effect that the *Sunday Times* – usually me – would either be carrying a story on an impending interest rate change or be calling for one. The rumours, started by money market traders anxious to close out a position or to do some business ahead of the weekend, were almost invariably false. But they meant that I spent many Friday afternoons either denying inventive market rumours or stonewalling.

Independence changed all that. Suddenly the market-movers were the members of the MPC, and, to be fair to the Bank, it made every effort to establish a dialogue between them and journalists. This took two forms. An interview with an MPC member became a property, while a lunch in the Bank's historic parlours was always a useful occasion. The losers in all this, from the moment Gordon Brown became chancellor, were junior Treasury ministers and senior Treasury officials. Standard practice for economic journalists before 1997 was to lunch Treasury ministers and officials, in the hope of getting snippets and stories. After 1997 Brown controlled the Treasury – usually his ministers knew less than advisers like Balls – and the Bank was where the decisions on interest rates were taken. A lunch in the Bank's parlours meant being greeted by one of its pink-jacketed doormen and being shown through a maze of corridors to a panelled room. At one time you would be offered sherry, followed by wine at lunch. Later the lunches became alcohol-free, perhaps unfortunately. Eddie George, a nice man, if occasionally prickly, was an affable host, though he was never very comfortable when he could not smoke or when making the many speeches required of a Bank governor. I once sat next to him at a lunch hosted by the House of Commons press gallery, at which he was the guest of honour. He confided that he never ate before making a speech. Given that many of a governor's speeches are made after dinner, this must have been uncomfortable.

Mervyn King, his successor, was much more at home making public speeches. We got on well. He, like me, came from the Black Country – in his case, Wolverhampton – and had an abiding interest in West Midlands sport, as a keen follower of Aston Villa football club and the Worcestershire county cricket team. He was also an enthusiastic tennis player. We probably spent too much time talking about these things. King was a noted academic economist. When he joined the Bank as chief economist in 1991, he was better known for his expertise on the British tax system than on monetary policy. At the London School of Economics, as well as many academic papers, he co-wrote with John Kay what was for many years the seminal work on Britain's tax system. He also attracted the attention of Nigel Lawson, becoming one of a small group of his 'Gooies' (group of outside independent economists) who advised informally on policy. Eddie George said he could have won a Nobel Prize had he stuck with academic economics. He knuckled down at the Bank, however, and when the Conservative government adopted an inflation-targeting regime after sterling's expulsion from the ERM, King was instrumental in its design. Though he was not regarded by the Brown government as an automatic choice to succeed George in 2003 – and the Labour government deliberated before renewing his appointment in 2008 – he more than anybody ensured that the Bank could make the successful transformation to independence. He was also famously gloomy. When we did get on to talking about the economy, particularly in the wake of the global financial crisis, King usually saw large black clouds on the horizon. On the MPC, he was usually the most pessimistic voice around the table.

Bank independence opened up a dialogue with Bank insiders such as Charlie Bean, Paul Tucker, John Gieve, Rachel

Lomax, Ian Plenderleith and Spencer Dale. It also introduced a new breed of decision-maker, the so-called external members of the MPC, the 'outsiders'. From the start the Treasury, which initially appointed the MPC's external members by calling them up and giving them a short time to decide whether they wanted to take up the offer, and later publicly advertised vacancies on the committee, has always managed to attract high-quality candidates. Some, such as the Dutch-born economist Willem Buiter, brought personality as well as expertise inside the Bank's grey walls. Buiter had a string of one-liners. 'Market intelligence' – the views of the financial markets – was a contradiction in terms, he said. When the financial crisis broke, he said it had exposed the uselessness of most monetary economics taught in universities since the 1970s. Buiter was not afraid to change his mind, one month in 1998 refusing to join the MPC majority in voting for a rate cut and the next pressing for a bigger one than the committee as a whole. These public jousts on interest rates were fascinating, and MPC members quickly became labelled as 'hawks' or 'doves'. DeAnne Julius, the American-born former chief economist at British Airways, feared deflation and was an early dove. The calibre was high.

The MPC attracted (though not all at the same time) three former chief economists at the Confederation of British Industry: Kate Barker, Andrew Sentance and Ian McCafferty. While on the committee, Barker was commissioned by the government to examine the issue of housing supply in Britain and produced an influential report. Richard Lambert, a former *Financial Times* editor, only left the MPC when he took up the job as CBI director-general. Sushil Wadhwani, a highly regarded economist who on leaving the MPC established his own hedge fund, was another leading light, as was Steve Nickell, one of Britain's top labour market economists. The names changed, but the MPC continued to attract a high standard of economist: names such as Tim Besley, Charles Goodhart, David

Miles, David Walton and Martin Weale. Though the outsiders – four in number at any one time – could always be outvoted by the five insiders on the MPC, in practice it did not work out that way. Mervyn King was outvoted on a number of occasions, as some of his insiders joined forces with some outsiders. He maintained this was a sign of the health of the framework. There was never a Bank block vote.

Many of these MPC members became, as well as good contacts, firm friends. Though they were always discreet about how they had voted until it was made public, in the early days of independence this was a tricky task. Then, taking a leaf out of the practice of the Federal Reserve in the USA, there was a six-week delay between MPC meetings and the publication of the relevant minutes. Members were thus required to stay silent about how they had voted for a month and a half. Later the delay was cut to two weeks.

Bank of England independence was not the only factor in the long recovery from the early 1990s until 2008. The recovery was clearly already established under the pre-independence policy arrangements. Later the Bank was criticised for keeping interest rates too low rather than too high in the run-up to the crisis, allowing dangerous imbalances and excessive borrowing to build up over a number of years. Independence was, however, a big, important and generally beneficial change. It took interest rate decisions out of the hands of politicians, and it ensured that those decisions were taken on economic rather than political grounds. Businesses and households could plan on the basis of sudden lurches in interest rates being a thing of the past; the average Bank rate came down to 5 per cent rather than the 12 per cent of the 1980s, and changes were small and gradual. It helped foster strong and sustained economic growth.

Flexibility pays off

The long upturn also owed much to the delayed impact of the 'supply-side' reforms of the 1980s. One of the reasons why Britain had in the past been unable to sustain prolonged periods of economic growth was that falling unemployment, and rising demand for labour, allowed the trade unions to exercise their leverage over employers. The wage-price spiral – higher wage demands being followed by rising inflation, and often accompanied by industrial disruption – was the typical pattern. The authorities found themselves being forced to apply the brakes prematurely. If it was not always boom-bust, it was certainly stop-go. This changed. After the great battles of the 1980s the unions were a pale shadow of their former selves in the 1990s and beyond. Politically, they lost power and influence in the 'New' Labour party of Tony Blair and Gordon Brown. For Labour, keen to present itself as pro-business and very different from the 'Old' Labour of the past, the unions were a little like an embarrassing cousin from the backwoods turning up at a smart family wedding. Suddenly, smart-suited young men started outnumbering T-shirted trade unionist activists at Labour conferences. Union membership was in decline, and the union bosses no longer called the tune, even when they and their members were still responsible for a significant slice of the party's income.

One theory is that a combination of the union reforms of the 1980s and the recession of the early 1990s 'shocked' pay increases down to permanently lower levels. Earnings tended to increase in real terms – they rose faster than inflation – but not by much, and barely at all towards the end of the period. Industrial disputes became, if not quite a thing of the past, increasingly rare. The British disease, or at least one important aspect of it, had been cured.

There were other examples of the 'new' British economy of the 1990s and 2000s. In the 1960s and 1970s Britain experienced annual net migration in most years. More people left the country on a long-term basis than arrived, even in a period in which there were high levels of immigration from the Commonwealth. This began to change in the 1980s, though not dramatically. In most years there was annual net immigration, but the numbers were typically less than 40,000. From around 1994 onwards, however, Britain began to be a magnet for migrants, typically attracting 140,000 or 150,000 a year, a number that swelled to more than 200,000 with the expansion of the European Union to include ten Eastern European countries in 2004. Not only did net migration on this scale signal that Britain had become an attractive location for foreigners, usually in response to job opportunities, but it also had a direct impact on the economy. Inward migration was part of the economy's flexibility, a safety valve when the job market threatened to tighten up, which could have pushed up wage increases to a level that could have endangered low inflation. Britain was able to draw on a pool of imported labour. As the long recovery went on, this became increasingly important.

When Tony Blair came into office in 1997, after eighteen years of Conservative government, Britain was also a country in which taxes were lower than in most competitors, and in which deregulation and privatisation had transformed a once over-regulated economy with an over-sized state sector. Though the new government began to re-regulate – one of its earliest acts was signing up to the EU working time directive – it took time for those advantages to be eroded. The World Economic Forum, which hosts the annual Davos meeting in the Swiss Alps, produces a global competitiveness index, ranking some 200 countries on a range of measures intended to reflect factors that matter to international companies: ease of doing business, regulations, tax, skills and education, infrastructure and so on. In 1998 Britain was ranked fourth, a very different proposition from the economic wreck of two decades earlier, though it subsequently slipped back. But this was a country that had changed for the better, in a remarkably short time. It was a place where the world was happy to do business.

Economic competence

Though their reputations have since suffered, and though their relationship later foundered on the rocks of intense rivalry – which came to be known in Westminster as the 'TB-GBs' – Tony Blair and Gordon Brown exuded confidence, and competence, when they came to power. One immediate issue was whether Britain should join the European single currency, which was yet to be christened the euro, but which was likely to come into being at the start of 1999. At the time Brown was in favour, but he was later to change his mind. Blair favoured membership in principle but did not want to be in the first wave of members. There were good political reasons for this: memories of the ERM humiliation were still raw, and the public would have taken some persuading. There was another reason, as Derek Scott told me. He was the former Denis Healey adviser who was lured from the City to be personal economic adviser to Blair (where he was to have battles with the Treasury that recalled those of Alan Walters under Thatcher). Scott told me that one reason why Blair did not want to join the euro during Labour's first term was that he was determined to demonstrate that a Labour government could run the economy competently, without outside influence or support. The record was not good – the devaluations of the 1945–51 Attlee and 1964–70 Wilson government and the IMF crisis of the 1974–9 Wilson–Callaghan government – and the new prime minister wanted to show that the party had changed. I knew Blair reasonably well. In the early 1990s he had invited me to his House of Commons office and said that we should keep in touch and exchange ideas. In 1995 I was at the event in Australia at which opponents and critics said he had made his 'devil's pact' with Rupert Murdoch. Roughly every three years Murdoch gathered senior executives from across his media, film and publishing empire to exchange information and hear outside speakers. For this one we had travelled by plane and boat to Hayman Island, off the coast of Queensland and close to the Great Barrier Reef. Paul Keating, the Australian prime minister, gave a speech and provided air transport for Blair. Keating, as it emerged later, told Blair that Murdoch was 'a bastard', though Blair took the second bit of Keating's advice, which was that he was also somebody you could do business with. Blair was guest of honour, astonishingly for an opposition leader just a year into the job and with two years to go until the general election. His speech to the assembled executives made the right noises about New Labour's pro-business approach, and was beamed back to be broadcast live by Sky TV. It sealed the support for Labour in 1997 by the News International tabloids, *The Sun* and the *News of the World*. After the speech a relieved Blair seized on me as a friendly face among hundreds of strangers, before being whisked away to meet more important people.

Towards the end of 1998, not long into the Labour government, I was invited to a Downing Street seminar, the subject of which I have forgotten, followed by drinks. Blair was working the room and came up to the small group I was in. He asked me how I thought the economy was doing. I said so far so good, and that Bank of England independence was working well but that I feared the effects of international developments. At the time the US hedge fund Long-Term Capital Management had just failed, Russia had defaulted on her debts and Asian economies were mired in crisis. Business confidence in Britain had fallen sharply, normally a harbinger of recession. I told him I feared that Britain could go into recession and that his government would be blamed for it. This was not what he wanted to hear. A mid-term recession would have scuppered his hopes of demonstrating Labour's economic competence. He did not stay long to discuss it. Fortunately for him, and for the country, I was too gloomy. Aggressive interest rate cuts by the Bank of England and by the Federal Reserve in the USA helped ensure that 1999 was a year of growth, not recession. The economy sailed on. Indeed, figures now show that it grew by more than 3 per cent in 1999. Labour held on to its new reputation.

Nor was this just an accident. In the years following the unexpected and disappointing defeat in 1992 Labour had thought long and hard about what it would do when in office, and nobody had thought about it more than Gordon Brown and his team, and most notably Ed Balls, his key adviser. When they arrived at the Treasury on 2 May 1997, to the applause of officials, they arrived with a plan. At initial meetings with senior officials, when Whitehall conventions normally dictate that wide-eyed ministers are told about the conventions of running a government department, Brown gave them his plan and told them to get on with it.

Avoiding boom and bust meant gaining the trust of the markets. Labour had never won such trust. Its record was one of battles with financial markets, battles it usually lost. This had to change, not least by taking some key decisions out of the hands of politicians. At a time when the academic debate was over 'rules' versus 'discretion' Balls came out firmly in favour of rules. Without such rules politicians would always be tempted to use their discretion for short-term political advantage rather than for the medium- and long-term benefit of the country. It sounded logical, and it was. Rather than selling the pound at the prospect of a Labour government in 1997, currency dealers bought it, and in the main carried on buying it for the duration of Brown's chancellorship. A strong pound was, if not unknown for a Labour government, certainly unusual. It appeared, indeed, to be a vote of confidence from the markets for Labour's rules-based approach to economic policymaking. This was different.

Balls, with whom I was in regular contact, was for several years one of the most influential people in the country, despite at that time only being an adviser. He had laid out the economic approach that Labour should adopt, was instrumental in the timing and framework for Bank of England independence and quickly became the conduit between Treasury officials and a chancellor who was not keen on getting bogged down in too many meetings. Balls had just turned thirty in May 1997. Many young men would have become unbearably pompous after such achievements – I remember a young David Cameron as a rather arrogant special adviser to Norman Lamont in the early 1990s – but Balls, to his credit, was not. He was good company, and remained as good a source for stories in government as he had been in opposition.

Freed from day-to-day decisions on interest rates, Brown set about his own version of the supply-side revolution of the 1980s. There was a productivity agenda, measures – and frequent reports – to raise education and skill levels and the commissioning of experts to offer advice on raising Britain's competitiveness. There was a strengthened competition regime, through the Office of Fair Trading and Competition Commission, designed to ensure markets operated efficiently and brought the maximum benefit to consumers. It felt like a government that was firing on all cylinders. It felt like a government that knew what it was doing, and that bred confidence.

A housing boom after all

One problem was that it bred rather too much confidence. The combination of low interest rates and an economy that had apparently turned into a perpetual motion machine was just too tempting as far as the housing market was concerned. In the mid-1990s, when the market was suffering the hangover from the price collapse, wave of repossessions and negative equity left over from the price crash of the early 1990s, there appeared to be little danger of a repeat of the damaging booms of the early 1970s and late 1980s. But the market had not, as was hoped, changed fundamentally. It was merely dormant. To the Labour government, and to the newly independent Bank of England, this was disappointing. The hope was that the new stability in growth and inflation would mean stability in all aspects of the economy. In fact, and housing was not alone in this, the stability in the wider economy bred instability, or at least over-exuberance, in other areas. From their low point in December 1995 until they began to fall in October 2007 with the onset of the global financial crisis, house prices rose by more than 260 per cent, according to the Nationwide Building Society. The average price rose from what now looks like a very low £50,798 to £186,044. Prices at the end of the process were more than 3.5 times higher than when they had started. Some of that reflected general inflation – even in a low inflation era the cumulative effect of twelve years of inflation was not negligible – but even after adjusting for that, 'real' house prices were more than 2.6 times the level at which they started. Just as the economic upturn from the early 1990s to 2008 broke previous records, so did the housing boom. The rise in house prices from 1995 to 2007 was the longest and largest on record, bigger than the Lawson boom of the 1980s and, indeed, any period of rising prices in the twentieth century, all of which had been brought to a halt by deliberate policy, usually higher interest rates.

The boom in house prices did not occur quietly. In a quiet week a good topic for my *Sunday Times* column, with a guaranteed response from readers, was the housing market. Those responses divided roughly equally into two camps: those who thought prices were always about to crash and those who expected them to rise for ever. My position was always that house prices did not spontaneously combust; it needed something, usually a sharp rise in interest rates or a recession, to send them falling fast. That provoked anger among those who wanted to see prices crash, while my suggestions that the rise would eventually run out of steam were criticised by the eternal optimists. For a while I had a weekly column on the housing market in the newspaper's Home section, imaginatively called Home Economics. Debating house prices, either in print, online or in public became a significant part of the job. I was not alone in taking an interest. Indeed, the media was widely blamed for the boom. There were television programmes on housing, labelled by critics 'property porn', such as Channel 4's *Location, Location, Location*, presented by Kirstie Allsopp and Phil Spencer; and *Property Ladder*, presented by Sarah Beeny, another Channel 4 programme, featuring amateurs who renovated and developed properties for profit.

More important was buy-to-let. Over many decades leading up to the 1990s Britain's private rented sector had been in decline, squeezed to a fraction of its former size by owner-occupation, social housing and rent controls. Most remaining landlords were either businesses or relatively wealthy individuals. In the 1990s they were joined by a new breed, the buy-to-let landlords. Specialised buy-to-let mortgages were launched in July 1996 following pressure from the Association of Residential Letting Agents. The name describes well what they are: mortgages for the purpose of buying property to let out, not to live in. Just over a decade later, in September 2007, there were nearly a million such mortgages, and their combined value was £116 billion. When the financial crisis hit, some predicted the demise of the buy-to-let landlord. But they survived and at time of writing are poised to become more important than social landlords (councils and housing associations). A spectacular example of this new breed of landlord was provided by Fergus and Judith Wilson, two former maths teachers from Maidstone in Kent who had accumulated a portfolio of 900 properties worth £250 million. In 2009 it was reported that the Wilsons were proposing to sell their portfolio and cash in the estimated £70 million profit on it. They were not immediately successful. Similar stories appeared again in 2014. Buy-to-let landlords may have been a new breed, but they were not universally popular, being blamed for driving up house prices and snapping up properties young first-time buyers coveted. A 2008 assessment by the official National Housing and Planning Advice Unit concluded, however, that the effect had been relatively modest.

House prices boomed because interest rates were low and stable, and because confidence was high. The key calculation for potential home-buyers is the 'front end' cost of ownership. If they can afford the initial monthly repayment, almost irrespective of the price of the property in relation to their income, they will buy. When mortgages were also easy to come by, and could be quickly arranged, there was little to hold buyers back. Prices also rose because of a shortage of supply, and it was this that also preoccupied a Treasury concerned that low-inflation stability did not extend to the housing market. In April 2003 Gordon Brown and John Prescott, the deputy prime minister, commissioned Kate Barker, a member of the Bank's MPC and former chief economic adviser at the Confederation of British Industry, to investigate the country's housing needs. Her final report, published in July 2004, was clear on the remedy: more houses. For years, additions to the housing stock – new houses and flats – had been running at a slower rate than the rise in the numbers of households. That rise, projected at more than 200,000 a year for the two decades following the publication of the review, was occurring because of population growth, migration, divorce and young people setting up home earlier. Importantly, it was set to continue. Reducing the annual rise in house prices to just over 1 per cent a year, in line with the EU average, would require an additional 120,000 new homes annually. A big expansion of social housing was also among her recommendations. Barker did not argue that the limited supply of new housing was the only factor pushing up prices, but it was a significant one. Soon, far from booming, the supply of new homes was about to slump.

Spending like there was no tomorrow

The first half of the long upturn was characterised by reasonably tight control over public spending. The budget deficit left over by the recession of the early 1990s had forced the Conservative government to increase taxes and exercise spending restraint. This continued under Gordon Brown. For his first two years at the Treasury he was the 'iron chancellor' or 'Prudence Brown', a fiscal conservative, attacked by some in the Labour Party and by the unions for not spending. I remember a press conference he and Ed Balls held ahead of a big international meeting at which even the journalists were criticising him for being too parsimonious, given the healthy state of the public finances. That was to change, and it was to change dramatically. Brown's prudence, as he made clear, was for a purpose. He used to give his budget documents thematic titles, and the March 2000 budget was called 'Prudent for a Purpose', the purpose being huge increases in public spending.

Brown in 1997 had inherited public spending plans described by Kenneth Clarke, his Conservative predecessor, as 'eyewateringly tight'. He raised taxes in his first budget, including a £5.2 billion windfall tax on the privatised utilities and a £5 billion annual 'raid' on pensions through the abolition of the dividend tax credit, which had shielded pension funds from tax on the returns they received on their shareholdings. He also increased personal taxes by stealth, partly by abolishing well-established reliefs such as the married couple's allowance and mortgage interest relief. Brown and Tony Blair had learned from the history of previous Labour governments.

They, on taking office after a period of Conservative rule, typically relaxed government spending, thus cheering supporters among public sector unions and their members. The problem with spending first and asking questions later was that it usually ran into financial trouble, as the devaluation crisis in the 1960s and the IMF crisis in the 1970s had clearly shown. So Brown went about it in the opposite way. First he raised the taxes and squeezed spending, to provide the cushion of very healthy public finances. These were helped by the April 2000 auction of third generation (3G) mobile phone licences, which raised an astonishing £22.5 billion: £380 per head of the UK population. Then, and only then, did Brown relax spending. This was his prudence for a purpose.

The spending increases announced in the March 2000 budget were foreshadowed, much to Brown's disgust, in a television interview Tony Blair did on 16 January 2000 with Sir David Frost for his Sunday-morning *Breakfast with Frost* programme on the BBC. Blair, responding to a winter crisis in the National Health Service, pledged to raise health spending in Britain to the EU average. Such was the rivalry between the two, even at that early stage, that Brown, who had been happy with the idea of merely raising NHS spending to the European average, was soon aiming higher. In 2001 he commissioned Sir Derek Wanless, former chief executive of National Westminster Bank, to quantify 'the financial and other resources required to ensure that the NHS can provide a publicly funded, comprehensive, high quality service available on the basis of clinical need and not ability to pay'. Wanless delivered his interim report in November 2001 and his final report in April 2002. The first set out the scale of under-funding and the extent to which Britain fell behind other advanced industrial countries on a variety of health outcomes. The second detailed the additional resources needed over a twenty-year period under three different scenarios: 'solid progress', 'slow uptake' and 'fully engaged'.

All three built in real increases in NHS spending of more than 7 per cent a year for the first five years, even though Wanless warned that such rises were 'at the upper end of what should sensibly be spent'. His concern was over the ability of the NHS to absorb an increase in funding of this magnitude without huge waste. He also warned that 'higher spending inputs do not necessarily imply better health outputs and outcomes'. Despite the caveats, the review was interpreted by Brown as a green light for substantial increases in health spending. If health was getting substantially more, it was hard to exclude other priority areas, such as education. Indeed, it was hard to exclude any areas at all. Some of this largesse was paid for by higher taxes, including an unpopular 1 per cent rise in National Insurance contributions for employees and employers, announced in 2002. Much of it, however, was based on the assumption that the room for manoeuvre Brown had given himself during Labour's first term made years of big public spending increases affordable.

Those increases were considerable. In the case of the NHS, founded in 1948, Brown delivered the biggest sustained increases in its history, averaging 6.6 per cent a year in real terms from 2000 to 2010. Health was not alone. The Institute for Fiscal Studies calculated that overall government spending rose by 4 per cent in real terms between 1999–2000 and 2007–8, with the increase split between a huge 16.4 per cent annual rise in investment spending (schools, hospitals, roads etc.) and a 3.6 per cent average increase in current spending. The increases for health were outstripped by that for transport, at 8.4 per cent a year. Education (5.4 per cent), law and order – the Home Office (4.8 per cent) – and housing (4.3 per cent) were also winners. It was clear, long before the global financial crisis hit at the end of Brown's chancellorship, that not only could spending on this scale not be sustained but that it was already excessive. Brown, however, insisted that he had not replaced his earlier prudence with irresponsibility, and he did so by pointing to his own fiscal rules.

Breaking the rules

If there is one thing you learn from following economic policy over a very long period, it is that rules are made to be broken. When governments say they have nailed themselves to the mast of fiscal responsibility by adopting rules that will never be broken, you know that they have done nothing of the sort. When they say the money supply will be strictly controlled within pre-set limits, you should be down to the bookmakers and bet that it will not be. When they say they will never devalue the pound, it is time to move your money into that Swiss bank account. So it was with Gordon Brown and his fiscal rules, which he put in place in 1997 and which had a better run than most. Though they were under pressure even before the crisis hit, it was that which killed them off. The first rule was the 'golden rule': balance, or better, the current budget over the cycle – in other words, only borrow for investment. The second was to keep the public sector's net debt below 40 per cent of GDP and was known as the sustainable investment rule. The rules were self-imposed and self-policed (though the Treasury checked its assumptions twice a year with the National Audit Office).

The crisis saw both Brown's fiscal rules buried, or rather suspended (never to be resurrected), though they had been under pressure for some time. Once, in the early 2000s, the chancellor moved towards rapid increases in spending, it was only a matter of time. Subsequently, international organisations such as the International Monetary Fund (IMF) and the Organisation for Economic Co-operation and Development (OECD) suggested that by the time of the crisis the Labour government was running a 'structural' budget deficit of 5 per cent of GDP. A structural or underlying deficit is one that remains even when the economy is operating normally: in other words, when there is full employment. The public finances had initially looked very good under Brown, helped by special factors such as the

£22.5 billion windfall from the auction of the 3G mobile phone spectrum. It did not take long after the spending relaxation for the effects to begin to be felt. In November 2002 some of the gloss went off Brown's iron chancellor reputation when he was forced to announce a doubling of annual borrowing from £11 billion to £20 billion. Given what happened later, this looks almost like small change, but it marked the start of a long battle between the Treasury and many outside economists and commentators over whether the rules were being followed. Martin Weale, then director of the National Institute of Economic and Social Research, later a member of the MPC, was a persistent critic. It was said later that Weale, appointed to the MPC in 2010, would never have got the post had Brown still been at the Treasury.

After 2002 official projections of the budget deficit were more likely to be revised up than down. Prudence was replaced by a series of upward revisions of the official borrowing forecasts. One of the difficulties about talking to Brown at those 11 Downing Street breakfasts, or to his advisers and officials, was that they were usually in complete denial about this. For his first five years, after adjusting for the economic cycle, Brown barely borrowed at all. For the next five years, borrowing averaged close to 3 per cent of GDP. Even with the economy growing strongly, borrowing was high, though tiny compared with what would happen later. But borrowing should have been lower when the economy was growing strongly. Part of the problem was that Brown was reluctant to acknowledge that anything was wrong. 'Fiscal policy is underpinned by clear objectives and two strict rules that ensure sound public finances over the medium term while allowing fiscal policy to support monetary policy over the economic cycle', the Treasury said in the 2007 Budget. This was a bold claim. Before too long it became nonsensical.

The long recovery from the early 1990s to 2008 was not perfect. Near its start there was a major policy reversal and national humiliation: the ERM exit. Near its end the strains were clearly showing. For its first few years households and businesses took some convincing that things were genuinely getting better. In the history of UK recoveries that is not unusual. What was rather unusual was for a government in power for more than five years of good recovery to get voted out of office by a landslide, as the Conservatives did in 1997. The long upturn also saw the introduction of a big important change in the way economic policy operated: Bank of England independence. It also saw a determined effort by the government to correct Britain's chronic instability, its tendency towards high and volatile inflation and a boom-bust economic cycle. Both the Conservatives, before they left office in 1997, and Labour, after 1997, also took steps to try to improve Britain's long-run economic performance – a version of the supply-side revolution of the 1980s. There was a mortgage-fuelled housing boom and excessive growth in public spending. Too much debt was taken on, taxes went up, though not excessively, and there was more regulatory red tape after 1997. But Britain, for a period, did very well. It did not, could not, last for ever, and it ended in tears, as we shall see in the next chapter, but this was the closest we came – in the time I have been following these things – to prolonged economic success. For a while, quite a long while, it seemed Britain had finally cast out her economic demons. No longer, it seemed, did we need to look for the next set-back, or, when it appeared, the economy was robust enough to take it. For once, sustained growth alongside low inflation became the natural order of things. For almost two decades the economy seemed to be doing well. It was a big disappointment when this turned out not to be the case.

8

The biggest crisis

The financial services sector in Britain, and the City of London at the centre of it, is a great example of a highly skilled, high value-added, talent-driven industry that shows how we can excel in a world of global competition. Britain needs more of the vigour, ingenuity and aspiration that you already demonstrate that is the hallmark of your success.

Gordon Brown, Mansion House speech, 20 June 2007

The economic times we are facing are arguably the worst they've been in 60 years. And I think it's going to be more profound and long-lasting than people thought.

Alistair Darling, *The Guardian*, 30 August 2008

There have been many times over the decades when things have looked very bad for the British economy. There have been plenty of occasions when it was never quite clear how it would find its way out of the hole it was in. Crises have come and gone. Mistakes have been made. Governments have succeeded and then spectacularly failed. Most of those episodes have been recounted in this book, including the devaluation of 1967, the

IMF crisis of 1976, the winter of discontent, the stock market crash of October 1987 and Black Wednesday in 1992. The 9/11 attacks on the USA in September 2001 must rank as the most shocking set of events of my lifetime, which did more than anything else to shape the early part of the twenty-first century.

In terms of an economic shock, however, nothing compares with the global financial crisis which began in the summer of 2007 and reached its deadliest phase between the autumn of 2008 and the spring of 2009. This was the biggest crisis of my lifetime, one whose effects are still clearly with us as I write this, and will be for some years to come. This was the time when we were on the edge of the economic abyss, when we stared disaster in the face. Set against this, previous economic crises seemed like parochial affairs, mere errors that needed to be, and would be, corrected. This was close to the collapse of capitalism and the near-death of a functioning banking system needed to hold any economy together. This was the time when we almost did not have a banking system, when in practical terms cash machines – ATMs – almost were not refilled, wages were almost not paid and supermarket shelves almost were not restocked. However much governments had to hold their noses before rescuing the banks – and, as we shall see, dithering over such rescues caused some damage – there was no alternative. Banking collapse would have been followed by economic collapse and civil breakdown. Those who argued that the banks should have been allowed to fail had no idea of how much more serious it would have been if that had happened. The fact that this was avoided was no small triumph, though avoiding disaster rarely brings the kudos for policymakers that it should.

For two years from the autumn of 2007, and the run on Northern Rock, through the banking and market meltdown, it felt as though all the reassuring certainties had gone. There was a mini-industry among pundits of predicting that, no matter how bad things were, they were going to get much, much worse.

I never joined in with that, always insisting that the world would come through this crisis, but there were plenty of times when I doubted my own reassurances. I lost count of the number of people, including work colleagues, who asked whether their money was safe in the bank and, if not, how to make it safe. That itself was extraordinary: until the crisis few would have questioned whether their deposits were safe. In the atmosphere of near-collapse, however, it was a highly relevant question. My standard response was that, if people wanted additional security, they should ensure that their money was spread between different banks, to take advantage of the deposit guarantee scheme (the financial services compensation scheme). Though it subsequently became more generous, at the outbreak of the crisis the scheme guaranteed only the first £2,000 of an individual's deposits in any one bank, and 90 per cent of the next £33,000. Beyond £35,000 you were on your own. In reality, if a big bank had collapsed, even that relatively small compensation scheme would have been overwhelmed.

There is not room here for a blow-by-blow account of the financial crisis. Its importance, as far as this book is concerned, was not only its severity but also the fact that it demonstrated, much more effectively than any of the many other set-backs the British economy has suffered over the decades, that pride does indeed come before a fall, and that we are never so vulnerable as when we think things are going really well.

9 August 2007

There are some pieces you write that hit the spot, with immaculate timing, and there are many that do not. When I wrote my column for Sunday 5 August 2007, I was probably scratching around for a theme. Though August is unfairly labelled these days as the silly season, when no real news happens, it can be a struggle for economic commentators. So I chose to focus on the jitters in the financial markets, warning that they could be telling us something important. 'Problems in the American subprime mortgage market – loans to borrowers with dodgy credit histories – have been apparent for months', I wrote.

> But the defaults have been getting bigger and more frequent. Think of it as an inverted pyramid, resting on these dodgy, subprime loans, which were sliced and diced and turned into a range of sophisticated financial derivatives, notably collateralised debt obligations (CDOs). If the base is rotten, the pyramid risks collapse, and fears of this have grown, widening spreads (increasing the cost of borrowing) across a range of markets. Deals that looked good when spreads were narrow, such as leveraged buyouts, are no longer viable.

I am not pretending for a moment that I saw the crisis, in all its Technicolor glory, coming. There are plenty of financial episodes that, however serious they may seem at the time, pass with relatively little effect. Markets may fall off a cliff, but most times they do not drag the economy with them. I have lost count of the number of times since the worst phase of the crisis when people claiming expert knowledge have warned that something similar is going to happen again, only perhaps worse. Some kind of crisis may have been inevitable in 2007, but it could have panned out in any number of ways.

Anyway, just four days after that fortuitously timed piece it was clear that a significant financial crisis was occurring. On 8 August economic journalists had gathered, as they do each quarter, at the Bank of England for its quarterly inflation report press conference. There were questions about the worries in financial markets and about the fears of a crisis emanating from the USA's subprime mortgage market – the toxic loans to borrowers with poor or non-existent credit histories which had been bundled together or 'securitised' into sophisticated financial instruments. The abiding memory of that press conference was the reassurance offered by Mervyn King, the Bank's governor. 'It is not an international financial crisis', he insisted, but rather a more realistic pricing of risk by the markets. 'Our banking system is much more resilient than in the past', he added, noting that 'the growth of securitisation has reduced fragility significantly'. King, reflecting what at the time was the conventional wisdom among central bankers, thought the banking system was safe. He was to change his view very dramatically as the crisis unfolded.

On 9 August 2007, the day after his reassuring comments, the problems in the USA's subprime mortgage market went global and became, in particular, a crisis for Europe's banks. Central banks usually supply large-scale liquidity to the financial markets only in extreme emergencies. They did so in the aftermath of the 11 September 2001 attacks on the USA. As far as financial markets were concerned, 9 August 2007 was even bigger. The European Central Bank, in a brief announcement from its headquarters in Frankfurt, said it would supply sufficient liquidity 'to ensure orderly conditions in the euro money market'. Whether, in making that announcement, the ECB was aware just how much liquidity would be needed is not clear, but almost 95 billion euros were demanded by forty-nine separate European banks. They needed the ECB's help because the money markets had ceased to function. Suddenly, banks and other institutions which had been happily dealing with each other for generations decided it was too risky to carry on doing so. The banks no longer wanted to lend to each other. Without such flows liquidity dries up, and without liquidity banks can no longer function.

At that moment, too, it became clear that we were talking about a global phenomenon. The ECB was not responding to some distant threat. It was dealing with a crisis on its own doorstep. BNP Paribas, France's biggest bank, announced that it was suspending withdrawals from three of its investment funds. One Dutch bank announced that it had lost tens of millions of pounds on its subprime investments, and others began examining their books to see how much damage they had suffered. The ECB's decision to supply liquidity was followed by the USA's Federal Reserve. Central banks were fighting a fire that was beginning to rage. That fire, burning only in the financial markets for now, would soon begin to affect the real economy. To use the American expression, events on Wall Street would start to hurt Main Street. The surprise was that the Bank of England, sitting in the heart of the financial capital of Europe, if not the world, chose not to react. Talking to Bank officials at the time, indeed, it was hard not to detect a strong sense of contempt for the ECB, a new kid on the central banking block, which had over-reacted, perhaps even panicked, because it lacked experience in these matters. Such snootiness did not last. Soon the Bank had to defend the fact that it was too slow off the mark.

The hazards of moral hazard

The Bank of England's tactics in the days and weeks following the outbreak of the crisis caused bemusement and anger. Britain's banks were every bit as desperate for liquidity as their European counterparts, and told the Bank of England so. Some, who had European subsidiaries, took advantage of the liquidity being offered by the European Central Bank. The strong belief was that the Bank was waiting to see whether the storm would blow over before acting, perhaps for fear that it would make a difficult situation worse by weighing in prematurely. Later, stories began to emerge that King, the governor, had locked himself in a room with a large pile of reading material while he worked out what to do. King himself gave a different version when a guest on *Desert Island Discs* on BBC Radio 4 in 2013, insisting that he knew exactly what to do when the crisis broke.

That was not how it looked from the outside, or to many on the inside. To the markets and the City's banking community the Bank's hesitation was due to the fact that, despite nearly two decades at the Bank, King was fundamentally an academic economist, lacking the market 'feel' of his predecessors, including Eddie George. Not for King bank boardrooms or City lunch rooms: the Bank should keep its distance. Later, some of his most senior colleagues revealed their disquiet with the Bank's response. Sir John Gieve, one deputy governor, said subsequently that the Bank's footwork in the early stages of the crisis owed more to John Sergeant (one of the less skilful contestants on the TV programme *Strictly Come Dancing*) than Fred Astaire. Paul Tucker, the Bank's most senior interface with the markets, was also perturbed.

The strongest argument for not coming to the aid of the banks was the one closest to King's heart: moral hazard. If the banks were immediately helped out, there would be nothing to stop them engaging in risky behaviour over and over again in the future. They had to be taught a lesson. Others disagreed, arguing in essence that, when the world was collapsing around you, philosophical arguments should be put to one side and that there would be time for punishment later. Sir Callum McCarthy, chairman of the Financial Services Authority (FSA), the banking regulator, acknowledged that there was an argument to be made about moral hazard but said he was more concerned about the impact of the crisis on 'innocent bystanders', including the banks' customers. 'My own view of the balance between the moral hazard arguments and the other instances is slightly different.' He and Hector Sants, chief executive of the FSA, had unsuccessfully pleaded with King to change policy. The House of Commons Treasury committee, reporting on the events of August and September 2007 a few months later, was particularly critical of the Bank: 'The Bank of England, the European Central Bank and the Federal Reserve each pursued a different course of action in response to the money market turmoil in August 2007', it said.

> Only the Bank of England took no contingency measures at all during August, in order to protect against moral hazard, that is, the fear that an injection of liquidity would offer incentives for banks to take on more liquidity risk, secure in the knowledge that the Bank of England would step in to resolve future liquidity crises ... We are unconvinced that the Bank of England's focus on moral hazard was appropriate for the circumstances in August. In our view, the lack of confidence in the money markets was a practical problem and the Bank of England should have adopted a more proactive response.

This was not just a technical argument about difficulties in the money markets, as McCarthy's 'innocent bystanders' – bank customers – soon discovered.

The run on the Rock

Most people in Britain had never seen a run on a bank. There had been banking failures, such as the collapse in 1991 of Bank of Credit and Commerce International (BCCI) and in 1995 of Barings, as a result of the actions of Nick Leeson, its infamous Singapore-based trader. Smaller banks and building societies had occasionally got into difficulty, including the New Cross and Grays societies, often as a result of unorthodox behaviour by their executives, but had been effortlessly swallowed up by bigger competitors, with the support of the authorities. The closest most had got to a bank run was the fictional account in *Mary Poppins*. For a proper bank run, in England at least, it was necessary to go back to 1866 and the City bank Overend, Gurney & Co. We had, it seemed, consigned these things to the history books.

Or not. On 9 August it was not just in Europe that the pressures were starting to be felt. Traders at Northern Rock reported that its markets for funding were suffering 'a dislocation': in other words, it was finding it difficult to raise money. Northern Rock, a Newcastle-based former building society, had become Britain's most aggressive mortgage lender. Its products included the notorious 'Together' mortgage, under which customers could borrow up to 125 per cent of a property's value, apparently safe in the knowledge that rising house prices would soon pull them out of negative equity. Northern Rock's business model was based on borrowing significant amounts in wholesale money markets – rather than relying on customer deposits – and lending those funds out in mortgages. It was, in the jargon, 'borrowing short and lending long'. On 9 August it was no longer able to borrow short. Adam Applegarth, its chief executive, and Matt Ridley, its chairman, having been contacted by the FSA along with all other banks to see whether they were experiencing funding difficulties, had to admit that they were. Northern Rock, Britain's seventh-largest bank and a FTSE-100 firm – one of the 100 largest firms quoted on the stock market – was no minnow, and it had been growing by 20 per cent a year since being converted from a building society, 'demutualised', in 1997.

When Applegarth and Ridley realised that they were in difficulty, they looked at three possible solutions. One was to manage their way out of it, selling some assets and hoping that investors would take on 'securitised' bundles of their mortgages. That was ruled out by the sharp deterioration in market conditions. Another was that it would be secretly supported by the Bank of England, Treasury and FSA until conditions improved, while hoping that word did not get out about its difficulties.

That, however, was ruled out by King's moral hazard concerns, though such secret support was just over a year later provided to Royal Bank of Scotland and Lloyds Bank. The third route was the tried and trusted one of organising a takeover of the troubled bank, in a way that had happened in the past. Northern Rock would be bigger and harder to swallow than the building societies and smaller banks rescued in the past, but it was not impossible for a larger bank to do so. The hastily arranged marriage between Lloyds Bank and Bank of Scotland in the autumn of 2008 did not have a very happy outcome but showed what could be done.

On 16 August, Applegarth and Ridley found themselves on the receiving end of King's moral hazard arguments. A formal request to the Bank to provide it with temporary liquidity, supported by the FSA, was rejected. To do so would be futile, King also argued, because everybody in the markets would quickly realise that Northern Rock was in trouble. To do so secretly, he claimed, would be against EU rules (though they were not drawn up to deal with conditions of financial crisis). Northern Rock had one last option: to sell itself to the highest bidder. Conditions in the money markets calmed a little, though they did not allow Northern Rock to resume its funding operations. But it secured a deal to be taken over by the larger Lloyds Bank, run by an American, Eric Daniels, at a knockdown price of just £2 a share. There was one snag: Lloyds needed £30 billion of credit from the Bank of England, to be paid back after two years, to make the deal work. King, however, again provided the obstacle to a deal, saying he could not recommend such a deal, and that it would only be done against his objections, which the government could not ignore. Northern Rock, it seemed, was on its own. Soon everybody would realise how dangerous that was.

On the evening of Thursday 13 September, at around 8.30, the BBC's then business editor, Robert Peston, reported the first in what was to be a series of scoops during the financial crisis. Northern Rock was to be given emergency support by the Bank of England, acting as lender of last resort. The implication of this, that Northern Rock could keep going only with official support, was not lost on viewers and listeners. There is an interesting question about whether things would have been different if the Bank of England had been able to stick to its original plan, once the option of allowing Northern Rock a 'safe haven' with Lloyds Bank had been vetoed. That plan was to announce the lender-of-last-resort support first thing on Monday 17 September, together with reassuring statements about this being only a temporary difficulty and there being no question of depositors' money not being safe. By Thursday afternoon, however, the rumours were swirling around Northern Rock even before Peston broke his story. Because of those rumours the announcement was brought forward to the morning of Friday 14 September. Had it held until then, it would have been the main news for the following day's newspapers. As it was, most led on Friday with the story of the bail-out of the Rock. By Saturday they had another story: the run on the Rock.

It was the first British bank run since the 1860s, but it was a very modern one. As soon as the news broke of Northern Rock's difficulties, its customers began trying to move their money electronically, by accessing their internet accounts. Once the bank's website became overwhelmed and impossible for many to access, the effect was merely to add to the panic. Though the reason was technical, the impression was that Northern Rock had already closed for business. So a modern bank run turned into a traditional one. Unlike its rivals, Northern Rock had a relatively small number of branches, seventy-two, and soon they too were overwhelmed by customers wanting to get their money out. This looked bad, and it was. Not until the evening of Monday 17 September, when Alistair Darling, the chancellor, announced that the government would guarantee all the deposits of the Rock's customers, did the panic subside.

The damage was done. Pictures of panicked customers trying desperately to get their money out of a British bank flashed around the world. Britain looked like a country in trouble, a theme picked up by Richard Lambert, the former *Financial Times* journalist and Bank of England MPC member, who a year earlier had become director-general of the CBI, the business organisation. In September, just after the run on the Rock, he happened to be giving a speech in Newcastle, the bank's home town, and he didn't pull his punches. 'It's not just the north-east that has been damaged by this episode', he said. 'The reputation and standing of the UK as a world financial leader has also been tarnished. Outside the movies, a run on a bank is something that happens in a banana republic. That one should have happened, under our noses, in a mature and prosperous country like the UK, is almost unimaginable.'

Alistair Darling

The man with the job of dealing with this fast-unfolding crisis was Alistair Darling. He was appointed chancellor by Gordon Brown, taking over on 28 June 2007, when Gordon Brown became prime minister. Darling had had a string of Cabinet jobs under Tony Blair, including at the department of work and pensions, transport, Scottish secretary and secretary of state for what was then the trade and industry department. He was known as the archetypal safe pair of hands, quietly competent and capable of ensuring that his departments did not make the news for the wrong reasons. This was one reason Brown appointed him. The other was that he did not want somebody at the Treasury trying to extend his reach across government, as he had done. Darling would run the Treasury quietly and competently, leaving all the big initiatives to emanate from Brown's 10 Downing Street. It did not quite work out like that.

Darling was the most accessible of all the chancellors I have reported and commented on, and entirely straight to deal with. Even during the crisis he made time for meeting economic journalists socially, as well as for formal interviews. At one such occasion, when we invited him to Soho House, then achingly trendy, he let slip to me that there was no question of the Labour government holding a public spending review before the general election, so great were the uncertainties. Voters would thus go into the polling booth without knowing much about Labour's plans. It made for a very good story, and, to his credit, the Treasury denials were at best half-hearted. On another occasion he invited a small group of us to 11 Downing Street for drinks. It was an informal evening, the opposite of most such parties. In the absence of waiters, Darling himself and his wife, Maggie, were on hand to top up glasses and hand around the crisps. You felt that, if he had never gone into politics and this had been a quiet little drinks party in their Edinburgh town house, it would not have been much different. I liked him a lot.

Though appointed by Brown, Darling had a tense relationship with him. In the summer of 2008 he invited a *Guardian* journalist to the family croft on the island of Lewis in the Outer Hebrides. There, in the company of Darling and his wife, she put together a magazine profile of the chancellor. As he was musing on the crisis he would be returning to when his holiday was over, Darling said that the economic times the country was facing 'are arguably the worst they've been in 60 years, and I think it's going to be more profound and long-lasting than people thought'. It made front-page news in *The Guardian* and was widely followed up. Brown was furious, accusing Darling of pulling the rug from under the economy. The prediction was, of course, right, but Darling was required to do a round of the television and radio studios insisting that he was referring to global economic conditions and the scale of the challenges policymakers were trying to deal with. Relations with Brown were never very good again. The old tensions that had characterised the Blair–Brown era returned. Often Darling would ask what Downing Street was saying. Often Brown would claim credit for initiatives carefully put together by Darling and his Treasury officials. As the 2010 election approached, Darling restrained Brown from committing even more emergency public spending to boost the economy, knowing it would add to the fiscal mess he or his successor would have to clear up. At one stage Brown made a serious attempt to displace Darling from the Treasury and replace him with Ed Balls, until he was warned that this would add to the uncertainty and instability the economy was facing.

Darling was also frustrated and angered by Mervyn King's behaviour. King was 'slow to recognise the nature of the crisis', Darling wrote in his memoir *Back from the Brink*, in which he implied that during the crisis the Bank governor had leaked sensitive material to George Osborne, the Conservative shadow chancellor. The impression was of a chancellor who was fighting internal battles at a time when he was trying to prevent the economy succumbing to the worst financial crisis in a century. He did pretty well.

The collapse

For Darling and his Treasury officials, and for Mervyn King at the Bank of England, it soon became clear that Northern Rock was merely an appetiser for the much bigger and graver events to come. It was clear that the housing market in Britain was taking a big hit, and it was clear to me that the economy was also slowing. During the spring of 2008 it was, as I wrote at the time, grinding to a halt. The problem was, not for the first time, that the official statistics were misleading. Britain's job market was holding up remarkably well, with employment, admittedly a lagging indicator, continuing to grow until the summer of 2008. So, it seemed, was the broader economy. The first estimates for GDP in the second quarter of 2008 suggested a small rise, which was later revised to a sizeable fall. The fact that the economy appeared to be slowing rather than falling off a cliff meant that the Bank of England, for one, was distracted. A sharply rising oil price – crude oil reached a record $147 a barrel in the summer of 2008 – pushed inflation above 5 per cent, one theory being that speculators had turned their attention away from other troubled financial markets and piled into commodities. As late as August 2008, one member of the Bank's monetary policy committee, Tim Besley, was voting for an interest rate hike.

Very soon, nobody was talking of raising interest rates. Central banks, including the Bank of England, were scrambling to cut them as quickly as possible. In March 2008 one prominent Wall Street investment bank, Bear Stearns, had got into trouble and had been rescued, the US authorities coming up with a $30 billion sweetener to ring-fence Bear's most toxic assets –subprime securities and other financial instruments that were trading at very large losses – a condition that its rival J. P. Morgan, run by Jamie Dimon, one of the few Wall Street winners from the crisis (for a while at least), insisted on. It was reasonable to expect that a similar sort of rescue would occur when the next bank hit the rocks. Over the summer it became clear that the most vulnerable such bank was Lehman Brothers. I had known Lehman Brothers for some time, mainly through visits to its London headquarters in Canary Wharf. Everything about it spoke of solidity and permanence, from the building itself, with its expensive art works on the floors where it entertained visitors, to the quality of its research. Its economics team was headed by John Llewellyn, formerly one of the OECD's senior officials. Before the crisis Lehman, which could trace its history back to the 1840s, appeared indestructible. Soon it was anything but. It was run by Richard 'Dick'

Fuld, known as 'the gorilla' for his imposing physical presence and occasional tendency to engage in fist fights, mainly when he was younger, though he astonished an audience just before the crisis by saying that he felt like tearing the heart out of any investor selling Lehman's stock short 'and eat[ing] it before his eyes while he's still alive'.

Lehman's demise owed quite a lot to Fuld's personality. Despite repeated warnings that the firm either needed to be sold, or raise a huge amount of capital from outside, he seemed determined to maintain the bank's independence. A collapsing share price – by early September 2008 it was barely a tenth of its level a year earlier – told its own story. Two separate announcements in early September – that a proposed partnership with Korea Development Bank had broken down, and that a separate capital-raising exercise had failed – sounded the death knell. Even then the expectation was that some kind of rescue would be orchestrated, as had happened with Bear Stearns.

This time, however, was different. Hank Paulson, the US Treasury secretary, was under pressure over bank bail-outs and over the rescue earlier in September of Freddie Mac (the Federal Home Loan Mortgage Corporation) and Fannie Mae (the Federal National Mortgage Association), the USA's mortgage guarantors. As the key weekend of the financial crisis approached, 13–14 September 2008, it was clear that Lehman needed a private rescue, a takeover. It did not happen. Paulson and his colleagues went into the weekend believing that they had two potential saviours for Lehman, either of which would take a nasty problem off its hands. By Sunday 14 September both suitors had dropped out. Bank of America instead bought Merrill Lynch, one of Lehman Brothers' Wall Street rivals. Barclays, the final hope, dropped out of the bidding altogether, under pressure from the authorities in Britain. What should have been a collective effort to stave off disaster ended up with the USA's biggest corporate bankruptcy and, despite frenzied attempts to limit the damage, a catastrophic shock for the global financial system.

Falling off a cliff

Though policymakers tried to put a brave face on it, it was clear that something dramatic had changed. The crisis, which up to Lehman Brothers had been something of a phoney war, suddenly became a very real one. On the weekend after the Lehman collapse, under the headline 'Welcome to the New Age of Austerity', I wrote:

> Lending feast has been replaced by lending famine, and that famine will last. People in Britain have become accustomed to easy money. Over the past year they have seen the credit taps being turned down and it has hurt. Last week's crisis tells us that is not going to change for a long time. Combine that with the likelihood of higher taxes and slower growth in government spending and it does not look like a comfortable picture. Welcome to the new austerity.

For a first stab after Lehman that was not bad. First, however, policymakers had to try to catch an economy that was falling off a cliff. I cannot overstate the drama of the months after the Lehman collapse. This was genuine economic theatre. Businesses likened it to a switch suddenly being turned off. Orders were cancelled and credit lines pulled. There was a collective drawing in of horns. The statistics show that Britain's economy shrank by 1.7 per cent in the third quarter of 2008, 2.2 per cent in the fourth and 1.8 per cent in the first quarter of 2009. Each one of those quarterly falls was big enough to constitute a significant recession in its own right. Unemployment rose by nearly a million in the space of a year. Even those numbers do not, however, capture the sense of it, the sense being that it was going to be hard to stem the tide. Alistair Darling tried his best, announcing a temporary cut in VAT from 17.5 per cent to 15 per cent in November 2008, as well as a boost to infrastructure spending (though the government bemoaned the lack of 'shovel-ready' projects). The Bank of England took its time to respond to the Lehman bankruptcy, waiting until 8 October to cut interest rates from 5 to 4.5 per cent. It then got with it, reducing rates to 3 per cent in November, 1.5 per cent in January 2009 and just 0.5 per cent in March. Bank Rate had never before been below 2 per cent, let alone within a whisker of zero.

Around the world there was something close to panic. Testifying to Congress in early 2009, Ben Bernanke, chairman of the Federal Reserve, the USA's central bank, and thus one of the most powerful officials in the world, reported on a US economy that was contracting at a 6 per cent annual rate and in which businesses had shed 600,000 jobs in January 2009, roughly the same as in November and December. The 'Detroit Three' – General Motors, Ford and Chrysler – lobbied Congress in November 2008, and again in December, pleading for aid to prevent collapse. They warned of the loss of 3 million jobs, from a collapse in car sales from 16 million to just 10 million. The old saying that what was good for General Motors (GM) was good for the USA had never seemed more apt. The big car companies were given government aid, though this did not prevent GM succumbing to temporary bankruptcy. Across the Pacific in Japan, Toyota reported its first loss for fifty-nine years. In Britain, Woolworths was on the brink of celebrating its centenary, having been brought over from the USA in 1909 by Frank Woolworth as a variation on his US 'five and dime' operation. Woolworths in Britain was, according to him, 'a penny and sixpence store' and a staple of the country's high streets. But, having limped through Christmas 2008, it finally closed the doors of its more than 800 shops. Some stores were bought by other retailers, including the newly ubiquitous pound shops. Others remain empty to this day.

Woolworths' demise was a symptom of a wider malaise. The economy had changed dramatically. Gordon Brown, in his swan-song budget speech as chancellor in March 2007, was able to report on a British economy which was the fastest-growing in the G7, with that growth set to continue. There would, he repeated, be no 'return to the old boom and bust'. Two years later it looked very different. The economy was in its worst recession in the post-war period. GDP fell by 6 per cent from peak to trough – worse than the recessions of the 1970s, early 1980s and early 1990s. In 2009 the world economy recorded its first post-war annual contraction. This was the biggest of all busts.

Meltdown

After the Lehman collapse, the rest of the autumn of 2008 and the following winter brought wave after wave of grim news. At the time I likened it to having twenty years or more of huge stories compressed into a few weeks. We could barely keep up. Stories that in normal times would have been preceded by weeks of speculation and weeks or months of analysis, such as the shotgun marriage between Lloyds Bank and Halifax Bank of Scotland (HBOS), came and went. A few weeks before it happened, the rescue by the British government both of the expanding Lloyds Banking Group and of Royal Bank of Scotland – then the biggest bank in the world – was the stuff of fantasy. It soon became the normal run of things. To paraphrase Lewis Carroll, there were times when we had to believe six impossible things every day. It was fortunate, during that period, that the *Sunday Times* had moved to more flexible deadlines. There have been times when the newspaper's Business section went to press on Friday evening, on the assumption that there was not much live business and financial news on Saturday. The crisis proved conclusively that there was. In the autumn of 2008 it seemed that every weekend brought a new phase of the crisis, and a new gathering of worried finance ministers and central bankers. Treasury and Bank of England officials got used to very late nights and giving up their weekends, and so did their City advisers and the bankers.

Mervyn King, by now fully engaged with the crisis, described it a few weeks after the Lehman collapse as 'an almost unimaginable' sequence of events. They included a $700 billion bailout of the US banking system by the USA's Treasury Department under the Troubled Asset Relief Programme (TARP), a plan only approved after a tough battle with Congress. George W. Bush, when he was pleading with Congressional leaders to back the White House's banking bail-out package, two weeks after the Lehman collapse, was typically blunt: 'If money isn't loosened up, this sucker could go down.' Rescuing the banks cost governments hundreds of billions in providing capital, liquidity support and guarantees for the banking system. In Britain the response included the nationalisation of much of Bradford & Bingley, a mortgage bank, and the emergency merger of Lloyds TSB and Halifax Bank of Scotland (HBOS) with the government waiving competition rules to allow the deal through. On 8 October, two weeks before King's speech, Abbey (owned by the Spanish bank Santander), Barclays, HBOS, HSBC, Lloyds, Nationwide, RBS and Standard Chartered were named in a package that would provide up to £50 billion of capital, and hundreds of billions of taxpayer-funded liquidity and credit guarantees.

Banks were in trouble, and had to be rescued. Merrill Lynch, another Wall Street giant, was forced into a merger with Bank of America. AIG, the USA's biggest insurer, had to be rescued by the US government. Several European banks, including the Belgian-Dutch Fortis Bank and Germany's Hypo Real Estate

Bank, got into trouble. UBS (Union Bank of Switzerland), a pillar of the country's banking establishment, was knee-deep in toxic assets. In mid-October the Swiss government agreed to inject $5 billion into the bank, alongside an officially backed fund to take up to $60 billion of its toxic assets. In 2008 UBS lost more than $17 billion, the largest corporate loss in Swiss history. ING, the big Dutch bank, had to be helped out at the same time by a €10 billion capital injection from its government. It was a dangerous contagion. Before it came to an end both Lloyds and Royal Bank of Scotland were substantially owned by the state. Fred Goodwin, the abrasive, ambitious chief executive of RBS, became a pariah and was stripped of his knighthood. Nicknamed 'Fred the Shred' for his ability to cut costs ruthlessly, he was the Icarus of the banking crisis. Nobody tried to fly higher, and nobody got more badly burned. Northern Rock, which started the rot in Britain, had been nationalised even before the crisis entered its worst phase. Decades of privatisation – selling off state-owned industries – were reversed by the forced nationalisation of leading British banks.

Saving the world

Though Gordon Brown's behaviour had Alistair Darling fuming, the crisis may have been his finest hour, its closest rival probably being his successful intervention in the Scottish referendum campaign of September 2014, when he campaigned passionately and successfully to preserve the union. Britain's rescue plan for the banks in October 2008 was widely praised for being clear-sighted and logical, even as the USA was struggling to get its rescue plan in place. Though the British plan was a product of the hard work by Darling and his officials at the Treasury, and by King and his at the Bank, together with an array of other experts, Brown was its figurehead, and received international plaudits. It was not just a question of rescuing the banks. Economies desperately needed stabilising too, and Brown came to be seen as being in the vanguard of a traditional Keynesian response to the crisis. All the old rules, including the government's fiscal rules, had to be abandoned. It was a time of crisis. 'I guess everyone is a Keynesian in a foxhole', said Robert Lucas, the University of Chicago economist, and anything but a Keynesian. He was joking, but not that much.

In November 2008 the IMF called for a global fiscal stimulus equivalent to around 2 per cent of GDP, equivalent to some $1.3 trillion. Even that was based on a mere slowing of the global economy, to 2 per cent growth in 2009, rather than the outright recession that occurred. In fact, in the post-war period the IMF had come to define a global recession as a 'growth' recession: a slowdown to around 2 per cent, which happened in the 1970s, early 1980s and early 1990s. The crisis also saw the elevation of a previously obscure body, the G20, which included the G7 countries of the USA, Japan, Germany, Britain, France, Italy and Canada but also, importantly, the big emerging economies: notably China, India, Brazil, Indonesia, Mexico and Turkey, as well as Saudi Arabia. The G20 held its first big crisis meeting on 15 November 2008 in Washington. Though it was hosted by George W. Bush, he was by then very much a lame duck president, in his final few weeks in the White House. Barack Obama had just won the presidential election, defeating John McCain. Obama did not attend the meeting, pointing out that Bush was still president, but the G20 meeting nevertheless endorsed fiscal measures to stimulate demand 'with rapid effect', while pledging also to take steps to ensure that 'fiscal sustainability' would be achieved again when the crisis was over. Larger budget deficits would be temporary, though for many countries, including Britain, 'temporary' meant very many years. The biggest stimulus was in China, $586 billion (though Obama announced a $789 billion package – spread over many years – shortly after he took office the following January), but every country came up with something. Britain committed to a £20 billion stimulus, despite the country's lurch into large budget deficit, mainly a temporary VAT cut from 17.5 to 15 per cent, with effect for thirteen months from 1 December 2008. A car 'scrappage' scheme gave motorists an incentive to trade in their old cars – which would be broken up – for new ones. There was no political consensus on these stimulus measures. Though the Conservatives were electoral beneficiaries of the crisis, they did not cover themselves in glory in this period, opposing even a temporary fiscal stimulus on the grounds that the public finances were too fragile to take it.

The November 2008 G20 meeting marked the start of the process of stabilising the global economy, but there was still work to do. When Britain assumed the presidency of the G20, at the start of January 2009, Gordon Brown was determined to seize the moment. In April 2009 the G20 met again in London's Docklands, in a vast exhibition centre well away from potential protesters. Given that the G20's mission was to preserve growth and jobs, the motivations of the protesters were a little puzzling, though anything that propped up what they saw as a broken system was perhaps unjustified in their eyes. Attending that G20 meeting was a somewhat surreal experience, though not as surreal as some. The participants were actually there, unlike at some summits, where they are many miles away from the journalists. The G20 claimed 'a concerted and unprecedented fiscal expansion' amounting to $5 trillion, which would boost the global economy by 4 per cent. The $5 trillion was the product of a certain amount of creative accounting, mainly consisting of the combined deterioration in fiscal balances in the global economy, most of it due to the recession's impact on tax revenues and government spending. But there were also explicit Keynesian fiscal measures. And, perhaps more by luck than judgement, the April 2009 G20 meeting did more or less coincide with the low point for the global economy.

Soon it was possible to report that the world economy had stabilised and was tentatively returning to growth. In the case of countries such as China, which had briefly paused at the end of 2008, there was never any doubt. In 2009 the Chinese economy grew by more than 9 per cent, while advanced countries had their biggest drop in living memory; including a fall of nearly 4.5 per cent in the euro area. Most of that fall happened in the early months of the year, however. By mid-year things were looking up. Surveys also suggested that was the case in Britain, though there was an agonising wait before that was confirmed by official figures. At time of writing, official GDP figures show that growth returned in the third quarter of 2009. At the time, the official verdict was that Britain's growth did not return until the final three months of 2009, and then only by a whisker, and this was not announced until January 2010. There was plenty more drama to come, most notably the crisis in the eurozone and the threat of a fiscal crisis in Britain. The abyss was still too close for comfort. But the economy had stopped falling off a cliff.

Why did we not see it coming?

The financial crisis was both an exhilarating and a depressing time. It ushered in a period in which I probably wrote more than ever before. The normal pattern for these things is that crises and the excitement surrounding them blow up but then soon subside, as does the interest in them. My weekly column in the *Sunday Times* trundles on, whether we are in a period of high excitement and anxiety or not. The crisis of 2007–9 and beyond was, in contrast, relentless. It just carried on, week after week, month after month, column after column, 2,500-word article after 2,500-word article. There was a lot happening, and the interest was enormous. It was also, however, a time of soul-searching, when I wondered whether I should give up. We were supposed to know about these things. Why had we not seen it coming? It was not hard to see parts of the story, and indeed it was clear that something serious was happening in the summer of 2007. Nobody, however, predicted that it would turn out as it did. It was clear even before the Lehman Brothers collapse that Britain's economy had stopped growing, but even then the full scale of what subsequently happened was not obvious. One prominent economic commentator, fortunately not me, wrote in early September 2008 that there was virtually no risk of Britain having a serious recession.

One defence was that the crisis could have panned out in a number of ways. Lehman Brothers did not have to collapse, generating near-meltdown in the Western banking system and a dive in the world economy. Some say that if it had not been Lehman it would have been another bank. Even so, allowing Lehman Brothers to fail because the politics of rescuing it were not right, only to trigger a round of much bigger bank rescues, in the USA and globally, was a big mistake. The other defence, and it is not much of one, is that we simply did not know what was happening within the banks. The fact that such blindness extended to bank boards, supervisors and auditors is an excuse. But we all should have known. We treated banks as if they were safer than they were, and as if the people running them still put such safety at the top of their list of priorities.

Perhaps the biggest misjudgement was over the treatment of so-called derivatives, the financial instruments that caused much of the trouble. In the past, a crisis in the USA's housing market would have stayed in America, causing problems for lenders but – apart from its impact on US growth – not many for the rest of the world. In 2007–9 it was different, because of what turned out to be an alphabet soup of derivatives. They started straightforwardly enough: mortgage-backed securities (MBS) were simply pools of mortgages put together for securitisation purposes – in other words, turned into a security, so investors could buy them. An MBS bundle of mortgages, as long as the underlying loans were of good quality, provided a good investment for fund managers, with a secure long-term return. The problem, of course, was that many of the subprime mortgages bundled together in this way were not of good quality. The ratings agencies, which gave many of these securities AAA, 'Triple-A', ratings, had much to answer for.

MBS were just one type of asset-backed security (ABS). If it had stopped there, the crisis might not have been so serious. There were, however, plenty of others. Collateralised debt obligations (CDOs) were more sophisticated, splitting the 'debt', or borrowing, into tranches reflecting the different risks of default. CDO-squared (CDO^2) instruments were CDOs consisting of other CDOs and became notorious, not least because on one calculation an investor would have been required to read a million pages of documentation to do due diligence on such an instrument. There were more acronyms in this alphabet soup. Credit default swaps (CDS) were a type of insurance contract. A firm wishing to minimise its credit risk gets somebody else to take on that risk, the risk of default, and pays a premium to it to do so. It buys a CDS from another firm, in some cases an insurance company (the American insurance giant AIG got into huge difficulty because of its exposure to CDS). It was not alone. When the global financial crisis broke in 2007, they were worth $55 trillion, nearly equivalent to the world's gross domestic product, though this was only a fraction of the $500 trillion trade in all derivatives. Another important acronym, the SIV, or structured investment vehicle, was used by the banks to parcel up and issue debt.

Policymakers got derivatives badly wrong – not least Alan Greenspan, the chairman of the Federal Reserve, from 1987 to the eve of the crisis in 2006. 'What we have found over the years in the marketplace is that derivatives have been an extraordinarily useful vehicle to transfer risk from those who shouldn't be taking it to those who are willing to and are capable of doing so', he told a Congressional committee in 2003. 'Prior to the advent of derivatives on a large scale, we did not have that capability. And we often had, for example, financial institutions, like banks, taking on undue risk and running into real, serious problems.'

Why did it happen?

Derivatives ensured that the risk was spread, but the effect was to amplify losses and damage to the financial system, not limit them. They were not the only cause of the crisis. Famously, when the queen visited the London School of Economics (LSE) in November 2008 to open its new academic building, her apparently throwaway question provoked a huge debate. The global financial crisis, she said, was 'awful', and she asked: 'If these things were so large, how come everyone missed it?' Professor Luis Garicano, director of the LSE's management department, who was showing her around, offered an answer. He referred to declining lending standards, particularly in the USA's housing market, and the herd instinct in financial markets. But he conceded that the warnings should have been louder. 'We economists and academics should have been louder in our warnings and more proactive in suggesting solutions', he wrote later. 'Particularly problematic and subject to a serious rethink are the short-term and one-sided incentives prevalent in the financial industry – and the failure by those who took the risks to bear the risks. The public is right to be outraged.'

Garicano was greatly overstating the extent to which 'economists and academics' had seen the crisis coming, but his reply provided the template for others. Even Mervyn King took to saying that he should have shouted louder. In June 2009 the British Academy assembled a star group of economic and financial experts, including seven people who were either serving or had served on the Bank of England's MPC: Tim Besley, David Miles, Paul Tucker, Sir Alan Budd, Sir John Gieve, Professor Charles Goodhart and Sushil Wadhwani. Sir Nicholas Macpherson, permanent secretary to the Treasury, and two of his predecessors, Sir Douglas Wass and Sir Gus O'Donnell, then Cabinet secretary, were there, along with many others. I was not at the first meeting but did attend a second, follow-up gathering. Tim Besley and Peter Hennessy, both professors and fellows of the British Academy, summed up the group's conclusions in a letter to the queen. It at least admitted that 'the exact form it would take and the timing of its onset and ferocity were foreseen by nobody'. Why did nobody properly assess the risks the banks were taking? The letter noted that plenty of people were employed specifically for that purpose – the assessment of risk – including 4,000 risk managers in one of Britain's big banks (RBS) alone. The problem was that these experts could not see the woods for the trees. 'The difficulty was seeing the risk to the system as a whole rather to any specific financial instrument or loan', they wrote. 'Risk calculations were most often confined to slices of financial activity, using some of the best mathematical models in our country and abroad. But they frequently lost sight of the bigger picture.'

The British Academy's response to the queen's question was not the only one – there were very many others – but it stands the test of time pretty well. Economists like to think they can cut through the complexity and stand back, but they get caught up in the mood too. Most of all, they did not know very much about what was happening within the banks.

'Most were convinced that banks knew what they were doing', the British Academy said.

> They believed that the financial wizards had found new and clever ways of managing risks. Indeed, some claimed to have so dispersed them through an array of novel financial

instruments that they had virtually removed them. It is difficult to recall a greater example of wishful thinking combined with hubris. There was a firm belief, too, that financial markets had changed. And politicians of all types were charmed by the market. These views were abetted by financial and economic models that were good at predicting the short-term and small risks, but few were equipped to say what would happen when things went as wrong as they have. People trusted the banks whose boards and senior executives were packed with globally recruited talent and their non-executive directors included those with proven records in public life. Nobody wanted to believe that their judgment could be faulty or that they were unable competently to scrutinise the risks in the organisations that they managed. A generation of bankers and financiers deceived themselves and those who thought that they were the pace-making engineers of advanced economies.

The crisis was also the product of a very long build-up. The so-called 'shadow' banking system dated back three decades to around 1980 in the USA. Shadow banks performed functions similar to the banks but escaped, and were designed to escape, at least some of the regulatory oversight. The shadow banking system, which included off-balance-sheet subsidiaries, was as big as the formal banking system by the time of the crisis. Not only that, but the world was hungry for credit. A paper put together by Andrew Sentance, then a member of the Bank of England's monetary policy committee, and a Bank economist, Michael Hume, tracked the global credit boom back to the early 1990s. Initially it was a US-led corporate credit boom, led by the rise of dot.com businesses. Then consumers took over. Behind it all, the financial sector itself was expanding. Two-thirds of the rise in private debt in Britain from the early 1990s was in the financial sector, though there were also big increases in corporate and household, particularly mortgage, debt. An accident was waiting to happen, and it did.

Economies get through even the most severe financial shocks, but not without changing, and not without having the stuffing knocked out of them. In some ways the global financial crisis and 'great recession' were unusual. The numbers were terrible, as were the consequences, not least for the budget deficit. But life went on, the banks kept their doors open and breakdown – civil and economic – was avoided. For this, though they were by no means perfect in their responses, a lot of credit has to go to ministers and officials. The system came through its biggest modern-day test and, thanks to some extraordinary interventions, survived. But it was a close-run thing. We will be talking about the crisis for decades to come, and fearing another one. Capitalism, meanwhile, faced more questions during and after the crisis than for a very long time. Where do we go from here? That is what I shall try to answer in the final chapter.

9

Something will turn up

Within just fifteen years we have the potential to overtake
Germany and have the largest economy in Europe. Five
years ago, that would have seemed hopelessly unrealistic;
economic rescue was the limit of our horizons. Today, our
goal is for Britain to become the most prosperous of any
major economy in the world in the coming generation,
with that prosperity widely shared across our country.
George Osborne, budget speech, 18 March 2015

The world has always been more interconnected than we think.
For most people, the idea might have seemed fanciful that
dodgy mortgage loans to poor people in Florida and Detroit
could trigger a run on, and the near collapse of, Britain's high
street banks, factory closures in the Black Country and elsewhere, and the years of austerity. This was, however, the reality,
and to a certain extent it always had been. All big financial crises
are global in nature, and all take longer to get over than we hope
and expect. It took a while for the fear of renewed collapse to
be removed. The most powerful aftershock of the banking
crisis was in Europe, with the euro coming close to break-up,
as Greece (twice), Ireland and Portugal were forced to accept

bail-outs and tough economic programmes. The scars of the crisis were felt – and will be felt – for a very long time.

With hindsight, we were too impatient for the nightmare to be over, too anxious for normality to be restored. This was to ignore the lessons of history, most clearly set out by Carmen Reinhart and Kenneth Rogoff, in their book *This Time Is Different: Eight Centuries of Financial Folly*. The title is, of course ironic: the two economists mean that crises follow a certain pattern. As they put it:

> It can be inferred from the evidence of so many episodes that recessions associated with crises (of any variety) are more severe in terms of duration and amplitude than the usual business cycle benchmarks of the post-World War II period in both advanced countries and emerging markets. Crises that are part of a global phenomenon may be worse still.

In and after a crisis, asset prices – shares and housing – fall, unemployment rises, per capita gross domestic product falls and government debt rises. The worst of these effects can last for ten years, though the post-war experience of milder crises had been better, with an average duration of four and a half years. Averaging these out, it was reasonable to expect the worst effects of the crisis that began in 2007 to last for perhaps seven years, maybe slightly less. People hoped for too much too soon. When the world economy bounced back sharply in 2010, growing by more than 5 per cent, with world trade up more than 10 per cent, the hope was indeed that this time was different. The reality was that there was a long way to go. Ignoring these lessons of history, and the fact that both a fall in living standards and a period of financial convalescence were inevitable, meant that Britain embarked on a strange debate, one in which it was almost as if the crisis had not happened.

The aftermath of the 2007–9 crisis was one in which, not for the first time, economists did not cover themselves with glory. Having failed to see it coming, they then embarked on a long debate about the appropriate response to it. Much of that debate was like a re-run of the ancient battles between Keynesians and monetarists, over which a truce had been called some years before the crisis. Keynesians insisted that the temporary fiscal boost provided by the Labour government during the worst phase of the recession should be maintained until the economy had fully recovered. It was cheap for governments to fund their debt, so why should they not fund more of it to achieve stronger growth? Just as economists had ignored the role of finance in the run-up to the crisis, however, they were ignoring it in its aftermath. I cannot say that Britain would have definitely faced a fiscal and financial crisis had it tried to expand its way out of trouble by increasing public spending in 2010, 2011 and beyond. Those who advocated such a course cannot, however, say that it would not have done. In 2010 officials I spoke to in the Bank of England and the Treasury were genuinely very worried that Britain, badly exposed to the crisis because of its large financial sector, would be seen as its weakest link. The commitment to reducing the budget deficit was essential to keep the markets on board. The alternative could have been the kind of crisis of confidence Britain faced in 1976, and the IMF bail-out, which came after the Labour government tried to expand its way through the first OPEC oil crisis. The risk of not having a programme of deficit reduction was too great. I would have backed such a programme if it had been implemented by Alistair Darling (though he would almost certainly have been forced out of his job by Gordon Brown had Labour won the 2010 general election). I backed it, though I disagreed with a lot of the detail, when it was implemented by Darling's replacement, the Conservative chancellor in Britain's first peacetime coalition since the inter-war years, George Osborne.

George Osborne

George Osborne is the last of my chancellors, and probably the one I had the most distant relationship with. Under every previous chancellor there was a constant dialogue, either directly with them or by proxy through their advisers. Not so with Osborne. It may be that this reflected his personality, or the fact that, as an intensely political chancellor, he saw his natural constituency as political rather than economic journalists. It may also have been that his media advisers saw his time better spent in television news slots – usually on a building site or in a factory wearing a helmet and high-visibility jacket – than in chewing the fat with economic journalists. After the regular contacts with Alistair Darling and his team, and with Gordon Brown and his advisers, this was a change for me.

I knew Osborne, of course. Soon after he was appointed shadow chancellor in 2005 I was invited in to chat with him. He was very young, only thirty-four at the time, and looked it. For most people in public office age is not an issue, and soon it was not an issue for Osborne. At the time, however, he did seem very young indeed. He had clear ideas about what he wanted to do, which was to get the Tories into a position in which they could credibly campaign in a general election for tax cuts. His predecessors, he said, had been guilty of making promises of tax cuts too late, so voters saw them as gimmicks. He would, instead, build the case for lower taxes over the course of the parliament. Instead of fiscal largesse being almost entirely directed towards higher public spending, which was what Labour was doing, the Conservatives would 'share the proceeds of growth' between lower taxes and higher spending.

It did not, of course, turn out like that. The Labour government was thrown badly off course by the financial crisis and, despite responding comprehensively to it, suffered badly politically. The Conservatives were, however, also blown off course. Once the economy was hit by the crisis, the idea of sharing the proceeds of growth was no longer remotely relevant. It took Osborne and David Cameron a long time to regroup, and in the meantime they struggled to respond adequately to the crisis. One reason my relationship with Osborne was never particularly good may have been that I wrote a piece in January 2009 attacking the fact that the shadow chancellor appeared to feel obliged to respond to every minor bit of economic news by releasing an e-mail (there were sometimes several a day). At that time Osborne's strategy appeared to be to criticise everything the authorities were doing. So he attacked what were then suggestions – two months later they became a reality – that the Bank of England was considering quantitative easing (QE): purchasing assets with electronically created money to boost the economy. Despite the fact that QE was supported by many economists, including many of the free market economists at the Institute of Economic Affairs and elsewhere who were normally close to the Conservative Party, Osborne felt obliged to attack it. 'The very fact that the Treasury is speculating about printing money shows that Gordon Brown has led Britain to the brink of bankruptcy', he railed. 'Printing money is the last resort of desperate governments when all other policies have failed. It can't be ruled out as a last resort in the fight against deflation, but in the end printing money risks losing control of inflation and leads to all the economic problems that high inflation brings.'

He did change his mind, and before too long was as chancellor acceding to Bank of England requests for permission to undertake more QE. At a time when the onus was getting the country through the banking system's near-death experience, it showed both inexperience and crass political opportunism. There was something of that when Osborne became chancellor. Soon after the May 2010 election he had a small reception at 11 Downing Street, a rare occasion. He told me he had recognised quite early on the likelihood that the Conservatives would not get an overall majority in the election, and thus the need to form a coalition. That was to his credit. Less so was the over-confidence of him and his colleagues. With his mantra that 'we're all in this together' his first big announcement in his June 2010 Budget was a hike in VAT from 17.5 to 20 per cent, to take effect at the start of 2011. This VAT hike, coming at a time when inflation was accelerating anyway, hit the recovery. The last thing the economy needed was a big and visible tax hike. Gordon Brown was criticised for his 'stealth' taxes, which were meant to escape people's attention. But 2010 and 2011 were probably a time for stealth taxes. The other early error was that the coalition's spending review, intended to set the parameters for most of the deficit reduction during the parliament, was done too quickly, and despite a change of Treasury chief secretary – the minister in charge of spending – during the process. David Laws, the Liberal Democrat first appointed, had to resign because of an expenses scandal, and was replaced by Danny Alexander.

Osborne did, however, show considerable grit. When his policies came under intense criticism and pressure when the economy failed to recover decisively in 2011 and 2012 – the expression used by his Labour shadow Ed Balls was 'flat-lining' – he stuck to his guns. He brushed off being booed by the crowd when he presented medals at the London Paralympics in 2012. He also showed considerable determination in getting the man he wanted as governor of the Bank of England: Mark Carney. Paul Tucker, one of Mervyn King's deputies, was widely expected to be given the job on King's retirement in 2013, but Osborne had other ideas. In particular, he appears to have wanted somebody who was not associated with the Bank's occasional failings during and after the crisis.

A Canadian at the Bank of England

Mark Carney, the first non-Briton to head the Bank of England in more than 300 years of its existence, soon demonstrated why he was the object of Osborne's desire. The new Bank governor, who had had a good crisis in a similar position at Canada's central bank, had an excellent reputation internationally as chairman of the G20 Financial Stability Board. He was also exactly what Britain needed in 2013: an optimist at the helm. While Mervyn King, his predecessor, was widely thought of as the gloomiest person with the Bank, Carney approached his new job with confidence. He believed Britain's economy could properly recover, and he was determined to do his best to make it come about. Under King, the Bank's approach was that it took one meeting of its interest rate-setting monetary policy committee at a time. People might hazard a guess, but it was impossible to pre-judge what the MPC might be doing in three or six months' time. Carney's approach was different. In August 2013 he launched his 'forward guidance' on interest rates, saying that the MPC would not even consider raising interest rates, then still at their crisis level of 0.5 per cent, until the unemployment rate – which was then nearly 8 per cent – had come down to 7 per cent, which the Bank did not expect to happen until 2016. The guidance did not go quite as planned. Unemployment fell more quickly than the Bank expected, and just over a year later had fallen not to 7 but to 6 per cent, without triggering a rise in interest rates. Carney had, however, got his message across, despite some criticism from the financial markets: interest rates would not rise until the recovery had had plenty of time to breathe. It would not be put at risk by a premature rise in interest rates.

Carney, whom I met shortly after his arrival from Canada for a cup of tea in the Bank's parlours, was an impressive character. Good-looking and neat – some likened him to the actor George Clooney (appropriately, he arranged for a Nespresso machine for the Bank's parlours to replace its traditionally insipid coffee) – he exuded quiet confidence. Though King was undoubtedly a better economist, Carney came over as a more competent and more rounded character, and certainly a better manager. Though he was new to the UK when I first met him, he had read into his subject and knew all the important issues. He could be prickly, though, in public and in private. A year later, when I interviewed him, he was fuming about a piece I had written a couple of weeks earlier, and said so. Carney took up the appointment of governor for five years rather than the eight stipulated when the job was advertised. But he was determined to leave his mark on an occasionally sleepy institution, undertaking a huge institutional shake-up and bringing more women into senior positions.

A crisis of confidence

The years after the financial crisis were different from what had gone before. Perhaps because of that Reinhart and Rogoff rule, that big financial crises take a long time to get over, Britain suffered from a collective hangover, in common with most other countries. Its direct effects, on unemployment, mortgage repossessions, business failures and other measures of economic distress were less than after many earlier recessions. The rise in unemployment in 2008–9 was much smaller than if the pattern of previous downturns had been followed. Soon employment started growing and unemployment started falling. But trust was gone – in the banks, in politicians and in the system – and confidence was shot. During the crisis a phrase by a senior Indian official, used during a panel at the Davos World Economic Forum – a somewhat surreal annual event in the Swiss Alps I attended for many years – came into popular use. 'Confidence grows at the rate that a coconut tree grows, but confidence falls at the rate that the coconut falls', said Montek Singh

Ahluwalia, deputy chairman of India's Planning Commission. So it did in Britain. For firms and individuals, the world they had come to believe in no longer seemed secure. After the crisis, the fear was of another one, perhaps even bigger. The longer it took for anything like normal conditions to return, the greater the reasons for caution. For two or three years after the crisis it felt as though a switch had been turned off.

Britain suffered in the period after the crisis not mainly because the coalition government increased VAT and cut public spending. The biggest single factor in the economy's slow recovery was probably the weakness of money and credit growth, which would have been no surprise to students of previous crises. The term went out of fashion as the years passed but it was, in many ways, just an old-fashioned credit crunch. Britain moved from easy credit availability – a time of 10 to 15 per cent credit growth when people could get a mortgage in ten minutes over the phone and run up tens of thousands of pounds of zero-interest balances on credit cards – to a time when credit growth was zero at best. Credit is the oxygen of a modern economy. When there is no credit growth it is hard to have economic growth. Mortgage lending dried up, and lending to small and medium-size businesses fell. Banks went from lending freely, and bending over backwards to do so before the crisis, to barely any lending at all after it. Some of this was forced on them by the need to rebuild capital. Some of it was an abrupt change in behaviour and psychology. The banks went from rewarding employees for their success in lending to rewarding them for their success in not doing so. The old adage that bankers only lend you an umbrella when the sun is shining was never more convincingly demonstrated. Meanwhile, the vision of an economy being led out of recession by exporters taking advantage of sterling's big fall during the crisis was dashed by events elsewhere. The crisis in the euro area, which had the side-effect of knocking confidence in financial markets badly, also prevented firms delivering the export-led growth that a 25 per cent fall in the pound (which occurred from the autumn of 2007 to the early part of 2009) should have guaranteed.

Another big factor was the performance of wages. Britain's labour market performed in an unprecedented way in the aftermath of the crisis. Employment was unexpectedly strong – in spite of public sector job cuts – and unemployment fell relatively early by past standards as the economy recovered. The contrast between the recovery in employment, which was stronger than in previous cycles, and the recovery in GDP, which was weaker, was striking. Five years after the economy's crisis trough, in the middle of 2009, employment was up by 2 million to nearly 31 million – a record – with the proportion of the workforce in jobs also at a record of more than 73 per cent. The unemployment rate fell below 6 per cent, with the wider measure dropping below 2 million and the narrower claimant count falling below 1 million. Wages, however, were unusually weak. The normal relationship between falling unemployment, implying a tighter labour market, and the growth in wages broke down. For nearly six years wages consistently increased at a slower rate than prices. Real wages fell by roughly a tenth, partly because inflation was mainly above the official 2 per cent target, even in a post-recession period, and partly because wages themselves were notably weak. The normal relationship in Britain, that wages tended to outstrip inflation in fair weather and foul, disappeared.

There were technical reasons for the weakness in wages. Some of the growth in employment was in low-wage, low-productivity jobs. Productivity – the growth of output per worker or output per hour – was also notably weak. At the top end of the scale big City bonuses, which had boosted average earnings before the crisis, even though they were received by relatively small numbers, either became a thing of the past or were paid in different ways. It was also possible, however, that something fundamental and lasting had happened. The recession of the early 1990s was too early for the full effects of the labour market reforms and the reductions in union power under Margaret Thatcher to be properly felt. The deep 2008–9 recession and its aftermath were in a period of limited union power and labour market flexibility. Once wages had been 'shocked' down to a new level, or a much slower rate of increase, there was nothing to bring them back up again. A tight job market would eventually result in labour shortages and rising wage pressures. The fact that it took so long suggested something had changed. The age of the automatic annual pay increase was over. Strong employment growth alongside weak wages was better than the alternative, and the rise in employment meant additional wages and salaries were going into the economy, but the change took some getting used to.

Where did we go from there?

In 2010, when Britain was still in the grip of the global financial crisis, my book on it, *The Age of Instability*, was published. There were many other books on the crisis at the time, there have been many since, and there will be many more in the future. J. K. Galbraith's classic *The Great Crash 1929* was not published until the 1950s, and books on the Great Depression were still coming out in the 2000s. One thing I tried to do was to set out how Britain was likely to do in the years after the crisis. There were ten predictions, most of which were right but some of which turned out to be pessimistic or misplaced. The predictions were: first, what I described as a jobs-light recovery; second, reluctantly big government; third, higher taxes; fourth, a slowing of globalisation; fifth, constrained consumer spending; sixth, risk-aversion; seventh, 'staying green' – a continued commitment to the environment; eighth, suspicion of markets;

ninth, greater equality; and tenth, that the world economy would tilt faster towards the East.

For some of those predictions it will take time before we know whether they are right or not, but for others quite a lot of evidence is already there. The prediction of a jobs-light recovery certainly fitted much of Europe, where unemployment remained stubbornly high and youth unemployment rates – which peaked at more than 50 per cent in Spain and Greece – were national scandals. Britain, however, did surprisingly well on this score. Despite a smaller fall in employment and rise in unemployment during the recession than was feared, subsequent job growth was stronger than hoped, as noted above. Another prediction, that the commitment to the environment would survive the crisis, was also questionable. In the aftermath of the crisis, the Conservatives' stance on the environment moved from 'vote blue, go green' to one where David Cameron – under pressure over rising living standards – was pushing through changes which would 'get rid of all the green crap' from energy bills. Internationally, governments remained committed to reducing greenhouse gas emissions, but the crisis undoubtedly diverted attention.

Otherwise, so far, things have largely followed the predicted pattern. Governments found, in the main, that the bank stakes they had acquired during the crisis were harder to dispose of than they had hoped. In Britain most of Northern Rock was sold to Virgin Money for £747 million. Part of the government's holding in Lloyds Banking Group was subsequently sold to City institutions. Hopes that the official majority holding in Royal Bank of Scotland would be sold before the 2015 general election, which the coalition thought would draw a line under the crisis, proved over-optimistic, however. The lesson from previous crises, such as those in Sweden in the 1990s, that it could take a decade or more to dispose of the stakes acquired during crises, appeared to be a valid one.

Globally, even though there was not the feared rise in protectionism, the crisis appeared to mark the high-water mark of rampant globalisation. World trade bounced back sharply in 2010, after collapsing in 2009, but then grew very slowly, and much more slowly than in the pre-crisis period. Many of the international banking flows that had dominated before the crisis fell to a fraction of their previous level. This, described in 2014 as 'financial deglobalisation' by Kristin Forbes, a member of the MPC, was a significant change. In 2007 international capital flows had been equivalent to 15 per cent of world GDP; seven years later they were just 1.6 per cent. The main reason was that the banks had sharply cut back the amounts they were moving across borders. Forbes, who offered the interesting observation that part of the reason for sterling's 1967 devaluation was the loss of foreign earnings when the Beatles stopped touring America in 1966, cautioned that the sharp drop in these flows would leave Britain vulnerable to the whims of foreign investors. 'A reduction in international bank flows could make it more difficult, and possibly even more expensive, for the UK to fund its current account deficit', she said. Though she did not put it quite as bluntly, sterling weakness could come back to haunt the authorities, as on so many occasions in the past. Mark Carney's idea that interest rates could rise gradually and to a lower level than was the norm in the past could be blown out of the water if the Bank of England were to find itself defending sterling. It has happened before and it could happen again.

Union blues

Where does the British economy go from here? This book has taken us on a journey through crises, plenty of them, a loss of global economic influence and profound geographical and sectoral changes. The north–south divide has always been with us, but in the middle of the second decade of the twenty-first century it is arguably wider than it has ever been. The Scottish referendum of September 2014 almost resulted in break-up of the United Kingdom, despite the gaping holes in the economic programme for independence presented by the Scottish National Party (SNP). Though the referendum eventually resulted in a 55:45 per cent vote in favour of preserving the union, it was followed by the devolution of significant tax-raising powers to Scotland, with pressure for similar devolution to Wales, Northern Ireland and the regions of England. Most economists believe such changes will make the economy harder to manage. The lesson of the eurozone's difficulties is that it is hard to construct a happy marriage from centrally set monetary policy and fiscal decisions taken away from the centre – in the euro's case, by individual governments. Though the countries and regions of the UK will have less fiscal independence than EU member states, it will be a complication future chancellors could do without. Nor has Scottish independence necessarily gone away. The September 2014 vote was sold by both sides as a once-in-a-generation opportunity for Scots to decide on their future, but it quickly became clear that a resurgent SNP was reluctant to take 'no' for an answer. The prospect loomed of a so-called 'neverendum': repeated votes on independence until, for the nationalists at least, the right answer is achieved. It is not a happy prospect.

If one worry about the UK economy is that there will no longer be a UK economy – I would put the chances of break-up over the next two decades at around 40 per cent – another is that Britain will no longer be part of the European Union. For some people, and some businesses, that is less a worry than a fervent hope. Exit from the EU would, however, generate considerable uncertainty, and any euphoria would probably be short-lived. Over more than four decades Britain has had a stormy relationship with the EU. It included an early vote on whether to remain part of the European Economic Community (EEC), in 1975, just two years after entry on 1 January 1973. The vote to stay was clear-cut: two to one. Some who look back on it, and voted yes, now say they did so under false pretences. Instead of the free trade area they thought Britain had joined, the next forty years saw creeping federalism, greater EU influence over British laws and regulations and, particularly once the EU welcomed the former Soviet bloc states of Eastern Europe, large-scale immigration to Britain from poorer countries. It was probably this, in combination with the eurozone crisis, which resulted in an increase in Euroscepticism, and the rise of the UK Independence Party (UKIP). In the 1990s, after Britain's troubled period as a member of the ERM and the humiliation of Black Wednesday, Eurosceptical parties remained on the fringes. In the May 1997 general election the Referendum Party, a Eurosceptic party formed by the billionaire businessman Sir James Goldsmith, received only 2.6 per cent of the vote. UKIP scraped just 0.3 per cent. Voters opted for a pro-EU Labour Party under Tony Blair, and voted out a Conservative Party badly divided on Europe but with its fair share of noisy Eurosceptics.

This changed in the 2000s, for the two reasons touched on above. Immigration into Britain from Eastern Europe, and in particular from the so-called Accession countries (the A8) which joined the EU in 2004 – the Czech Republic, Estonia, Hungary, Latvia, Lithuania, Poland, Slovakia and Slovenia – became a huge political issue. This was despite the fact that in the ten years from 2004 net migration from these countries was relatively small in relation to overall immigration. In the 2004–13 period net migration (arrivals minus departures) from the A8 economies totalled 437,000, less than half of all net migration from the EU (899,000), and just over a fifth of non-EU net migration (1.98 million). Perceptions were important, however, and the perception that Britain was open house to immigrants from Eastern Europe provided a powerful boost for UKIP and other Eurosceptic parties. So did the failure of the eurozone. Suddenly Europe was not a place to envy, which had long been Britain's default position. A eurozone teetering on the edge of the abyss, as it did in 2011 and 2012, with several economies requiring rescues, was not the picture of success traditionally associated with Europe. Nor was it, when euro entry was the hottest economic topic of all as recently as 2003, when Gordon Brown eventually steered Britain away from entry, what people thought they might be joining. A lucky escape turned into something like contempt for the eurozone, with anybody advocating membership risking ridicule. Europe's very slow growth, meanwhile, provided a strong argument for redirecting Britain's economy, and its exporters, towards the faster-growing BRICs (Brazil, Russia, India and China) and other emerging economies, though Germany had been very successful in exploiting such markets from the heart of the EU, and as the euro's pivotal member.

What about membership of the EU? In a speech in Berlin in 2014, Sir John Major, the former prime minister, set it out clearly:

> I put the chance of exit at just under 50 per cent. But if the negotiations go badly, that percentage will rise. Conversely, with genuine reform, it will fall. I ask our European partners to realise we are close to a breach that is in no one's interest. Britain's frustration is no game. It is not a political ploy to gain advantages and concessions from our partners. There is a very real risk of separation that could damage the future of the United Kingdom – and Europe as a whole.

Were Britain to leave, Major suggested, there would be no coming back. Divorce would be final. The evidence is that most Britons – and most British businesses – do not want to leave the EU. The rise of UKIP, paradoxically, was accompanied by an increase in support for continued EU membership, which in one 2014 poll hit a twenty-three-year high. The theory was that

UKIP had pushed some voters previously sitting on the fence into the pro-EU camp. There are circumstances in which voters could decide to leave the EU in a referendum. One would be if voters move even further away from the mainstream and come to regard a vote to leave the EU as a vote against the establishment. It is much more likely than not, however, that membership will continue.

Dealing with debt and deficits

Though Britain's economy had in many respects put the worst of the crisis behind it as I completed this book, important sources of vulnerability remained. The first, touched on above, was the deficit on the current account of the balance of payments. The story of the balance of payments is, at least in part, the story of manufacturing. The shift in the early 1980s from an economy which had always paid for its food, raw material and energy imports by exporting finished products to the rest of the world was profound. For a while that shift was masked by the rise of North Sea oil, which for a few years in the 1980s restored the health of the balance of payments. It was, however, a temporary phenomenon. By 2013 Britain's overall trade in goods, including oil, was in deficit to the tune of £110 billion, partly offset by a surplus on services of £78 billion. Britain's financial account, which reflects the balance between UK earnings from investments overseas and those earned by foreigners on their investments in the UK, was also in deficit, however, giving an overall current account deficit of £72 billion, 4.2 per cent of GDP, which widened to a record 5.5 per cent in 2014. This raises one of those questions politicians often put: can we pay our way in the world? Or, in one of the most frequent questions I have been asked by readers over the years: why do we not make things any more? And its close relative: how long can we keep running a trade deficit?

The answer to the second is: for a very long time. Official figures show that Britain's last current account surplus was as long ago as 1983. The recent deficits have been larger – the last comparable figures were during the Lawson boom of the late 1980s – but the fact of current account deficits is not unusual. For some, including senior government and Bank of England officials, that offers reassurance. Britain has always run a deficit and been able to fund it by attracting capital inflows, so why should that not continue? There is a sense, however, that 'paying our way in the world' could become more important in the future, as it was at the start of our story in the 1950s and 1960s. The trade deficit appears destined to widen inexorably, unmoved by helpful changes in the pound or other factors. North Sea oil is a shadow of its former self, and, while there are hopes that Britain, like the USA, could have a shale oil and gas revolution – reducing energy imports – it would be unwise to rely on it. Most importantly, perhaps, as far as the balance of payments was concerned, Britain successfully replaced actual engineering with financial engineering. The City, and the wider financial services industry, was a highly successful exporter and manager of money. Britain enjoyed a surplus on investment income to offset the deficit on trade. In the aftermath of the crisis, however, that surplus on investment income went into significant deficit. Add the fact that international capital flows have been hard hit by the crisis, and Britain starts to look vulnerable. That could mean the need for fundamental, even painful, adjustment, with the country reducing its appetite for imports and finding a way of increasing exports of goods and services.

The second vulnerability is the public finances. The story of Britain's adjustment from the crisis is one in which the government has taken on debt even as the debt burden of households and firms fell. By late 2014 public sector net debt was £1,450 billion, or almost 80 per cent of GDP, £1,000 billion – a trillion – higher than its level less than a decade earlier. Public sector borrowing was running at just under £100 billion a year. These were large numbers, and while the deficit was gradually – if unevenly – coming down, progress was very slow. George Osborne argued that most of this was due to factors outside the government's control, including the unexpected weakness of wages but also the eurozone crisis, and that it would have been folly to try to stick to his original deficit reduction targets in the face of these factors. In the jargon, he allowed the so-called 'automatic stabilisers' – when growth is weaker, tax revenues will undershoot and some government spending will be higher – to operate. In some ways, however, the coalition operated a strange kind of austerity, which included a generous and costly rise in the personal income tax allowance to £10,600, a reduction in the main rate of corporation tax to 20 per cent, repeated postponements of planned increases in the excise duty on petrol and a reduction in the very highest rate of income tax from 50 to 45 per cent. Though that reduction was officially estimated to have cost little or nothing in lost revenue, and while it was widely welcomed by business, it did not quite chime with the chancellor's 'we're all in this together' message. There was also considerable generosity when it came to pensioners, with their pensions and allowances protected, partly because pensioners tend to vote, and when they do so, tend to do so for the Conservatives more than any other party.

Largesse directed towards pensioners in the 2010–15 parliament highlighted one of two long-term problems associated with Britain's public finances. The first is that without fiscal repair the economy becomes more vulnerable to the next downturn, and less able to take Keynesian action – through temporary tax cuts and higher public spending – to deal with it. The 2007–9 crisis and recession pushed Britain's budget deficit from £36 billion in 2006–7 to £153 billion in 2009–10. Entering a downturn with a deficit of close to £100 billion could easily mean that it would be pushed to £200 billion or more, and even more the next time. Running a balanced budget, or something close to it, is no guarantee of immunity from crises and recessions, but it does leave an economy in better shape to tackle it. All the parties fighting the 2015 general election had plans to reduce the budget deficit, of course, but experience suggests that a little healthy scepticism is the right way to treat such plans.

Getting older

The long-term challenge is arguably greater, even if the deficit is brought down in the next few years. The Office for Budget Responsibility (OBR), established in 2010 as the government's independent fiscal watchdog, produces an annual report on Britain's long-term fiscal sustainability. Its 2014 report repeated the broad conclusions of previous ones, that long-term pressures for higher public spending, principally age-related spending on pensions and healthcare, will not be matched by a stream of higher tax revenues. It concluded: 'In the absence of offsetting tax rises or spending cuts this would widen budget deficits over time and eventually put public sector net debt on an unsustainable upward trajectory. The fiscal challenge from an ageing population is common to many developed nations.'

This is the fate of Britain, and of most advanced economies (and also of some emerging economies, such as China). How to manage when living to a hundred becomes unexceptional and when a smaller working population has to support a growing number of dependents? Over the fifty years to the early 2060s, state pensions, the NHS budget and long-term care costs will together add to public spending by between 5.5 and 6 per cent of GDP. This is in spite of an expected increase in the state pension age to seventy over the period, although on one set of projections the OBR budgets for a state pension age of seventy-five. The driver of all this is, of course, something we should be positive about: greater longevity. The effects are, however, striking. In the period covered by this book the ageing of the population has already occurred at a pace that surprised even demographic experts. In 1961 just 0.7 per cent of the UK population was eighty-five and over. By 2014 it was 2.3 per cent and by 2064, on the central projection used in the official fiscal projections, it will be 7.7 per cent. Almost a fifth of the population will be in the 65–84 age bracket in 2064, compared with just over a tenth in 1961. The 'core' of the workforce, those in the 16–64 age group (though 16 is young these days for people to start work), was between 63 and 64 per cent of the population in 1961, as it was in 2014. By 2064 it will be 55 per cent. Take out young people staying in education, and those of traditional working age will in effect be only half the population.

The good thing about demographics is that they come upon you slowly, allowing time for adjustment. The bad thing is that they are the kind of long-term challenge that it is easy for politicians, with their limited time in office, to duck. Some things have been addressed. There is now a process in place for increasing the state pension age. George Osborne took advantage of the crisis to legislate for an increase from sixty-five to sixty-six in 2020, to sixty-seven in 2028 and sixty-eight in 2046. These increases could be accelerated. It is also the case that the workforce is adapting all the time. In 1961 only a minority of women were in work. By 2014 more than 73 per cent of women in the 25–34 age group, and nearly 78 per cent of those aged 35–49 were employed. A more recent trend has been for greater numbers of older people to stay in employment, partly as a result of age discrimination legislation and partly because of the realisation that earlier pension expectations were not going to be achieved. In 2014 more than 1.1 million people aged sixty-five and over were in work, up by half a million on their levels before the crisis, with the numbers increasing all the time.

Some of this suggests that we will adjust to these demographic challenges, partly as a result of government policy and partly because people are already responding. In the golden age of pensions in the UK, which was probably the 1990s, the vogue was for early retirement. Those days have gone. An ageing population is a challenge, as is dealing with Britain's twin deficits: the balance of payments and public borrowing. None of these challenges is, however, insurmountable.

Reasons to be cheerful

It is easy for economists to be gloomy. Indeed, this is often the default position. Since the financial crisis there has been no shortage of such gloom. Economists, reviving an idea developed by the Keynesian economist Alvin Hansen in the 1930s, fear 'secular stagnation', or permanently slower growth. Others, notably the American economist Robert Gordon, fear that advanced economies have lost the key ingredient that fuelled growth: innovation. The great innovations which were labour-saving (which in the case of household appliances enabled women to join the workforce) and changed production processes are behind us. What we think of as innovation now is often just the means of delivering entertainment. Neither seems particularly plausible to me. Hansen predicted secular stagnation for the USA in 1938, but the post-war period saw the full flowering of the American dream of strong growth and rapidly rising living standards. The second half of the twentieth century, despite its periodic crises, was a period of rapidly rising living standards for all. Living standards in Britain doubled between the end of the Second World War and the mid-1970s, and doubled again over the following decades. Growth is more of a challenge in a period after a big financial crisis, and when there is a large hangover from that crisis, when the banks need to be financially strengthened, which typically limits their lending, and the public finances brought back to health with tax increases and spending cuts. One of the features of Britain's economy in the post-crisis period was very weak productivity growth. Plenty more people were in work, but economic output per head did not rise. That, however, is more likely to be a temporary adjustment rather than a permanent condition. The longer people stay in the workforce, up to a point at least, the more productive they are likely to be.

As for innovation, it is not only economists who underestimate what is still in the pipeline. The pace of technological change, which was hot in the twentieth century, has reached boiling point in the twenty-first. Half a century on, perhaps this really is Harold Wilson's white heat of the technological revolution. Technology is changing the way industries operate, and it is changing the commercial world fundamentally, and in a way that is hard to equate with stagnant productivity. Nor should we be dismissive about the creative industries. The creative industries – which include advertising, marketing, design, fashion, film and television, computer games and museums, galleries and libraries – account for 5 per cent of Britain's GDP directly, and 10 per cent when indirect effects are taken into account, and are growing at a faster rate than other sectors. With roughly 2.5 million people employed in these sectors, which account for 11 per cent of exports, these industries are ones in which Britain appears to have comparative advantage. Nor are they exclusively London-based. A report by the CBI, 'The Creative Nation', predicted that Britain could cement her position as the world's creative industries' hub by 2025 and cited regional successes such as MediaCityUK in Salford and the Titanic Quarter in Belfast. While traditional industry has seen its share of the economy decline, creative industries have seen their contribution rise.

As with traditional manufacturing, however, the danger is of complacency. A report by Nesta (formerly the National

Endowment for Science, Technology and the Arts), 'A Manifesto for the Creative Economy', set out some of the risks:

> The UK's creative economy is one of its great national strengths, historically deeply rooted and accounting for around one-tenth of the whole economy. It provides jobs for 2.5 million people, more than in financial services, advanced manufacturing or construction. This creative workforce has in recent years grown four times faster than the workforce as a whole. Behind this success, however, lies much disruption and business uncertainty, associated with digital technologies. Previously profitable business models have been swept away, young companies from outside the UK have dominated new internet markets, and some UK creative businesses have struggled to compete. UK policymakers too have failed to keep pace with developments in North America and parts of Asia. But it is not too late to refresh tired policies.

It was a useful warning, and politicians have responded, though perhaps not enough, with tax breaks and other incentives. But it would be wrong to be too pessimistic. The English language is a big advantage in many of these creative industries, and, after failing in the era of personal computers, Britain is succeeding in the digital age and should continue to do so.

The biggest economy in Europe

One very likely change, as we move through the twenty-first century, is that the relative size of the British economy will increase, partly as a result of stronger growth than in most of continental Europe and because of rising population. Population growth, while controversial when associated with immigration, is strongly associated with economic growth. Migrants tend to be of working age – when they arrive, at least – and add to the productive workforce. They are often attracted by a strong economy and rising employment, creating a virtuous circle, particularly when compared with the alternative of slow growth and declining population. According to population projections from the United Nations, taking the UN's central estimate, the UK's population will increase from 63.1 million in 2013 to 67.2 million in 2025, 73.1 million in 2050 and 77.2 million in 2100. Projections by the Office for National Statistics are, if anything, higher than this. Germany, currently the European Union's most populous country, with 82.7 million people, is projected to see its population decline to 80.9 million in 2025, 72.6 million in 2050 and 56.9 million at the end of the century, a huge population decline. France will overhaul Germany, according to the UN, its 64.3 million population in 2013 rising to 68 million in 2025, 73.2 million in 2050 and 79.1 million in 2100. Italy will see its population decline from 61 million to under 55 million by the end of the century. Spain's population will peak at just over 48 million.

Given the projected population difference, Britain seems certain to overhaul Germany in GDP terms. France, with its population increase, should also do so. Whether Britain is a bigger economy than France depends whether the current growth advantage persists. The Centre for Economics and Business Research, in a December 2013 report, predicted that the UK will become a bigger economy than France around 2018, largely because of this stronger growth, and that it will overhaul Germany in GDP terms around 2030. A similar message came from PricewaterhouseCoopers (PWC), a leading firm of accountants, in a July 2014 report. 'The UK is projected to gain ground against its major Western European rivals. Not only do we expect it to overtake France within the next few years, but we also expect it to narrow the gap with Germany.' By 2030, PWC predicted, UK GDP would be significantly larger than

France and within sight of Germany, with the momentum in the UK's favour, largely for population reasons.

Becoming the largest economy in Europe, which seems likely for Britain in the twenty-first century, would bring echoes of the country's successful past, long before the painful dismantling of empire and two world wars provided a powerful drag. The trends, however, have been in that direction for some time. Earlier in the book I described the turning point around 1980 from when the economy began to record faster growth in GDP per capita than other leading advanced economies. That, of course, is what matters. Having a bigger GDP spread over a much larger population is not of much use. Here the weakness of productivity growth – GDP per worker – in the immediate post-crisis period was a cause of concern. The assumption has been that this weakness is only temporary and that productivity will recover to something like its long-run average rate of growth. If not, then on the familiar dictum that 'productivity isn't everything but in the long-run it is almost everything' the UK outlook would be correspondingly bleaker. There is not a bright future as a low-wage, low-productivity economy.

The other factor is that being the biggest economy in Europe will not mean as much in the future as in the past. The rise of the so-called emerging economies is transforming the world economy. I like to think of two-thirds of global growth coming from emerging economies in the twenty-first century and one-third from the advanced world, whereas in the twentieth century it was the other way round. So, even as Britain overtakes France and closes on Germany, it gets overtaken by India, with countries such as Brazil and Indonesia also fast making up ground. Succeeding in the twenty-first century will mean engaging with these fast-growing economies.

Something will turn up

It is easy to be pessimistic about the outlook for the British economy. The global financial crisis hit hard and left a legacy of large budget deficits and debt, as well as a big current account deficit, all of which will take years to work off. Add low productivity and you can sink even lower. The challenge of an ageing population, and the pressure it will put on public services, will be considerable. On the other hand, Britain is in a better position than many countries to face up to these challenges. Growth in the post-crisis period came back quicker and more strongly than in many other countries, particularly in Europe. The labour market has shown itself to be genuinely flexible, a tribute to the reforms of the 1980s, which many competitors have yet to undertake. There is the possibility, perhaps no more than that, of a new energy revolution in the form of shale oil and gas. There is a dynamism about parts of the economy – particularly technology, advanced manufacturing and the creative industries – which offers a lot of hope for the future. Above all, the lesson of many decades is that, however bad it seems, something will turn up, though sometimes only for it to disappear again later. Wilkins Micawber was right to hope. The £2 coin issued in 2012 to commemorate the bicentenary of the birth of Charles Dickens – when the economy was going through a tough time – had Mr Micawber's most famous quote inscribed along its edge. It was very appropriate. Something will turn up. It always has done, and it probably always will.

Back to the Black Country

During the writing of this book I made many visits back to Birmingham and the Black Country. Without any of my family left there, these visits were as an outsider: a stranger, often to attend conferences and other events, sometimes just out of curiosity. Two-thirds of my life has been spent away from the

West Midlands, so the accent has almost gone. I might struggle to understand my younger self. This was not deliberate, just decades of immersion in other people's voices, other accents. Going back can be confusing; some landmarks have disappeared, while others have been built in their place. These days, regional cities – Wolverhampton became one of three Millennium cities in 2000 – are known as much for their universities as for their industrial and commercial might. Wolverhampton has a university quarter in its city centre, something I would never have expected fifty years ago. Get on a train from Birmingham to Wolverhampton, however, and some things are familiar, including some factories that were derelict when I was a teenager and which remain derelict now. Wolverhampton, like many town and city centres, is a shadow of its former self, with many empty shops. The bustling town centre of my childhood is quieter now. The experience of being taken to a department store like Beatties in Wolverhampton is not what it was. But the Molineux football ground, home of Wolves, has been completely rebuilt and is a fine venue, if not always with a team to match. The Grand Theatre, where pop groups played and where I used to see pantomimes, has had a makeover and is a successful regional theatre.

Birmingham has re-invented itself rather better than Wolverhampton. It now comes across as a moderately successful commercial centre, with lawyers and accountants dominating in place of the great industrialists of old. The political parties now come to Birmingham's international convention centre (ICC) for their annual conferences. The city has the largest German Christmas market outside Germany, a slightly strange boast; and the Bullring Shopping Centre, one of the great modernist developments of my childhood, has been rebuilt. Birmingham, and I am not sure I ever thought I would say this, has become an attractive place to visit.

There are also, as I write this, signs of revival in the area.

Austerity hit the West Midlands hard, with big cuts by Birmingham City Council, the largest local authority in Britain, indeed Europe. A strong recovery by Jaguar Land Rover following its acquisition by India's Tata Group had, however, revived spirits. Though based in Coventry, Jaguar Land Rover's influence extends across the West Midlands. In October 2014 the firm opened a new £500 million engine manufacturing facility near Wolverhampton. After decades of bad news, this was at least a step in the right direction. The workshop of the world is still in business, though it is a pale shadow of what it used to be.

Economies can never be preserved in aspic. The manufacturing industry I grew up with had many faults. It was arrogant, without good reason to be so, and uncompetitive. Foreign competition saw much of it off, while a terrible industrial relations climate did for much of the rest. Management did not manage, and often caved in to the unions in the interests of a quiet life, even as their German and Japanese competitors were investing for the future and making better products. Much of British industry, including much of it in the West Midlands, was competed out of existence. Over decades, the number of people working in factories has fallen sharply. These days, even in the Black Country, most of the fathers of any class of pupils would not be working in manufacturing, unlike in my day. This is the way things change. Services are more important to the economy than manufacturing, even in the West Midlands. As a country, Britain is more competitive – has a comparative advantage – in services rather than in mass manufacturing. That does not mean that some manufacturing, mainly high-value manufacturing, is not done very successfully. What remains is of significantly higher quality. There is not, however, enough of it; quantity is lacking. These are the forces of progress and of globalisation. Maybe manufacturing can revive in the Black Country, as part of a successful and diversified economy. Perhaps these things go in cycles, and perhaps the loss of manufacturing to China and other emerging economies went too far, and some of it will come back. There are some examples of this, known as 're-shoring', or 'the boomerang effect'.

Maybe, but a sustained revival of manufacturing and a rise in its share of the economy would break the pattern of many decades, and it is hard not to feel some regret. These old industrial areas, whether they are the Black Country, the Yorkshire coalfields or the South Wales valleys, never seem quite the same again when they have lost their essential purpose. On the sites where the great factories used to stand there is now another type of economic activity: big supermarkets, DIY stores or out-of-town shopping centres. People, by and large, find things to do. In 2014 the West Midlands, along with the rest of the country, was experiencing rising employment and a fall in the number of people out of work. No longer can it be said to be the beating heart of the economy, but it is doing better. There is, though, something missing. The manufacturing industry I grew up with, with its paternalistic employers and the apparent certainty that it would offer stable employment for generations, seemed strong and secure. People led busy and secure working lives and expected always to do so, doing more or less the same thing as their parents and grandparents had done. It was, sadly, an illusion. In most ways life is a lot better now than it was then. The air is cleaner, the smogs have gone, but so has a lot else. And it is hard not to feel quite a lot of nostalgia for those days.

10

A Political Postscript

'A traditional left-wing party competes with a traditional right-wing party, with the traditional result.'

Tony Blair, looking forward to the May 2015 general election, *The Economist*, 3 January 2015.

On 7 May 2015, something very surprising happened, at least for those who had not heeded the warning of Tony Blair, the former Labour prime minster. After five years of coalition government, and with every poll and every expert predicting another hung parliament, a Conservative government was elected with an overall majority. The majority was small, just twelve seats, but it was unexpected. Governments are supposed to suffer political wear and tear in office; to lose support between elections. In the event, that was indeed dramatically the case for the Liberal Democrats, the smaller coalition partner, which lost forty-nine of its fifty-seven seats and was reduced to a handful of MPs. It was demonstrably not true for the Conservatives, who added a net twenty-four seats to end up with 331; enough to be larger than all other parties combined. David Cameron, who continued as prime minister, became the first Conservative leader for twenty-three years to secure an overall majority, and the first for more than a century to increase his vote share after being in office for a significant period. For the Labour leader Ed Miliband, a long-time adviser to Gordon Brown, it was a catastrophic defeat and he immediately resigned the leadership. For Ed Balls, his shadow chancellor, an even more influential Brown adviser, it was even worse. In the space of twenty-four hours he went from expecting to stride back into the Treasury as chancellor to losing his parliamentary seat and facing a career beyond politics. The tragedy for him was that, having had his hands on the levers of economic power when in the Treasury, and having been almost promoted to the chancellorship by Brown in the dog days of Labour in 2009 to replace Alistair Darling, he may never get another chance.

The economy matters

What did the May 2015 general election tell us? Before it, the expectation was that the Conservatives' central charge, that Labour had been running the country when the economy crashed in 2008 and should not be trusted with it again, would work. Whether it was fair or not, polls showed a large and consistent Conservative lead on the question of economic competence; which party voters trusted to run the economy. Those polls also showed, however, that the Conservatives and Labour were neck and neck and, given the likely distribution of votes to the smaller parties, including a predicted Scottish National Party landslide (which duly occurred), Miliband was more likely to be prime minister. Labour's policies: a gentler pace of future austerity, rent controls, an energy price freeze, a 'mansion' tax for properties worth more than £2 million, the return of the 50 per cent top rate of income tax and the ending of so-called non-domicile tax status were all individually popular. Labour's counter charge, that the government was presiding over a recovery which was passing the majority of people by, appeared to be working. Perhaps there was genuine austerity fatigue. In an unguarded moment, which came out in a section of the Wikileaks' revelations, Lord (Mervyn) King had suggested to a contact that any party imposing the necessary austerity would be out of power for a generation. Perhaps this would be the fate of the Conservatives.

It was not to be, mainly because the headline verdicts of the opinion polls were so wrong. Whether the 2015 race was ever close, or whether there was a late swing to the Conservatives – even a swing that happened only when people were in the polling booth – will be the subject of research and speculation for years to come. The outcome, however, was one that should not have surprised anybody who believes that elections are, in the end, decided by the economy. There were complicating factors – the thought of a minority Labour government informally supported by the SNP deterred some English voters, and the Conservatives were able to profit from the weakness of their coalition Liberal Democrat partners by taking many of their seats – but the broad economic verdict still held. Voters saw austerity as a necessary evil to repair the badly damaged public finances, and many blamed Labour for that damage. They were also prepared to stick with the Conservatives because, while it had looked two years from the election that a weak recovery and falling living standards would be a poor platform on which to fight election, both came good. By May 2015 the Conservative chancellor George Osborne (who remained in post after the election) could boast the strongest growth among major economies, a 2 million rise in net new jobs over five years, zero inflation and, largely as a result, rising real wages. That was good enough for voters not to want to risk it.

The election was also an important test for economic philosophy. The philosophy of Margaret Thatcher, belief in markets, encouragement of enterprise, minimising direct intervention in business, and never assuming that government knows best, had survived more or less intact during the Blair and Brown governments from 1997 to 2010. Miliband was trying something different; a set of policies that involved greater intervention in markets and in business; that taxed the rich more heavily and which – through the attack on non-domicile status – Labour was prepared to risk Britain's attractiveness as a location for the footloose international wealthy and their investment. Blair's alarm about this shift in policy, encapsulated in the quote at the head of this chapter, was clear. After the Labour defeat his former New Labour colleagues queued up to denounce Miliband for tilting the party away from the policies that had given it three election victories, and for shifting it in an anti-business, anti-aspirational direction. Voters appear to have agreed that this was an error. Labour policies that were popular individually did not add up to an appealing whole. Whether that is true in future remains to be seen. Every election is different, though Labour is unlikely to repeat the experiment for quite some time. A broadly pro-business political consensus appears likely to survive the global financial crisis.

Déjà vu all over again

Almost before the final votes confirming a Conservative majority had been counted, some were predicting a grim few years for the new government. John Major, also a surprise election winner in 1992, spent the next five years trying to control a fractious party badly divided on Europe, ultimately without success. He crashed to a landslide defeat at the hands of Blair's Labour party in 1997. This time, Cameron would not only have the issue of Europe and the promise of an in-out referendum in 2016 or 2017 to cope with, but also pressure from a buoyant SNP for greater powers for Scotland, and the task of getting potentially difficult austerity measures through the House of

Commons with a tiny majority. Was this the election the Conservatives would have been better off losing?

History sometimes repeats itself. The history of the type of recovery economies can expect after severe financial crises has proved useful in recent years. Politics is less predictable. By the time you read this you may know whether chaos followed the Conservative victory in 2015. There were, however, four reasons to expect that it would not be. While, as in 1992, the victory was unexpected, the difference in 2015 was that the widely-expected alternative was a Labour minority government, not a Labour majority. Voters would not easily forgive a Conservative party that, having been given the gift of a majority, proceeded to squander it in a series of internal battles. Discipline could be expected to be stronger than in the 1992–7 parliament.

Related to this, the issue in the 1990s was Europe but it was particularly raw as a result of Britain's ERM (exchange rate mechanism) humiliation in 1992. And, while Major had negotiated opt-outs at Maastricht, so that there was no requirement for Britain to join the single currency, there remained intense frustration among Conservatives about Europe, not least because there was no question of an in-out referendum on the EU. This time there would be even greater frustration if for any reason the promised referendum does not occur. Assuming it does, and assuming even ministers are given a free vote, Conservative Eurosceptics will be given the opportunity to give vent to their frustrations. That still leaves the possibility of uprisings after the referendum, on the assumption that Britain votes to stay in, as I expect. Conservative MPs making trouble after EU exit had been rejected by voters – perhaps because there had been no meaningful renegotiation of the terms of membership – would, however, suffer by being seen as bad losers. The 1992–7 parallels look imperfect.

Scotland is a significant challenge, as discussed in the previous chapter, the more so because the SNP won an astonishing fifty-six of the fifty-nine seats in Scotland, making it the third largest party at Westminster. Though the SNP, led by Nicola Sturgeon (who is not an MP) had an extraordinary victory, it fell short of its ambition of preventing, or bringing down a Conservative minority government. It may yet be instrumental in bringing down a Conservative majority government but only time will tell. There are serious questions about how it will be possible to talk of a United Kingdom when there is a large nationalist bloc at Westminster, which has the ultimate aim of independence. It could be that independence is back on the agenda much sooner than was expected when the September 2014 'once in a generation' referendum resulted in a 55–45 per cent 'no' vote. The SNP has insisted, however, that it is not pushing for a re-run of the referendum, or even immediate full fiscal autonomy. Despite the SNP's May 2015 success, the September 2014 rejection of independence, coupled with a weak oil price that blows an even bigger hole in the public finances than existed before, may mean that Scotland remains part of the union.

What happens over the next few years depends, as you would expect me to say, on the economy. Interest rates will rise from the emergency 0.5 per cent level established by the Bank of England in March 2009. The assumption is that the vast majority of borrowers will cope but that has yet to be tested. There will be more austerity. In 2014–15 the budget deficit was a fraction under 5 per cent of gross domestic product; higher than the vast majority of countries, including even Greece. Getting it down to zero and beyond will require grit and imagination, though more than half of the task was accomplished in Osborne's first five years as chancellor. Without the Liberal Democrats to share the flak, the Conservatives may find it politically tougher to, as they put it during the election campaign, 'finish the job', though it will be a surprise if deficit-reduction measures are quite as draconian as was claimed during the election campaign. There will be no shortage of opposition in Westminster and from public sector critics. Expect frequent NHS crises. Growth is hugely important. If the economy has shaken off the worst of the crisis and is set for several years of good growth, austerity is easier to deliver (and may become less necessary) and normalising monetary policy – starting to raise interest rates – is more straightforward. If not, these things become more difficult. Indeed, in a fragile economy interest rates might not go up at all.

Whatever happens, another fascinating chapter has opened. Whether this is one where something does genuinely turn up, or whether there will be a lurch back into the kind of crisis that has characterised many of the periods described in this book, remains to be seen. As an optimist, I hope it is the former. As a realist, I know that we have not said goodbye to uncertainty, instability and policy mistakes. They are, after all, what makes it interesting.

References

1: The workshop of the world

Barnett, Correlli (1995), *The Lost Victory*, Pan Books.

Comfort, Nicholas (2012), *The Slow Death of British Industry, A Sixty-Year Suicide, 1952–2012*, Biteback Publishing.

Owen, Geoffrey (1999), *From Empire to Europe: The Decline and Revival of British Industry Since the Second World War*, Harper Collins.

Owen, R. J. (2005), *Memories of Rubery Owen*, Neate Publishing.

Wilson, Harold (1964), Leader's speech, Brighton, www.britishpoliticalspeech.org

2: Giving it all away

Daily Record (2013), 'Margaret Thatcher's Time in Power Destroyed Industries in Scotland and Still Casts a Shadow Over the Country', 9 April 2013: http://www.dailyrecord.co.uk/news/scottish-news/margaret-thatchers-time-power-destroyed-1819478

Dyson, James (2004), 'Engineering the Difference', the 2004 Richard Dimbleby Lecture: http://www.bbc.co.uk/pressoffice/pressreleases/stories/2004/12_december/09/dyson.shtml

Express & Star (2013), 'Legacy of Margaret Thatcher Will Live On for Years', 9 April 2013: http://

www.expressandstar.com/news/2013/04/08/
legacy-of-margaret-thatcher-will-live-on-for-years/

Koerner, Steve (2012), *The Strange Death of the British Motorcycle Industry*, Crucible Books. Extract: http://www2.warwick.ac.uk/knowledge/culture/stevekoerner

Red Pepper (2013), 'Dispelling the Thatcher Myths', April 2013: http://www.redpepper.org.uk/dispelling-the-thatcher-myths/

Rubery Owen (2013), 'History and Heritage': http://ruberyowen.com/rubery-owen-history.php

Thatcher, Margaret (1979), speech to the Conservative Party conference, October 1979: http://www.margaretthatcher.org/document/104147

3: Back from the brink

Bank of England (1978), quarterly bulletin.

Barnett, Joel (1982), *Inside the Treasury*, Andre Deutsch.

IMF Negotiations: Memorandum by the Chancellor of the Exchequer, 22 November 1976; The National Archive: http://filestore.nationalarchives.gov.uk/pdfs/small/cab-129–193-cp-76–111–1.pdf

Lipsey, David (2014), *In the Corridors of Power*, Biteback Publishing.

Sandbrook, Dominic (2010), *State of Emergency: The Way We Were, Britain, 1970–74*, Allen Lane.

Smith, David (1987), *The Rise and Fall of Monetarism*, Penguin Books.

'The Real Choices Facing the Cabinet': memorandum by the energy secretary, 29 November 1976: The National Archive: http://filestore.nationalarchives.gov.uk/pdfs/small/cab-129–193-cp-76–117–7.pdf

4: A close-run thing again

Conservative Party manifesto 1979; http://www.conservative-party.net/

Howe, Geoffrey (1979), budget speech, 12 June 1979, http://www.margaretthatcher.org/document/109497

Lawson, Nigel (1992), *The View from No. 11: Memoirs of a Tory Radical*, Bantam Press.

Lipsey, David (2014), *In the Corridors of Power*, Biteback Publishing.

Smith, David (1987), *The Rise and Fall of Monetarism*, Penguin Books.

Smith, David (2012), 'Sir Alan Walters', *Dictionary of National Biography*, Oxford University Press; http://www.oxforddnb.com

Walters, Alan (1986), *Britain's Economic Renaissance*, Oxford University Press.

5: A renaissance of sorts

House of Commons Library (1999), 'The Right to Buy', research paper 99/36, 30 March 1999.

Lawson, Nigel (1992), *The View from No. 11; Memoirs of a Tory Radical*, Bantam Press.

London School of Economics (2013), 'Investing for Prosperity: Skills, Infrastructure and Innovation'; http://www.lse.ac.uk/researchAndExpertise/units/growthCommission/documents/pdf/LSEGC-Report.pdf

Nickell, Stephen (2001), 'Has UK Labour Market Performance Changed?' Speech to the Society of Business Economists, May 2001: www.bankofengland.co.uk

6: Another fine mess

HM Treasury (2005), sterling withdrawal from the ERM, FOI disclosures, 9 February 2005.

Major, John (1992), speech to the Scottish CBI, 10 September 1992: http://www.johnmajor.co.uk/page1210.html

Neil, Andrew (1997), *Full Disclosure*, Pan Books.

Walters, Alan (1986), *Britain's Economic Renaissance*, Oxford University Press.

7: No return to boom and bust

Balls, Edward, and O'Donnell, Gus (2002), *Reforming Britain's Economic and Financial Policy: Towards Greater Economic Stability*, Palgrave Macmillan.

Barker, Kate (2004), review of housing supply: 'Delivering Stability: Securing Our Future Housing Needs', March 2004.

HM Treasury (2007), *Economic and Fiscal Strategy Report*, HMSO.

Keegan, William (2003), *The Prudence of Mr Gordon Brown*, John Wiley & Sons.

King, Mervyn (2007), 'The MPC Ten Years On', speech delivered to the Society of Business Economists, 2 May 2007, Bank of England.

Wanless, Derek (2002), 'Securing Our Future – Taking a Long-Term View – The Wanless Review', HM Treasury.

8: The biggest crisis

Bank of England (2007), opening statement to the inflation report press conference by Mervyn King, 8 August 2007.

British Academy (2009), 'British Academy Reveals Dangerous Recipe to the Queen', www.britac.ac.uk

Darling, Alistair (2012), *Back from the Brink: 1,000 Days at Number 11*, Atlantic Books.

House of Commons Treasury Committee (2008), 'The Run on the Rock', fifth report of session 2007–8, www.parliament.uk

King, Mervyn (2008), speech at the Royal Armouries, Leeds, 21 October 2008, www.bankofengland.co.uk

Lambert, Richard (2007), Newcastle speech, September 2007, www.cbi.org.uk

Smith, David (2010), *The Age of Instability: The Global Financial Crisis and What Comes Next*, Profile Books.

9: Something will turn up

CBI (2014), 'The Creative Nation: A Growth Strategy for the UK's Creative Industries'; www.cbi.org.uk

Centre for Economics and Business Research (2013), 'World Economic League Table', http://www.cebr.com/reports/cebr-world-economic-league-table

Forbes, Kristin (2014), 'Financial Deglobalization? Capital Flows, Banks and the Beatles', speech at Queen Mary University of London, 19 November 2014; www.bankofengland.co.uk

Major, John (2014), 'Britain and the EU: In or Out?', speech at the Konrad-Adenauer-Stiftung, Berlin, November 2014; www.johnmajor.co.uk

Nesta (2013), 'A Manifesto for the Creative Economy'; www.nesta.org.uk

Office for Budget Responsibility (2014), 'Fiscal Sustainability Report', July 2014; www.budgetresponsibility.org.uk

PricewaterhouseCoopers (2014), 'The UK's Standing in the World', www.pwc.co.uk

Reinhart, Carmen M., and Rogoff, Kenneth S. (2011), *This Time Is Different: Eight Centuries of Financial Folly*, Princeton University Press.

Smith, David (2009), 'Tories Out of Step as the Bank Wheels Out Its Big Guns', *Sunday Times*, 11 January 2009; www.economicsuk.com/blog

United Nations (2013), 'World Population Prospects: The 2012 Revision', www.un.org

Index